CHRISTIAN MISSIONARIES

CHRISTIAN MISSIONARIES

Owen Milton

EVANGELICAL PRESS OF WALES

© Evangelical Press of Wales, 1995
First published 1995
ISBN 1 85049 118 6

Cover design by Digby Williams

Published by the Evangelical Press of Wales
Bryntirion, Bridgend, Mid Glam. CF31 4DX
Printed in Wales by Bridgend Print Centre, Bridgend

CONTENTS

ILLUSTRATIONS

Photographs of J. O. Fraser and Isobel Kuhn by kind permission of OMF International (UK)

O'er the gloomy hills of darkness
  Look, my soul; be still, and gaze;
All the promises do travail
  With a glorious day of grace:
    Blessèd jubilee!
  Let thy glorious morning dawn.

Kingdoms wide that sit in darkness,
  Grant them, Lord, Thy glorious light;
And from eastern coast to western
  May the morning chase the night;
    And redemption,
  Freely purchased, win the day.

May the glorious day approaching
  End their night of sin and shame,
And the everlasting gospel
  Spread abroad Thy holy Name
    O'er the borders
  Of the great Immanuel's land!

Fly abroad, thou mighty gospel,
  Win and conquer, never cease;
May thy lasting wide dominion
  Multiply and still increase!
    Sway Thy sceptre,
  Saviour, all the world around.

William Williams, Pantycelyn, 1717–91

1
John Eliot
(1604 – 1690)

What is the difference between a missionary and a minister? When does a minister become a missionary? If given the option, should a man choose to be one rather than the other? And by what criteria should he make his choice?

Such questions would have been purely academic for John Eliot, who succeeded in combining both these honoured offices in a remarkable way. Nor could it be charged upon him that he spared himself in one vocation in order that he might discharge his responsibilities to the full in the other. In both respects he was a 'good and faithful servant'. Whether his work be evaluated in terms of his labours among the English settlers in New England or among their native neighbours the Red Indians, each community knew the privilege and benefit of being counted his responsibility.

John was born to farming parents who attended the Parish Church in Widford, Hertfordshire. Little is known of his early years, but it is evident that the valuable lessons that he learned at his father's hand stood him in good stead as he, later on, instilled those same principles in the Indians while he sought to train them in the ways of civilization. Whatever schooling he received in his childhood days obviously was fruitful, for in 1619 he entered Cambridge University, emerging four years later with the degree of Bachelor of Arts. Precise knowledge of details regarding his conversion to Christ is not available. What is known is that one of those whom God used in his Christian experience was Thomas Hooker. Cotton Mather permitted himself the rare Puritan diversion of a pun in commenting that this Hooker had 'angled' many sinners into the kingdom of God.

The relationship between the two men developed into a close friendship, particularly as Eliot was a schoolmaster at Little Baddow, near Chelmsford, Essex, where Hooker was Rector. Subsequently the teacher himself became a clergyman. Hooker, for his part found the persecuting policies of Archbishop Laud too much to take, and eventually, after spending some time in Holland, crossed the Atlantic and became one of the foremost Congregationalist ministers in Massachusetts before becoming one of the founding fathers of Connecticut. Eliot was to take a similar course, but went directly to America, and remained in Massachusetts.

No sooner had he arrived in Boston in 1631, a young man of twenty-seven, than he was preaching there and occupying the position of pastor during the absence in England of the regular minister, Mr Wilson. On Mr Wilson's return Eliot was asked to remain as his colleague but declined the offer. He wanted greater freedom than that afforded by the offer he had received; and also he had made a promise to friends in England that if they were to follow him out before he had settled in a pastorate he would be their minister. When a group did emigrate the following year, Eliot was ordained as their pastor. This was in a little township called Roxbury just outside Boston. There the first marriage registered was his own to Hannah Mumford in the same year.

His character as the minister of Roxbury was soon recognized and respected. In private he was a lover of prayer and the Scripture, and frequently kept seasons of fasting. He read Hebrew, Greek, and Latin with equal facility (believing that Hebrew should be the universal language!) The duty of mortifying sin was one to which he gave unsparing attention. In public he was generous, peaceable, but with an unflinching readiness to speak out for what was right, and warn his members. Finding a merchant with his books of business on the table and his books of devotion on the shelf he made the pointed remark, 'Sir, here is earth on the table, and heaven on the shelf; pray don't sit so much at the table as altogether to forget the shelf.' Good government and good schools seem to have been of great importance to him—for the white man and the red man alike.

Twelve years after his ordination John Eliot began to learn the language of the Indians of his neighbourhood. His concern for the natives had reached such proportions that he felt driven to do something about their condition. No one was doing anything to present the gospel to them, and he could not find it in himself to escape the responsibility. The Algonquin Indians to whom he was called were puzzled and distressed by the changes that they had seen since the coming of the strangers from across the sea. Their way of life to the immigrant white man was 'infinitely barbarous'. They were nomadic, moving about from one place to another when the supply of food and other creature comforts vanished. Hunting was the chief, if not only, employ of the men, while their squaws seem to have most of the work to do. If the coming of the English with their guns meant that the food supply was more easily secured it also meant that the Indians found themselves with much more time on their hands. In modern terms the rise in unemployment resulted in an increase in social problems. Along with this, illnesses that the English brought with them made devastating inroads upon them. This was fertile soil for a spirit of resentment to take root and flourish. It also provided the background against which John Eliot undertook his task.

Accompanied by two fellow ministers and an Indian interpreter, Eliot set out in the autumn of 1646 to preach to the Indians. This was to a district a few miles outside Roxbury. His first sermon in the newly learned language lasted an hour and a quarter. Taking his text from Ezekiel 37:3 he spoke of the creation of the world as well as of its judgment at the end. In between treating those two subjects he does not seem to have left much unsaid. A period of questions of over an hour followed during which it was clear that the preacher's efforts had met with no small degree of success, some of the hearers actually

11

inquiring as to how they could be saved. Further meetings were arranged in the next two months and as a result some Indians professed that they had been converted. It was undeniable that God's blessing was resting powerfully on Eliot's work. He began to publish the so-called 'Indian Tracts' which set out the account of his endeavours. One evidence of the progress of the gospel among these heathen was that at the Synod at Cambridge, Massachusetts in 1647, nine months after the first visit among them, it was decided that an extra address should be given—in the Algonquin tongue, for the benefit of the Indian converts.

Further encouragements were at hand. Before long the Indians asked if they might build a town of their own. This fitted in admirably with Eliot's scheme, for he believed that any real advance of the gospel depended upon the Indians adopting a settled way of life. The common Puritan opinion was that Christianity and civilization ought to march hand in hand, and this principle underlay all that Eliot sought to accomplish for his charges. He also was aided by the readiness of his brother ministers to step into the breach that was often left in Roxbury during his absence among the Indians. Nor was it only from the local Christians that he received assistance. In England the Society for the Propagation and Advancement of the Gospel in New England was established which was able to send financial support across the Atlantic. Their zeal in this enterprise may have owed something to the fact that there was abroad a belief that the Indians were descended from the lost tribes of Israel. Eliot himself shared this opinion. In consequence of all this enthusiasm the town of Natick was built, some twenty miles to the south-west of Roxbury, and if this was where he was most frequently to be found it was by no means the only place, for his travels took him among other Indians, some as far as sixty miles away. What these journeys cost him may be adjudged from these words in a letter he wrote:

> I have not been dry, night nor day, from the third day of the week unto the sixth, but so travelled, and at night pull off my boots, wring my stockings, and on with them again, and so continue. But God steps in and helps. I have considered the word of God in 2 Tim. ii. 3: 'Endure hardship as a good soldier of Christ.'

If Eliot enjoyed much support he also encountered opposition. The spirit of resentment dies hard and certain of the English settlers were not very happy at the rights being given to the Indians, on whose behalf Eliot appeared as a tireless champion. Some of the Indian leaders themselves were to prove a problem as they saw their dark powers over the people being whittled away as gospel light came in. In spite of discouragements he persevered and his vision never dimmed. There seems little doubt that he was involved in a scheme to put Indians into Harvard College and even to build an Indian College. Constantly he was trying to raise the standard of living of the recently enlightened Indians.

In 1649 he embarked on the task of translation. The first production was a catechism which appeared in 1654. It was the first Indian book ever printed. In the following year Genesis had been printed as had the Gospel according to Matthew. He pursued his task, completing the New Testament in 1661 and the Old two years later. This was by no means the end of his ventures as a translator: one of the people in England with whom he was in correspondence was Richard Baxter, whose permission he obtained to translate *Call to the Unconverted*. Through his efforts the Indians were able to read this work in their own tongue, and Eliot translated for them works by other contemporary writers as well, besides producing many books from his own pen.

It was not until some years after Eliot had preached to them that the first baptisms took place. Even then the 'Praying Indians' were not carelessly admitted to the privileges of church membership. When this did occur it was for a trial period at Roxbury and did not take place until 1659. Then they formed a church of their own at Natick. Once the precedent was set, other churches soon followed in the new Indian townships. The number of Christians grew apace; soon there were 24 Indian evangelists; and there were Indian pastors over some of the churches. Natives and settlers alike seem to have been fired by Eliot's example. John Hiacooms, 'that memorable Indian', writes Cotton Mather, 'was a very great instrument of bringing his Pagan and wretched neighbours to a saving acquaintance with our Lord Jesus Christ'. In the spirit of Eliot, Richard Bourn set out to rescue Indians 'from their worse than Egyptian-darkness'. The off-shore islands of Nantucket and Martha's Vineyard were evangelized. It seemed that nothing could halt the victorious advance of the gospel.

But the kingdom of darkness is not easily plundered. One of the chiefs who had welcomed the Pilgrim Fathers was Massasoit, and his people, the Wampanoags, benefited from the relationship with the English. On his death his son, Philip (or King Philip as he was called by the English), succeeded him—and he was not of his father's calibre. A cunning man whose actions belied his words, he was soon stirring trouble, his intention being to drive the foreigners from those shores. In 1675 matters came to a head. The outcome in terms of violence and carnage was of calamitous proportions. Had it not been for the Praying Indians it would have been far worse. Their forbearance and patience was a tribute and a testimony to the gospel they had received. They remained faithful to the settlers, fighting on their side, and by their contribution to the warfare saved the colony from what might well have been extinction. They were ill rewarded, and hundreds of them were interned on an island in Boston Harbour, with scarcely the barest of necessities. On the mainland the British made no distinction between one Indian and another, and so Eliot's flock suffered along with the others. When the war ended, settlements lay in ruins. It had taken enormous toll. The missionary's work was devastated—but not his spirit. He applied himself once more to the work but was not to see the same success as in the past. Before the war the number of Praying Indians had been 3,600. It was never to be as high again.

In 1685 he turned his attention to the negroes. Obviously his strength was not equal to the task as he saw it, but he arranged for negro servants to be sent to his home for instruction. One young boy who had been struck blind was taught to memorize whole chapters of the Bible. Although in his eighties he gave himself unsparingly to the service of his Master. In 1687, the year of his wife's death, he was still visiting the Indian townships. And never for a moment during all these years were his people of the church at Roxbury neglected.

He was 85 years of age when he died on 21 May 1690. As he awaited the summons from heaven he spoke of the decline of the work among the Indians and prayed that God would revive it; it was, after all, the work in which he had been engaged for so many years. When he spoke of his doings he reproved himself:

> But what was the word I spoke last? I recall that word, *my doings!* Alas, they have been poor and small, and lean doings, and I'll be the man that shall throw the first stone at them all.

14

John Eliot has earned the title, 'Apostle to the Indians'. A French missionary to the Iroquois had spent the night with the Eliots and both men had enjoyed each other's company. Apologizing that he could not accept the invitation to stay longer the visitor expressed his gratitude and sense of privilege at having been in 'the house of an Apostle'. This is probably the first time the name had been applied to him. It is a fitting tribute to the spirit of John Eliot that the man who gave it to him was a Jesuit.

2
Hans Egede
(1686—1758)

From Greenland's icy mountains,
From India's coral strand . . .

With these words opens what is probably the best-known of all missionary hymns, but whereas the names of missionaries, famous as well as unsung, who served God in India would roll off our tongues, the same could scarcely be said with regard to Greenland. The name at the head of this chapter, although unfamiliar, belongs to one of the earliest and greatest of such men.

It was in the Norwegian town of Harstad, once known as the 'Northernmost stronghold of Christianity', that Hans Egede was born. There inside the Arctic Circle, he was early fitted for the hard existence that lay ahead of him when he answered the call to one of the most inhospitable climates and environments that can be imagined. His Lutheran parents ensured him a Christian upbringing in which the spirit of German pietism was influential. His schooling was entrusted firstly to his mother's brother, who was curate in the church where Hans was baptized, and later to another clergyman who lived nearby. His formal education was completed at Copenhagen University. The choice of a course was not very easy, for he had wide-ranging interests extending from chemistry and geology through history and languages to mathematics and astronomy. Eventually, having set his mind on following his grandfather as a Lutheran minister, he gained a degree in theology. He was ordained in 1707 and appointed to a living in a district of the Lofoten Islands, still well within the Arctic Circle. His stubborn, sometimes violent, nature was not likely to endear him to people, and there were occasions when relationships in the pastorate were strained and stormy. In that same year he was married, his wife being thirteen years older than he was.

Greenland had long exerted a powerful influence upon him. Facts and legends had been mingled when he heard as a boy of the contact that had been made between that country and his own homeland. In the tenth century the renowned Norwegian, Eric the Red, had given it the name by which it was called. Various reasons have been suggested for what must have appeared to many to be one of the most colossal misnomers in history. Some have said it was because Eric reckoned it was an improvement on the country he had just left, Iceland; others that he thought that 'with such a name people will be more easily persuaded to go there!' Through Eric's son, Leif, Christianity had come to Greenland, and had made such an impact there that the country had eventually been granted its own bishop.

Over the centuries fewer and fewer visitors went to Greenland, and what had happened to those original settlers and to the gospel by the time of Hans Egede was shrouded in mystery. The young minister in the Lofoten Islands found his interest stirred, and became aware of a compulsion to go and discover for himself what was the condition of the descendants of those early Christians. The general opinion was that there were no descendants, and that all traces of a Christian presence had long since vanished. That kind of verdict Hans was not prepared to entertain. He determined that it was his responsibility before God to revive what he was persuaded was the declining cause of Christianity in the long-forgotten wastes of Greenland. From then on a new element intruded itself into his diligent pursuit of his parochial duties—a concern, a burden, from which he could find no release and, truth to tell, from which he sought none.

Response to his proposal was predictable—from coolness to downright opposition. He sought the support of bishops and of the King of Denmark himself. The Bishop of Trondheim professed that he was willing to do what he could. How much reliance could be placed on this kind of encouragement was exceedingly doubtful, since the bishop seemed to think that Greenland was 'not far from Cuba'! What must have been hardest to bear, however, was the reaction of his wife, who berated him for his foolish ideas, and even spoke of regretting that she had ever married him. Later she overcame her initial hostility and was to prove a tower of strength to him, to which be bore noble testimony.

Patience was not a virtue for which Egede was known and in 1718, unable to contain himself any longer, he resigned his living and with his family of four children sailed south to Bergen, the port from which he hoped to reach his ultimate destination. This journey was not without incident, for during its course he fell overboard and was rescued. While some might have regarded this as an ill omen he considered it as an indication of the divine approval on his venture. Two more years of chafing delay followed, during which he was granted an audience with the King, before he won the support of merchants and other influential people. The Bergen Company was formed, and with the King and Government prepared to assist with the cost he left Norway for the mysterious land whose call could not be stifled.

There were about 45 other people who sailed with him in order to found a settlement. This they did at a site near what grew into the town of Godthåb, the present capital of the country. They were there largely to serve the commercial interests of those who had financed the expedition. For his part Hans Egede never lost sight of the fact that its main purpose was 'the propagation of the pure and true doctrine of God', and he saw to it that the others were constantly reminded of this.

Excitement when they landed in 1721 soon gave way to a sense of foreboding. The Eskimos had greeted them in a friendly fashion, but when they realized that the party had come to stay the welcome cooled. Undeterred, Egede set himself to win the confidence of the natives. In this he was confronted by two difficulties that at the time seemed mountainous. One of these was the problem of language, for he had entertained hopes that he might find some similarity between their language and his. This optimism had been kindled by his belief that the heritage of the original settlers would have included at least some words that he might have recognized. There were no traces of this common vocabulary. The other obstacle was the lifestyle of the natives. There was an appalling lack of elementary principles of hygiene, and the smell of rotting meat and decaying fish inside their huts, along with absence of ventilation, was enough to test the strongest stomach. Hans Egede, who was of sterner stuff than most men, found his first visit to one of these homes a severe trial. Some of his companions failed the test abysmally, although on a later occasion one of them actually was able to stay and sleep there. This feat was accomplished mainly because an accident in childhood had robbed him of his sense of smell!

His frustration at the slow progress he was making with the language was offset by the ease with which his children advanced. Playing with their new friends was an obvious way in which relationships were established and understanding developed. Added to this was the ability of his son Paul to draw. The Eskimos were fascinated by this talent. His father could see how this gift could be turned to even greater advantage when he came to explain the gospel to them, for here were people who had never seen a lamb or a vine or a field of corn. As for Egede himself his contribution in this direction was music. By such means as singing the twenty-third psalm he gained their attention. His evangelism was of a basic but essential kind—the existence, power, and love of God, heaven and hell. They were horrified when Paul's drawing of the cross was presented and interpreted to them. To make matters worse superstition had a firm grip on the minds and hearts of the Greenlanders, a hold which was manipulated by the traditional enemy of any pioneer missionary, the *angakut,* and Hans Egede spoke with feeling of the 'devilish jugglery' of these 'soothsayers'.

Like David Livingstone there was much of the explorer as well as the missionary in him, and the hope of finding the lost colonists never seemed to desert him. His search for them, or at least for traces of them, involved him in many dangers and hardships, and although he never saw descendants of his ancestors, his diligence was rewarded when he came across remains of buildings, one of which had been unquestionably a church. When the natives inquired as to the interest of the white men in the building and what purpose it had served, it was with great eagerness that the Norwegian parson told them of a God who had loved them so much that he had sent his Son to help them and to die for them. It was with a heavy heart that he came to terms with the conclusion that it was not to be his privilege to discover the human evidence for his firmly-held persuasion, evidence which in fact did not exist. Greater things lay in store for him, however, for, as one of his biographers records: 'In those dark hours of defeat, frustration, and disappointment "The Apostle of Greenland", as he was one day to be called, was born.'

All the while, he was aware of his responsibility to the Bergen Company, and much of his time was taken up with seeking sites for new settlements and opportunities for trading. The task was made more difficult because of the presence of Dutch traders, who really had no business in a Danish colony. Eventually the tension between the Lowlanders and the Scandinavians reached a level which required the King to send an expedition to establish a military presence there. The improvement in the situation which was looked for with the arrival of the expedition did not materialize however, the new Governor and his second-in-command frequently quarrelling, and even coming to blows. As far as the missionary work was concerned Egede's changed attitude, unhampered by romantic notions, did not meet with immediate and outstanding success, but the first day of 1725 did mark a notable event in the baptism of the first believing Greenlander. A new threat appeared with the death of King Frederick IV in 1730, for his successor recalled the expedition, and a question hung over Egede's own future. After much heartache and a plea to the new King he and his small band of helpers were allowed to remain.

This period of uncertainty gave rise to a new crisis from an unexpected source. Under the mistaken impression that Hans Egede was giving up the work, the Moravian leader, Count Zinzendorf, sent a man called Christian David to carry on the work he had begun. Relationships between the two missionaries were far from cordial. Differences in personality and in background seem to have accounted largely for what ill feeling existed. David found Egede's approach to be lacking in love, while Egede thought David's gospel too sentimental. It was a contrast between the 'hard' and the 'soft' methods of evangelism. Missionary authority Stephen Neill thinks that this kind of conflict is not uncommon when a new missionary enterprise appears on the same field as an older one. 'The newcomers pick on the weaknesses of the old, with little regard for what the pioneers have endured.' The effect of such disunity on the natives is easy to imagine.

The frequently mysterious providence of God manifested itself remarkably in the year 1733. The ship that arrived in Godtháb carrying good news of the King's decision to support the missionary work carried something else as well—smallpox. A Greenlander visiting Denmark had contracted the disease and it was not until his return home that it was realized what the illness was. By then it was, of course, too late. Hans Egede revealed a side of his character and an aspect of the gospel that had remained hidden until that moment. He and his wife cared tirelessly for their people, going to homes that no one else dared enter, tending the sick, comforting the frightened, and above all receiving the orphans into his own home. The impression left upon the natives by such devotion became clear after the disease had finally receded. One dying Greenlander, who had disdained the gospel previously, now spoke of being able to 'die gladly' as a result of seeing evangelical words translated into actions. There is no doubt that he spoke for many others. The decimating effect of the plague resulted in the death of between two and three thousand out of a population of twelve thousand. It took its toll of Hans Egede, his wife never really recovering, and surviving only until 1735.

His own health declined at this time, so that he was not able to preach at the services at the settlement. His spirit too showed unhappy strains. Missionaries are as likely to have feet of clay as others, and Hans Egede showed an ugly bitterness at the prosperity that attended the efforts of the Moravians. He accused them of reaping where he had ploughed, apparently forgetting the great truth emphasized by the apostle Paul that one sows, another reaps, but God gives the increase. Depression and melancholy were no strangers to him. His time in Greenland was clearly drawing to a close, and in August 1736 he looked for the last time at its beloved 'icy mountains'.

His remaining twenty years, in Copenhagen, were by no means spent in idleness. He was appointed Superintendent of a seminary for training missionaries to Greenland, and he was employed in writing, including translation work. He and his son Paul produced an aid to the grammar of the language of Greenland and also a Greenlandic-Danish-Latin dictionary. He was happy as he saw all his children settle in Christian service, but there can be no doubt that his chief delight was in seeing the work in Greenland safe in Egede hands.

An experienced traveller, sent on an expedition to Greenland when Egede was there, found him to be something of an enigma. Why should a man spend his best years in the wastes of such a harsh country? What was the ambition that kept him there? Was it the desire to make a name for himself? Was it the hope to make his fortune by trading with the Dutch? The traveller's verdict is worth recording:

> I have come to the conclusion that he has no inclination for any such thing and only, as he says, wishes to live and die here in order to teach the savages the knowledge of God . . . such a man is worth his weight in gold.

3
David Brainerd
(1718-1747)

It may easily be forgotten that some people become missionaries without crossing the sea. David Brainerd is one of that company. Expelled from his college, constantly troubled by serious illness, dead before his thirtieth birthday—to be furnished with these bare facts alone is to wonder whether he could be called a missionary at all. Is he in all seriousness worthy to be held out as an example of one of God's profitable servants? However, when this skeletal information is clothed with flesh, the figure that emerges constrains us to put our hand upon our mouth. Horatius Bonar's lines may be perfectly applied in the case of Brainerd:

> He liveth long who liveth well!
> All other life is short and vain;
> He liveth longest who can tell
> Of living most for heavenly gain.

Brainerd was born at Haddam, a village on the banks of the Connecticut river. When he was only eight, his father died, and his mother died five years later, and so David found himself an orphan at the age of fourteen. How his mournful temperament coped with this sad fact may well be imagined, for he was a man given to periods of deep sadness. Failure to take account of this feature may well leave the reader dispirited in examining his diary, from which much of the material for his life is drawn. He confessed to being 'rather inclined to melancholy', while Jonathan Edwards refers to what 'may be called an imperfection in him ... that he was, by his constitution and natural temper, so prone to melancholy and dejection of spirit'.

He first became aware of soul concern when he was seven or eight years of age. He does not appear to have been greatly troubled, however, until he was thirteen. From then on religious duties were of critical importance to him. Not only was he concerned about his own condition, but he was distressed at the carelessness of others. Praying,

22

reading the Bible, meditating, guarding his thoughts, words and actions, he had a 'very good outside'. There was an air of anguish about him all this time. The sinfulness of his heart, the worthlessness of his efforts, the justice of God in condemning him, all these truths left him short of the rest and peace which are found only in Jesus Christ. Would there ever be an end to his searching? The answer came on a Sunday evening in 1739. He was granted such an experience that it is evident he found it impossible adequately to express it in words. The sheer pleasure he found in God completely captivated him, and whereas previously he had wished for another way of satisfying the demands of the law of God than that provided in Christ, now he could not understand why everyone else did not 'comply with this way of salvation, entirely by the righteousness of Christ'.

Even before this he had set his heart on the ministry. Now, in the same year of his conversion, 1739, he entered Yale College in New Haven. It was the time in the late thirties and early forties of an extraordinary spiritual awakening in New England through men like Jonathan Edwards, the Tennent brothers and George Whitefield. God drew near to him on a number of occasions during this period, and at the beginning of 1741 there was a remarkable work of the Spirit not only upon him, but also upon others in the college. Unhappily, this time of blessing proved to be the occasion of an incident which Brainerd was ever to regret. Although he was the last man one would have regarded as intemperate in zeal, he seems to have been a member of a company of students subject to enthusiasm. On being asked for his opinion of one of the tutors, Brainerd criticized unwisely and in an uncharacteristic way. The report came to the ears of the college authorities, and Brainerd was expelled in the following year with a few months of his course still to run.

From the time of his expulsion he went to live with a Mr Mills, a minister under whom he completed his studies. His diary for this period reveals a number of features. His feelings changed rapidly from one extreme to the other, from gloom in contemplating his spiritual condition to joy in the presence of God. Again, there was an intensity in his praying resulting in his sweating even in the cool breeze. It is hard to find in the records of the glorious history of the Church of anyone who prayed with greater fervour and passion, and with more exhausting physical effects, than Brainerd. Once more there were longings for heaven which could scarcely be contained. Perhaps most importantly other longings first become apparent at this time—those for the heathen.

In July 1742 he received his licence to preach, and in November was appointed to work among the Indians by the Society in Scotland for the Propagation of Christian Knowledge, one of several British missionary societies who supported the work of evangelizing the American hinterland. He took this as an indication that he should dispose of what had been left him of his father's estate. This he did by devoting it to the expenses for the training of a young friend for the ministry. He was enabled to do this to the end of his life and the completion of the young man's course.

It was in April 1743 that he came to a community of Indians in the forests at Kaunaumeek, and stayed in a rude cabin, a short distance from the Indian village. His mood at times was one of utter dejection. The immensity of the task and his own inadequacy combined to reduce his spirits to an unbelievably low plane. The recurring theme of his own vileness surfaces here, not for the first time, and before he had spent two weeks among the Indians, his diary recorded the astonishing words regarding his preaching, 'Longed to be excused from that work.' Nevertheless his sense of vocation had not entirely deserted him, and is reflected in his reference to the Indians as 'my people'.

His circumstances did nothing to relieve his darkness. His only conversation was with his interpreter, his diet was poor, his bed a bundle of straw. He was hated by the Dutch because he had come to preach to the Indians. It may well be that other missionaries suffered as much, perhaps more. What makes Brainerd's case so pathetic is that his temperament served only to plunge him into deeper gloom. This is not to say that he lay down under his burdens. It was at this time that he wrote, 'I felt contented with my circumstances, and sweetly resigned to God.' He was a tireless worker in spite of suffering illness and pain. He travelled extensively in pursuing his labours, scorning the most severe weather. Jonathan Edwards comments again on this feature, that he was 'excessive in his labours', and did not take sufficient account of his infirmity as he went about his task. He attempted far more than he ought to have done. During the years that he spent at Kaunaumeek he was refused his degree by Yale College, in spite of apologizing for his conduct, unless he returned there for another year. This was a blow he felt intensely.

When in the spring of 1744 he left Kaunaumeek it was not a case of abandoning his people. He persuaded them to move and to attend the preaching of another of God's servants at nearby Stockbridge. Nor did he seek a more comfortable existence. Declining invitations to a more conventional ministry as pastor in a pleasantly situated town at Long Island, he crossed the Hudson River and rode a further hundred miles through wild country to the vicinity of the Forks of Delaware. His first day was no more encouraging than at Kaunaumeek. The Lord's Day was not observed, the prospects appeared grim, and once more he was longing for death as his release from sorrow. Yet, despite his depressions, Brainerd was happy to be in the place of God's choosing. Preaching to the Indians meant removing prejudices against Christianity. To this he applied himself, as also to presenting the gospel to Irish and Dutch settlers in the area.

There was an interlude in his work while he was ordained at Newark, and then his return to Delaware was delayed by illness. The crippling alliance of physical pain and spiritual depression seem never to have been far away. Even then it is surprising and refreshing to discern shafts of light piercing through his longing for death, as in this entry in his diary, in July 1744:

> Last year, I longed to be prepared for a world of glory, and speedily to depart out of this world; but of late all my concern almost is for the conversion of the Heathen; and for that end I long to live.

Visits to the Susquehannah River, about a hundred miles to the west, and preaching to seven or eight tribes there, along with his evangelism at the Forks of Delaware, resulted in a readiness to hear, and also in some concern and conviction among the Indians. One of those so affected was the native who acted as Brainerd's interpreter, but mention of any conversions is not easy to find.

The summer of 1745 saw a significant turning point in his career. He travelled south-eastward for some eighty miles to a place called Crossweeksung, and there his yearnings for the people were to be abundantly gratified.

He was met with immediate encouragement. Although his first sermon was delivered to a small handful of women and children, when he told them he would preach again the following day, they travelled some ten or fifteen miles to inform their neighbours. This visit lasted for about two weeks. During that time the number who came to hear him increased from seven or eight to about fifty. Their eagerness was remarkable, and after a few days, they were asking him to preach to them twice a day. It appears that two of the Indians had been at the Forks of Delaware, and the report they brought back had kindled the interest of those at Crossweeksung. He was heartened still further on his return to the Forks of Delaware, where he baptized his interpreter and his wife, the first among the Indians. Whereas previously the truths he had been conveying to the Indians meant little to him, now when Brainerd had finished preaching, the interpreter would repeat and press home those same truths.

Longing to be back in Crossweeksung he was there again in August, having left at the beginning of July. The change in their conduct became very clear—they would not eat until he had said grace, and even that moved some to tears. Their conversation seemed to be all about the gospel, and their concern was that 'Christ should wipe their hearts, quite clean'. Tears were commonplace, and some were unable to sit or stand, but were prostrated, instances of occasions when the presence of the Spirit came with physical force. Old and young were humbled and bowed down. Not only drunkards, but little children were made very aware of their sinfulness. One woman who came out of curiosity and scoffed at the whole matter cried out for mercy before the sermon was over. Not only Indians but white people were similarly affected. On the last Sunday in August 25 Indians were baptized.

He now felt that he must go to Susquehannah once again. His request that the Indians at Crossweeksung pray for him was so eagerly received that after he left them before sunset, they prayed until morning. Passing through the Forks of Delaware he came to Susquehannah. Shaumoking, on the river, proved to be in the grip of the devil. Although the Indians were friendly to him, he was discouraged by their revelry and drunkenness. Even so he gathered fifty people together to hear the gospel. Juneauta, a town further down the river was much worse. A heathen sacrifice, with its associated dancing and extravagance left him greatly distressed, particularly when such behaviour occupied them for many hours on the Lord's Day.

Crossweeksung was a haven to him on his return after an absence of a month, especially when he remembered that those to whom he now came had once been as ungodly as those whom he had left. By November he could number 47 Indians whom he had baptized, 35 from Crossweeksung and the rest from the Forks of Delaware. Among the lessons that he learnt from this work of God was the fact that God began the work at a time when Brainerd had least hope. He was also constrained never to think after this that any man's salvation was an impossibility. One danger that did present itself was that now people were inclined to regard it as a matter of shame that they were not Christians, and therefore were tempted to appear to be so in order to be considered respectable.

Brainerd saw the necessity of having his Indians lead a more settled form of existence. Instead of hunting, cultivating the ground would prove a more secure source of food. Along with this would go the benefits of living together, worshipping on a more regular basis, and having a school which he proposed to establish among them. He was also made aware of the readiness of his people to partake of the Lord's Supper. Accordingly Sunday 27 April 1746 was set aside for this purpose. This was preceded by a day of prayer and fasting, two exercises upon which he laid much emphasis in his own personal devotion. On this day the people were reminded of the solemnity of the undertaking and were exhorted to pray for God's work, which Brainerd considered was in danger of decline. When the ordinance was observed, so near did God draw that Brainerd owned, 'Never did I see such an appearance of Christian love among any people in all my life.'

Another journey to Susquehannah was proposed. He was evidently physically unfit for the ride, for he was now coughing blood. Nevertheless he went, driving himself in spite of weariness and weakness, being forced sometimes to sleep in the open. Riding was now a great effort for him, and there were occasions when he was unable to preach, so infirm was he. On his return he could do little, being distressed at seeing how disconsolate the Indians were, having none to preach to them.

He determined to seek rest, and so rode to Elizabeth Town. He was so ill there that he could go no further. Here he remained for four months. He paid one more visit to Crossweeksung in March, spent a night with the Indians, and left them for the last time. His health now declined more quickly, although he was encouraged by doctors to continue riding. He stayed in Northampton, and was able to journey to Boston. He was struck with further illness, losing the power of speech, and on more than one occasion his friends gathered around what they thought would be his death-bed. His last months were spent in the home of Jonathan Edwards, at Northampton, Massachusetts, where he was visited by his brothers Israel and John. The night before his death, in spite of being in much pain, he spoke earnestly with John, who carried on the work, concerning the needs of the Indians. He was no stranger to suffering but what he endured that last night seems to have been unusually severe. It was not to be protracted, and at six o'clock in the morning it terminated. In his twenty-ninth year David Brainerd's longing to go to heaven had been granted.

Oswald Smith has a short biography entitled *David Brainerd, Man of Prayer*. It is right to indicate this feature of his ministry in this way. There can be no doubt that what enabled him to endure and what brought him such success as he saw was his utter dependence on God. In his last letter to his brother he writes:

> I must press you to pursue after personal holiness, to be as much in fasting and prayer as your health will allow, and to live above the rate of common Christians.

No one was better fitted to give such counsel than he was. But if he was a man of prayer he was also a man of suffering. Some bodily affliction is inescapable, but Brainerd appears to have brought much upon himself. It is to this attitude that Jonathan Edwards was referring when he remarked that Brainerd did not take enough care of himself. This poses the pertinent question that although it is good to be eaten up with the zeal of God's house, when does that zeal become irrational and intemperate, and do harm rather than good to the cause of God? But then, in today's generation that question may well be academic rather than practical.

Prayer and suffering may well be the two words that best express the life David Brainerd lived. It is significant that they are also two of the words most people would use to express the life of his Master. Let his own words describe the prevailing passion of his short life:

I saw so much of the excellency of Christ's kingdom and the infinite desirableness of its advancement in the world, that it swallowed up all my other thoughts, and made me willing, yea, even rejoice, to be made a pilgrim or hermit in the wilderness to my dying moment, if I might promote the blessed interest of the great Redeemer.

4
Christian Schwartz
(1726—1798)

To Martin Luther belongs the honour of breaking the chains that bound Germany in the prison of ignorance and superstition. The following century saw the land in danger of being overtaken by another captivity, that of a barren intellectualism. The great reformer would scarcely have recognized the legacy he had left to the world.

To the rescue came the spiritual movement known as Pietism. With it the warm, passionate heart of evangelicalism began to beat again and its dying form began to stir. The name chiefly associated with its beginnings is that of Philip Jacob Spener. Alarmed at the religious condition of people about him he gathered young men around him, prayed with them, and taught them the Bible. Soon he began to lecture on biblical subjects. In the year 1695 a university was founded at Halle and was soon to become the centre of Pietism. One of Spener's pupils and intimate friends was August Hermann Francke. He displayed a keen interest in the welfare of children and established an orphanage at Halle. John Wesley visited the orphanage and George Whitefield was encouraged by Francke's example to do a similar work in Georgia. Other similarities show that Methodism is a near kinsman to Pietism.

It displayed its pedigree as an authentic work of God in another direction. Missionary fervour soon became evident and men emerged from Halle with their hearts set on taking the gospel to other countries. India was perhaps foremost in their minds, but the German colonies in America were not forgotten. One of the first and most noble of this company was Christian Schwartz.

Born in Brandenburg in 1726 he made an early acquaintance with the hardships of life when his mother died before he was many years old. Even so he was privileged in that she was a devout and godly woman whose concern was that he should not be prevented from serving God in the study of theology if that should be his desire. To this end she extracted a promise from her husband and her pastor while she lay dying. From the course his life followed it appears that her longings for her son were fulfilled.

Under the influence of a tutor at his school he received a number of religious impressions. Two serious illnesses constrained him to make resolutions regarding his spiritual interests, but as is often the case these seemed to come to nothing. After leaving the school he was brought to the attention of the man who was, under God, to have a major part in directing his future, for he travelled to Halle where he studied under Francke at the university and lodged at the orphanage. At the Orphan House he was appointed to instruct the youth and to lead prayers, and in the course of his training Schwartz was selected to learn Tamil in order to help in translating the Bible into that tongue. The diligence with which he approached the task so impressed Francke that he encouraged him to become a missionary. Schwartz's willingness was soon translated into action and in July 1750 he arrived at Tranquebar in south-east India under the auspices of the Danish Mission College.

He spent many years here before moving to Trichinopoly, some miles to the west, where the work was under the direction of the Society for Promoting Christian Knowledge. A new mission station had been established there and Schwartz was asked to preside over it. The work proved demanding even for such an unrelenting spirit as his, and he found it necessary to appoint native converts as catechists, whose task included helping him in teaching and evangelism. His stay here, however, was not to be permanent. As he surveyed the surrounding districts and paid visits to some of them, he became increasingly occupied with one in particular. Tanjore attracted him more than any other. There was already a congregation there but he longed to make a greater impression on it. His first attempts to procure land there were met by rebuffs, but he was not a man to take such disappointments, and God was to reward his perseverance. For this was to be the scene of his most enduring triumphs, and as it proved, his last resting place on earth.

Both Scripture and history record that God's servants are to expect persecution, and it often proves to be the case that the more faithful the service the greater the opposition. Thus it was with Christian Schwartz, but the source of his opposition was not so much the Indians

Christian Friedrich Schwartz

as the Jesuits. While the latter sought to hinder his work the former for the most part 'heard him gladly'. There was one occasion when heathen hostility threatened the native Christians but Schwartz encouraged them to manifest a Christian demeanour and the enmity disappeared. This is not to say that the Hindus were converted readily. The missionary writes, 'They readily own the superior excellence of the Christian doctrine; but remain in their deplorable errors for various frivolous reasons.' This complaint he registered on more than one occasion.

He kept a very close and fatherly eye on the catechists in their demanding excursions. Every morning he gathered about him those who were within distance, instructing them how to present the gospel without arousing unnecessary antagonism, and to employ the soft answer that turns away wrath. After prayer and meditation on the Scripture he would send them on their appointed journey. The end of the day would see him awaiting their return so that he might share in their joy or their sorrow. The morning's devotional pattern would be repeated and they retired to their rest.

In true Pietist tradition he had a deep concern for the material welfare of the people as well as their spiritual state. Poor widows received his eager attention, and he was instrumental in erecting houses for them. The establishment of schools was of immense importance to him, and he had more than one end in view in his system of education. It was his intention that the children taught in the schools might learn English to facilitate their dealings with Europeans and enable them to avoid being exploited. Naturally he had evangelistic motives also, but it is important to realize that he was insistent that no unfair methods be employed and no undue pressure be brought to bear upon the pupils to influence them for the gospel. Schwartz was careful that this objection be removed before it arose and gained credibility.

He never married, and his attitude to those who did, particularly missionaries, would certainly raise a few eyebrows today, if not then. He urged the state of celibacy on his colleagues, and whatever disagreement his opinion on the matter might provoke his motive was of the highest possible order. Opinion and motive were both made plain when, on being informed of the arrival in India of a missionary accompanied by his wife, he wrote somewhat tartly:

> I confess, dear Sir, I was grieved at it . . . If one should enter into that state after he had become qualified for his office, the difficulty would be less; and, even then, he ought to be well assured of her real piety, otherwise she will be a sore impediment to him in the discharge of his duty.

His unmarried state did not mar his relationship with children. No doubt his early experience at Halle orphanage endeared them to him and, it appears, him to them. A letter written to the children of a friend of his who had recently died is very touching and reveals his eagerness that they should grow up to be Christian. It also contains much wisdom in the forceful encouragement it gives them to please their mother by their cheerfulness and willing obedience. As he lay severely ill a few months before his death it was his delight to have the children gathered about him for evening prayers.

It is remarkable how wide was his influence. He interested himself in the military garrison at Tanjore and gained serious attention from the soldiers, many of whom attended the Sunday services as well as the week-night lectures. The officers commented that 'corporal punishments had ceased from the time that the regiment began to relish religious instructions'. This contact resulted in his being asked to undertake a diplomatic mission to defuse a situation that looked like developing into something very dangerous indeed. On another occasion, when three years of famine and war brought devastating consequences, Schwartz came to the rescue. Joseph-like, he succeeded in setting aside a store of rice, and in time of deepest need was able to feed many who were at the point of starvation. Then there was the time when circumstances in Tanjore were such that the people left the country. When the situation improved and the people were encouraged to return they were very reluctant to do so. The efforts of the Governor, and even the Rajah, proved vain. Here again Schwartz showed his worth. Where the authority of princes and rulers had failed, his word accomplished the return of 7,000 in one day.

That anyone should want to criticize such a man seems strange, yet he found himself obliged to justify his work and his fellow missionaries. Montague Campbell, a man who had come out as private secretary to the Governor of Madras, found reason to make certain adverse comments which were later published. Schwartz was stung into action and stoutly defended himself. He rejected the unfounded accusation of theft of his property committed by a Christian; praised and vindicated his catechists and other Christians; spoke of how he had been asked to see that justice was administered correctly; and of how all agreed that conditions generally had improved largely through the efforts of the Christians. The water-courses had been cleansed under his inspection and profits had increased. He wrote:

No inhabitant has suffered by Christians; none has complained of it. On the contrary, one of the richest inhabitants said to me, 'Sir, if you send a person to us, send us one who has learned all your ten commandments.'

Christian Schwartz remained active until the last year of his life when his strength visibly declined. He was afflicted mentally and physically. He had the great satisfaction of having his European helpers around him as well as his beloved Indian colleagues. His conversation was constantly of spiritual affairs. 'Doctor,' he said to one who waited on him, 'in heaven there will be no pain. . . O! dear doctor, let us take care that we may not be missing there.' On 13 February 1798 he died aged 71. His deeds followed him even here on earth, for some years after his death the Rajah established homes and institutions for the care and maintenance of Christian children and handicapped folk.

The inscription on the monument erected in his memory at Tanjore by the Rajah is itself an eloquent testimony to the high regard in which he was held. It also serves as a compressed biography. Indeed, so concerned was he to decrease that his Master might increase that little material for an extended biography is available. His insatiable passion was that men and women might come to 'an interest in the atonement of Christ, and a participation in the graces of the Spirit'. An impression of the brevity of life meant that thoughts of heaven—and of hell—were never far from his mind, 'Eternity, awful eternity is at hand. Let us, therefore, not trifle away our time.'

Martin Luther would have approved.

5
Thomas Coke
(1747-1814)

It is sometimes held out—and quite rightly—as a tribute to George Whitefield that in the service of Jesus Christ he crossed the Atlantic on thirteen occasions. Whereas comparisons are odious, it is fitting to remember that another Methodist, Thomas Coke, accomplished the same feat on a further five occasions, and that it was on a voyage to India for the same purpose that he met his end. He may not answer to the traditional description of a missionary, but it is unquestionable that in his heart the impulse to evangelize was a fire that would not be quenched. It is to him, more than any other, that Methodism owes its missionary character, and from him that it learnt the far-reaching extent of the great commission.

The powerful evangelical forces that were released in the eighteenth century were already well under way when Coke was born in the pleasant Welsh rural town of Brecon. About ten miles away lay Trefeca, birthplace of Howell Harris. To the north was Builth, near which in 1736 the first of the society meetings in Wales was established. Two years later Harris records:

> Our country seems budding now. In our county 2 societies; 3 or 4 in Monmouthshire, some likely to be in Glam. and Montgomeryshire, 2 or more in Carmarthenshire, 1 in Herefordshire, vast many in Cardiganshire.

In South Wales in 1740 Harris reckoned that there were about fifty such groups meeting. It is perhaps not surprising that Coke should have become a Methodist, surrounded as he was by such influences. What is more surprising is that he should have become a Wesleyan Methodist rather than a Calvinistic Methodist like the majority of his countrymen.

He was born into a well-respected family, his father at various times serving as a doctor and later as a magistrate in the town. He grew up as an only child, following the deaths of two brothers who had died before his birth. He was educated at two famous institutions of that and the present day, the College in his home town and Jesus College, Oxford. Inevitably he became acquainted with the temptations of university life, but their attractions were cancelled by a sense of disgust when he encountered them in their grosser forms, and he was able to escape the snares to which many others fell victim. As well as the moral danger, another, not unexpectedly, threatened him. Although not a Christian at this time he held traditional views regarding the truth of the Bible. Now for the first time those beliefs were called in question, and while he sought to defend them he found himself becoming an object of scorn and laughter. For a while he surrendered his convictions, but before he left college he recovered them, and a change for the better was already becoming evident.

In 1768 he returned to Brecon where he was elected chief magistrate. He did not consider this a permanent arrangement, for during the three years for which he occupied this responsible post he never lost sight of his intention to take holy orders. Although his circumstances enabled him to purchase a situation to his liking he shunned such a dishonourable course, and refusing the easy options which were open to him became curate of South Petherton in Somerset. Like his godly mentor John Wesley he found himself in the ministry of the gospel before he had come under its saving power. But the great change was not far off.

The seriousness of his undertaking was not lost upon Thomas Coke. Very soon the awareness of his inability to discharge the responsibility was revealed to him. Again the likeness to Wesley became startlingly apparent. Both knew they had been sent to convert others but both knew that questions had to be asked about their own conversion. A book and a man were used by God in dealing with Coke. The book was Joseph Alleine's *An Alarm to the Unconverted* and the man was Thomas Maxfield, a clergyman who was staying in the neighbourhood. While he read the one and conversed with the other the light dawned upon him and he came to an assurance of salvation.

The consequence was soon evident. The fire so burned in his soul that he put aside his notes and gave his thoughts free utterance. The first time he preached in this manner three people found peace with God. The congregation wore a new aspect, and formality gave way to life. The building became too small to accommodate the worshippers, and the curate expressed his desire of adding a gallery to the premises. This enthusiasm was not at all to the liking of many of the leaders in the church, and they disapproved of the transformation in the character of the man whose virtues, when he first came, included being a 'clever whist-player'. By now, however, Coke was irrepressible, and so he employed a builder to make the necessary alterations, paying for the work out of his own pocket. This was not the last time that he was to use his own money to further the cause of the gospel.

Opposition continued to mount until his adversaries levelled against him what they must have thought was the worst indictment of all. They branded him a 'Methodist'. This was certainly something he had not bargained for—after all, he was not really sure what a Methodist was. He read the writings of Wesley and of John Fletcher of Madeley, and discovered that his heart was beating in time with theirs. In 1776 he met with Wesley for the first time, and his counsel was that he should remain in his present circumstances for the time being. His ministry was now conducted less along Anglican and more along Methodist patterns, with the result that he was dismissed by his rector at the instigation of his enemies, even though his congregation at this time numbered a thousand. Two alternatives were now before him—to seek a fresh charge or to throw in his lot with the Methodists. After further consultation with Wesley, he chose the latter course and in 1777 bade farewell to the Church of England. From this time the friendship of the two men deepened, and although Coke was nominally stationed at London, he was by no means confined there. He began a life of travelling and evangelizing, often in the company of Wesley. He must have appeared something of a godsend to Wesley, now in his eighties, and took much of the burden from him, acting frequently in the capacity of a secretary as he attended to much of his correspondence.

Methodism was nothing if it was not evangelistic, and if its evangelistic burden gave it a missionary ache, then its first mission field must be America. After all, John Wesley himself was a missionary, and that to America. After his return to England and his conversion he continued to show a great interest in the colonies and sent missionaries to work among and with the Christians there. The most important of these was Francis Asbury, whose contribution to American

Methodism was immense. A few years after his arrival in 1771, the Methodists were thrown into turmoil by the War of Independence. Wesley urged his people to be loyal to the crown, and all but one of the missionaries returned home, the exception being Asbury. This meant that the Church of England, from whom the Methodists had not separated, had to sever all its connections with America, and left the fifteen thousand American Methodists without an ordained minister. With no one to administer the sacraments, what was to be done for them? Wesley felt there was only one course open to him, and he took it. Thomas Coke was ordained superintendent of the Methodists in America and invested with authority to ordain preachers when he arrived in that continent.

Coke's first voyage to America was in 1784. No time at all was lost in setting to work, for on his first evening in New York he was required to preach, as he was on each of the following days. The period between his arrival at the beginning of November and the calling of the Conference on Christmas Eve in Baltimore was entirely occupied. He met Asbury who informed him that he had arranged an itinerary for him of a thousand miles, and his travels took him over Delaware, Virginia, and Maryland. At the Conference Coke's appointment was recognized and Asbury was ordained to serve as superintendent with him, the title 'superintendent' later to be changed to 'bishop'. Although most of his time was spent in evangelizing and pastoring, he also gave himself to the tasks of ordering the government of the new Methodist Episcopal Church, and the education of the young by promoting the establishment of a college (appropriately named Cokesbury) near Baltimore. The evil of slavery could not escape his attention, and he secured an interview with George Washington in order to discuss the problem.

His return to England in 1785 was certainly no respite, for he was as busy in Britain as he was across the Atlantic. Here again his travelling and preaching took up most of his time, and all the while there was the concern to make Christ known everywhere. Two years previously he had issued his *Plan for the Society for the Establishment of Missions among the Heathens.* Nor was he content simply to dream up schemes for others to adopt. While he brought before men the needs of Africa and India, he took the very practical step of raising funds by begging from door to door. He also made time to visit the

Channel Isles to prepare for missionaries to enter France, where the rumblings of discontent presaged the revolution that was to burst on the world before the decade was out. Involved as he was in so many journeys and voyages, it was to be expected that events would not always turn out as he had hoped. His second visit to America was to be by way of Nova Scotia. Plans had to be altered, however, when violent storms drove the vessel to the West Indies. Undismayed by this circumstance, he used the occasion to further the work already undertaken there. In fact, in 1792, while William Carey was still arguing his case in Kettering for missionary initiative, Coke had fourteen missionaries on seven West Indian islands, ministering to almost seven thousand communicants, only 136 of whom were white. He did not know what it was to hang his head in dismay when intentions were not realized. His purposes were never abandoned; merely amended.

The limitations of space forbid anything approaching a detailed account of Coke's nine visits to America. He and Asbury were the moving spirits behind a work which was to grow among the Indians. The Caribbean islanders welcomed him warmly and were grateful for his efforts on their behalf when, as sometimes happened, there were outbreaks of persecution. These efforts took him to Holland in order to plead the cause of the Christians on one of the Dutch colonies. But he not only brought encouragement; he received it as he saw the development of the work of God in their communities. A visit to France proved untimely. Ireland profited from his labours, and he was not forgetful of his native Wales. When he was not actually engaged in the work as a missionary, concern for those who served in that office constantly occupied him. He stirred up interest in them, solicited support for them, gave sacrificially his own money as well as time to them, and was in every respect what his biographer calls 'the pioneer or companion of the missionary'. He threw himself into the work of the infant Sunday school movement, and at the same time was attentive to the needs of soldiers and sailors. In the wars with the French he was most solicitous about the condition of the prisoners of war:

> There are now, I suppose, 60,000 French prisoners in England. Brother Toase is remarkably useful among many of them. Should he not be set at liberty to devote himself to their salvation here and there?

In the evangelistic enterprise nothing was beyond his compass. His first, indeed his only question, seemed always to be, How could Jesus Christ be suited to meet the circumstance? At home and abroad his sole design was to show that there was no situation to which the gospel was not the answer.

There were times when his zeal led him to make unwise statements and promises. After independence was gained by America he signed a congratulatory letter to Washington. This brought him under a cloud with the Americans, who thought this was a double-minded attitude for him to take, and with the British, who understandably felt aggrieved that one of their number should speak in such glowing terms of a 'glorious revolution'. On another occasion he dedicated himself entirely to the service of the brethren in America, in order to relieve the ageing Asbury of some of his responsibilities. At this time Wesley had died and the Methodists at home became increasingly aware of his value to them, and so he sought to be released from his commitment to the Americans. They were gracious enough to grant him his request. As well as revealing his willing spirit, this episode also displays clearly the high regard in which he was held on both sides of the Atlantic.

His ninth and final voyage to America was in 1803. If his busy life had not allowed him time for marriage, that was no longer the case. Indeed in the years that remained to him he was twice married. The change in his domestic circumstance did not mean entry upon a life of idleness. Turning his attention from the Atlantic Ocean was only the occasion for turning it to the Indian Ocean. There were two obstacles in the way of his going to India, one was the deep-rooted hostility of the East India Company, the other the inadequate finances of the Methodist Connexion. Once more Coke's rashness appeared. Hearing that there was the possibility of the Church of England settling a bishop in India, Coke offered himself for the bishopric. He scarcely thought that his breach with the Anglican communion and his devotion to the Methodist cause was any reason to deny him. Again he found himself the object of unjust but understandable accusations, one of personal ambition, and the other of treason against Methodism. Undeterred as ever, he saw hope in the fact that there was an open door in Ceylon. Through this door he thought he might eventually reach his goal. Attempts were made to dissuade him on account of his age and the inability of the Methodists to finance him. So distressed was he by this lack of support that a friend who walked home with him from the Conference meeting where the issue was debated reported that he wept in the street. Nothing could move him, however, and with others ready to sail with him he declared that if the cost was beyond the means of the Connexion he would be prepared to begin the enterprise at his own expense 'to the extent of six thousand pounds'. Overcome by his passion, eagerness, self-denial, there was nothing his brethren could do but give way to him.

True to character no time was lost, no effort spared in making final preparations. The enthusiasm of the man had been undiminished by the passing years. Those who were to accompany him could not fail to be infected by the energy that he generated. The time of farewell came, bringing with it its usual compound of emotions. There was an air of finality abroad. He preached his last sermon in England, and set out on his last voyage on the last day of the last month of the year. But his indomitable optimism was reflected in the text of that sermon, 'Ethiopia shall soon stretch out her hands unto God.' The journey was not half completed when the wife of one of his colleagues was buried at sea. Dismay grew when it was apparent that the health of the leader himself was in decline. At half past five on the morning of 3 May 1814 the customary knock on the door of his cabin was unanswered. Thomas Coke's voyage had been interrupted. His plans had been changed again, but this time it was not he nor circumstances that had altered them. It was God.

42

6
William Carey
(1761-1834)

'Let me see, Mr Carey, were you not once a shoemaker?' The sneer in the question of the government official was barely concealed. The answer came with telling effect, 'No, sir, only a cobbler.'

If the aim was to abase William Carey, attempts to exalt him were similarly dismissed. When at the end of his life he grew tired of hearing his name on the lips of the admiring and well-intentioned Alexander Duff, he requested the young man that after his days he would speak not of Dr Carey but of Dr Carey's Saviour. John the Baptist's desire to decrease so that Christ might increase was commendably matched in the self-effacing missionary from Paulerspury.

It was in this Northamptonshire village where he was born that Carey spent his boyhood. Brought up by Bible-reading Anglican parents, two features seem to have distinguished him from others. As is so often the case these developed as he grew to manhood and were largely responsible for making him the man he was. He had a thirst for knowledge which showed itself in the keen interest he took in nature as well as in his wide range of reading. Secondly, he possessed an unusual determination. His sister said that he always finished what he began. Without question this was to prove an invaluable characteristic in enabling him to complete the task to which God would call him. Discounting his many accomplishments, he himself was prepared to say only this of himself: that he could plod.

After leaving school Carey was apprenticed to a shoemaker in a nearby village. There he came under the influence of a fellow apprentice, John Warr. Warr came from a family of Independents, and although neither of the young men was converted, they argued vigorously over religion, Carey representing the Church of England and Warr the Dissenters. After a period of seeking God, Warr became a Christian. Immediately he became eager to win his younger colleague to Christ, and took him to the Dissenters' prayer meetings at Hackleton.

There Carey trod a path familiar to many before and since: he came under conviction of sin, sought to please God by his own efforts, and eventually abandoned such hopes by trusting in Jesus Christ. This last step occurred on 10 January 1779, a day appointed by the king for national fasting and prayer. The sermon Carey heard that day was based on the text in Hebrews 13:13, 'Let us go forth therefore unto him without the camp, bearing his reproach.' Carey took this as a divine summons to leave the Anglicans and make common cause with the Nonconformists. Even so, in later years he was only too ready to acknowledge his debt to the famous Thomas Scott, vicar of Olney: 'If there be anything of the work of God in my soul, I owe much of it to Mr Scott's preaching, when I first set out in the ways of the Lord.'

Another four years were to pass before Carey was baptized. That was a happy occasion. Another important event had taken place in 1781—his marriage to Dorothy Plackett, five years his senior. Sadly, for more than one reason, this proved to be a burden and a hindrance, rather than a blessing and encouragement.

All the while Carey was nurturing that talent which was to make such an outstanding contribution to his life's work. He proved to be a prodigious linguist, and the signs were already evident. His first excursion into the field of languages was through Latin. Coming across some Greek words in a commentary, he enlisted the aid of someone to teach him that tongue. Soon the pupil had outstripped the teacher. Neighbouring ministers helped him with Hebrew. He found a Dutch book in an old woman's cottage and by means of it set himself to learn Dutch. He bought a French book for a few pence, and in three weeks was writing in the language. In such ways was God preparing one of his greatest missionaries.

Encouraged by his friends at Hackleton, Carey began to preach and eventually was ordained, and inducted as the minister of the Baptist church in the village of Moulton, near Kettering. Here his stipend was so meagre that he was compelled to supplement his income by working as a schoolteacher. If his preaching prospered (and people were converted under it) the same cannot be said of his teaching. Maintaining discipline over his charges proved a task beyond him. Nonetheless his biographer records of these days that his pupils sometimes saw their teacher shedding tears in a geography lesson. Pointing to different places on the map he would cry, 'And these are pagans, pagans!'

That the fire kindled in Hackleton was already burning brightly in Carey's breast was apparent to visitors to his home at Moulton. On the wall hung a map constructed out of sheets of paper pasted together by him. This indicated not only the relative position of each country in the known world but also its moral condition. Captain Cook's *Voyages* was one of his sources of information.

By the time he became minister of the Baptist church at Harvey Lane, Leicester in 1789, his zeal had gathered still more momentum. It faced its greatest obstacle from within his own Particular Baptist denomination. There he had to break the chains of hyper-Calvinism, that firmly shackled many of the people to whom he belonged. In this the way had been prepared by his friend Andrew Fuller. His book, *The Gospel Worthy of All Acceptation*, challenged those who denied that the gospel was to be offered freely, not only to the heathen, but even to the people of England. Carey also took heart from the lives of the two outstanding missionaries in America, John Eliot and David Brainerd, as well as from the writings of Jonathan Edwards.

It was in 1792 that Carey published his *Enquiry into the Obligations of Christians to use Means for the Conversion of the Heathens.* Its importance in his scheme, and in the history of missionary activity is beyond dispute. Its contents may be divided into five sections. There is the duty incumbent upon the Church to evangelize. The commission given by our Lord to the apostles is still binding. Secondly, there is a review of previous endeavours to take the gospel to those outside the boundaries of civilization, with references to Eliot and Brainerd. Then the author presents a survey of the world, giving various statistics regarding population and religion. In the fourth place Carey pleads for action, citing scriptural promises and prophecies, and indeed shaming indolent Christians by pointing to the untiring efforts of merchants to increase their profits overseas. Lastly, Carey calls for the formation of a society to prosecute the grand object and so extend the kingdom of God on earth.

If the *Enquiry* was a historic document it was accompanied by a historic sermon. The author was now the preacher. Carey's text at the Nottingham meeting of the Baptist Ministers' Association was Isaiah 54:2-4. The substance of the sermon has been immortalized in the two pithy injunctions, 'Expect great things from God. Attempt great things for God.' Even then, men seemed unmoved. In desperation

Carey took hold of Fuller by the arm and challenged him—were they still to do nothing? Fuller was won over by this ardour that would not be quietened. The result was that four months later, on 2 October 1792, in widow Wallis's parlour in Kettering, the Particular Baptist Missionary Society was formed, the forerunner of the present day Baptist Missionary Society. Its first collection, taken up there among twelve ministers, a student, and a layman, amounted to £13-2-6. Carey's dream began to be realized. A missionary society—but where was the field, and who were the missionaries?

In the event, he himself volunteered to go down to what Fuller called the 'gold mine' of India, as long as those at home held the ropes, and so it was that he sailed to Bengal in June 1793. He took with him an unwilling wife, his children—including a baby about a month old—a sister-in-law, and a fellow missionary, a doctor called John Thomas, whose presence in all candour must have been a mixed blessing. This was scarcely an auspicious beginning for a frighteningly hazardous venture. On 11 November, he set foot in Calcutta, never to return to England.

Difficulties and handicaps encountered them immediately. There was opposition from the British East India Company; there was sickness; there was John Thomas with his eccentricities. Later his son died, his wife's mental health deteriorated, and Carey himself was at death's door. He found employment as manager of an indigo factory, but this ended in 1799. Everything was a constant struggle, and it appears that gains were hard won, and maintained by even greater endeavour. All this while Carey was engaged in preaching, translating, founding a school, and establishing a church. His spirits must have soared when he heard of the imminent arrival of new missionaries from England. Two of them were to be his partners in a work that was to prove of lasting benefit. They were William Ward and Joshua Marshman. With their arrival at the turn of the century the task of achieving his goal was accelerated. Ward, a printer, and Marshman, a schoolmaster, formed with Carey the 'Serampore Trio', according to one writer, 'probably the greatest missionary team in the story of Protestant missions'. Henry Martyn's tribute to them was: 'Three such men as Carey, Marshman and Ward, so suited to one another and their work are not to be found, I think, in all the world.' The three remained together until 1823 when Ward died of cholera.

Mention of Serampore indicates the next and last step in Carey's career. About sixteen miles north of Calcutta, it became the centre of operations for the missionaries. Being under the Danish flag it gave the three greater liberty to pursue their ends. Carey, now thirty-eight years of age, moved there in 1800, and one of the first decisions the various missionary families made was to live on a communal basis. This plan seems to have avoided the pitfalls of many such experiments amd the group appears to have lived together happily. A 'Form of Agreement' was drawn up according to which the affairs of the little community were administered.

The year 1800 was memorable for another reason. There is no doubt that Carey would have marked it as very nearly, if not actually, the climax of his life in India. After seven weary, demanding years, he saw the first Indian convert, Krishna Pal. He was baptized together with Carey's own son Felix. Others followed, and by 1804 forty Indians had been baptized, among them Hindus and Muslims. Needless to say this was an incredibly important step for these adherents of other religions to take. Carey had a great passion for preaching which was married to a passion for the subject of that preaching—Jesus Christ, the only Redeemer of the world. However, he saw the supreme need for the native Christians themselves to evangelize, and declared that the weight must rest upon their shoulders.

In 1812 the little company faced a disaster that would have defeated lesser men. Fire broke out, and their printing house was destroyed. Presses, paper, books, manuscripts—many items which could not be replaced—were lost. The measure of the man is seen in his comment as he was surrounded by ruin, 'The Lord has laid me low, that I might look more simply to him.' Never one to sink in adversity, Carey took advantage of the calamity to improve the Bible translations that had been destroyed. A year later he and his friends were persuaded that they had benefited from the distressing incident by an astonishing consequence of the fire. The loss they had sustained amounted to ten thousand pounds. This had the effect of arousing the sympathy of the people of Calcutta. More, when Fuller brought the matter to the attention of the people at home, in fifty days he had raised the sum that was lost, and had to ask that no more contributions be sent.

Education was an important plank in Carey's platform. From his settlement at Serampore his time was divided between there and

Carey and his helper revising the Bengali translation

Calcutta where he had been invited to become teacher of Bengali, San-skrit, and Marathi in the Fort William College. This was after just seven years in the country! In 1806 he was elevated to Professor. In 1818 he and his colleagues saw the fruit of years of planning when they built the Serampore College. Sanskrit and Arabic were taught there as were English language and literature. Carey taught Divinity, Botany and Zoology. This was a necessary progression as a result of the schools that had come into being within a twenty-mile radius of Serampore.

Allied to his devotion to teaching and learning was his immense work in the field of linguistics and translations. It is hard to think that his work here could ever be surpassed or even equalled. Tyndale-like, his earnest desire was that the lowliest and meanest of people might have the Scriptures to read in their own language. By 1801 the Bengali New Testament was completed by him. That was just the beginning. There followed some forty translations of the Bible or part of it into the principal languages and dialects of India and the East. Without question his was the genius behind these. Six completed translations of the whole Bible, and twenty-three of the New Testament came from his hand. Grammars and dictionaries seemed to flow from his versatile pen. Here is one day in his life at that time: it began at a quarter to six with a reading of a chapter from the Hebrew Bible, and ended after eleven o'clock with the writing of a letter. Compressed into that day were sessions of translating, learning a new language, teaching at the college, examining proof-sheets, preparing a sermon and delivering that sermon. The languages that occupied him in that one day numbered six.

Nor was he merely an academic. Indeed, words such as teacher, scholar, preacher, translator are of themselves inadequate to describe him. He created the Serampore Gardens, and was the inspiration of the Calcutta Botanic Gardens. He corresponded with the most famous of the botanists of the world. Perhaps it is the value of his work in this field that is indicated by the fact that he must be alone among the missionaries of the world in having a tree named after him. There was a practical side to all this as he contributed to the solution of providing for the starving by attending to the need to grow fruit and vegetables. He fought against the hideous custom of *sati,* the burning of widows. He campaigned against infanticide, the killing of lepers, and the various ills with which Indian society and religion were afflicted. In Calcutta he established a leper hospital.

He excelled as a missionary strategist, setting up missionary stations in areas that were Hindu and Buddhist strongholds. Each station had its own sphere of operations and was responsible for further expansion. He set a pattern for later endeavours, and the London Missionary Society, the Church Missionary Society, the Methodist Missionary Society were among a number that came into being after Carey's sailing, and probably on account of it. Reading one of the Periodical

Accounts sent home by him moved Robert Haldane to sell an estate so that missionary service might profit. So many rivers streamed from such an ordinary-looking source.

Towards the end of his life financial crisis struck Calcutta and Serampore, and this inevitably affected the mission. Carey's professorship at Fort William was terminated, and since the work of the gospel had depended largely upon his income, that ministry suffered. Nevertheless the emergency was once more met by help from England. The strains were by now telling on the aged, but still active, man. In his retirement he coupled increased exercise with a revision of the Bengali New Testament. He was aware that death was not far away and wrote to his sisters that this was probably the last letter they would receive from him. To say that such a life had been full is trite, and to Marshman he said, 'I have not a single desire ungratified.' It was entirely in character for him to give clear instructions as to what was to be inscribed on his gravestone:

A wretched, poor and helpless worm,
On Thy kind arms I fall.

Humble, industrious, visionary, persevering, here is the man who owned to one of his colleagues in England that he suffered from laziness, and to another admitted to lethargy. Towards the end of his life, while he called to mind the mighty achievements and transformations seen in India, his words were whispered, 'What God hath wrought!' William Carey would have been the first to disown the title history has sometimes sought to thrust upon him, 'the father of modern missions'. Perhaps he would not have quarrelled with the equally worthy description of Serampore as 'the cradle of modern missions'.

7
Samuel Marsden
(1764-1838)

The names of many of the missionaries whose lives are recorded in these chapters will be very familiar to readers, and it is scarcely possible to think of a Christian who has not heard of them. The names of others, no doubt, will be encountered for the first time. Among them probably will be that of Samuel Marsden. This may be surprising when one considers that among his friends and correspondents he numbered such distinguished people as William Wilberforce, John Thornton, and Charles Simeon. In the political realm his name was not unknown in the House of Commons, and he wrote to Mr (as he then was) Robert Peel, drawing his attention to the case of someone who was being unfairly treated. His extensive sphere of influence was matched by his sense of responsibility for the material as well as the spiritual concerns of men and women. And whereas most missionaries restrict their activities to one country, and one kind of people, Samuel Marsden served two—at the same time. To attempt to do any justice to his character and his work, one must ransack the vocabulary for words such as 'broad', 'large', 'wide', and their synonyms.

Although he was born into a family of Wesleyan Methodists near Leeds, it was on certain evangelicals in the Church of England that he made an early impression, and he was encouraged and helped by them in seeking ordination into the ministry. To this end he pursued his education at Cambridge, and it was while he was there that he came into contact with Simeon, and formed a friendship that was to deepen in later life. He did not complete his course, however, nor did he take his degree, for he was offered the influential post of chaplain to the convict colony of New South Wales in Australia. For a student to be approached in this way was most unconventional, and at first he declined, naturally wishing to complete his studies. The offer was renewed to him and he was persuaded to accept it. It is thought that the influence of Wilberforce lay behind these overtures —a striking indication of the respect and esteem he had already gained.

Australia had been discovered by the Dutch in the seventeenth century, but it was Captain James Cook, as a result of his voyages of discovery, who drew the attention of British politicians to its potential. Even then, that potential was limited to replacing the American colonies as a convenient destination where criminals might be deported, and according to one writer on Australia, 'For the first half of its existence, White Australia was, primarily, an extensive gaol.' Another statistic records that two generations after the first settlement '87% of the Austalian population were either convicts, ex-convicts or of convict descent'. The first contingent arrived in 1787. With them went a chaplain of the Church of England. Seven years later, accompanied by his new wife, Samuel Marsden stepped ashore to begin an unusual and memorable missionary work that was to end only with his death.

The voyage from England on a convict ship served to introduce him to the kind of man (and woman) to whom he had been sent. It was an experience that filled him with distress, and the degradation to which the passengers had fallen and which they manifested on their journey is better imagined than described. The traditional idea of the constituency of the missionary certainly did not obtain in this instance. These were not people to whom the benefits of civilization had not come: these had spurned and abused those benefits. It was not the case here of heathen who had never heard the name of Jesus: these openly profaned and blasphemed that holy name. Those to whom Samuel Marsden came were not savages who had never seen a white man: these were the white man.

Shortly after arrival the couple made their home at Parramatta, a few miles from what was then Port Jackson, present-day Sydney. He was immediately invested with the office of magistrate. This was not through choice but at the requirement of the governor, whose authority was absolute. Failure to comply would have meant his enforced return to England, and sooner than that should happen he was prepared to add this burden to what was obviously going to be a demanding vocation. It needed no great gift of foresight to predict that the criminal character of the colony would mean his having to abdicate some of his spiritual responsibilities in favour of his enforced civil duties, but he had no alternative. In the event the attempt to combine both posts in one person succeeded in involving the missionary in one controversy after another. Constantly subjected to false accusations, he was obliged often to defend himself, not for the sake of his own reputation but for that of the gospel. One of the charges levelled against him was that of greed because he had availed himself of the opportunity afforded by the authorities of acquiring land. He had succeeded in developing this until it became a profitable enterprise. But how else was he to provide for himself? And furthermore it was conveniently forgotten by his accusers that much of what he gained from his efforts was used in the extension of missions in the South Sea Islands and in promoting worthwhile causes in his adopted country. The skies were further clouded for him by two tragic accidents which resulted in the deaths of infant members of his family.

It was the custom after seven years for convicts to be released. On the land that was allotted to them by the government they built their homes, and communities were established. So it was that amongst people during and after their time of punishment that Marsden applied himself with characteristic zeal. Adequate provision for female prisoners ranked highly on his list of priorities as he became aware of the abuses to which they were subjected. In this he was encouraged by no less a person than the renowned prison reformer Elizabeth Fry. His concern was not confined to the immigrants, however, and he sought to right the wrongs suffered by the Aborigines, in particular establishing a school for their orphans. His attempts to uphold principles of justice were far from gaining him universal approval, bringing his life under threat, and prospects of improvement were so meagre that a visit to England was necessary in order to call the attention of the governmnent to the state of affairs and to secure its intervention. During his stay in Britain he had the ear of some of the most powerful men in the country, and was introduced to King George III himself. His presentation of the grievances that were festering was heard and his suggestions approved. Among these was the neglected opportunity of making full use of the advantages the new colony offered. To this end he was instrumental in persuading merchants and manufacturers of the importance of developing Australia as a wool-producing nation. Most importantly in terms of his missionary achievements, this period of two years' absence proved vital. His biographer is in no doubt:

During this short visit he may be said to have planned, perhaps uncon-sciously, the labours of his whole life, and to have laid the foundation for all the good of which he was to be the instrument.

By now his vision had extended, and his purposes and hopes were not confined to Australia alone. His mind was set also on the conver-sion of the cannibals of New Zealand. He had a first-hand acquain-tance with some of the natives, for on their visits to Australia their leaders had stayed at the parsonage at Parramatta. When he shared his concern with the officers of the Church Missionary Society he found them in complete sympathy with him, differing from them on one major point. In this debate it is clear that they had the mind of Christ rather than he, for he could not be shaken from his opinion that 'noth-ing . . . can pave the way for the introduction of the gospel but civil-ization'. Notwithstanding this divergence of views, when Marsden sailed from England in 1809 it was with two colleagues. He was returning to Botany Bay; they were bound for New Zealand. In the providence of God there was another passenger destined to play an important part in the work in the new mission field—a New Zealand chieftain called Duaterra.

He was greeted by further trials, involving him in disputes with the new governor. While these inescapably diverted his attention he still threw himself into the work of the gospel. He was an early riser in order to achieve all that he had set before him for the day. This some-times meant walking fifteen miles between Sydney and Parramatta in order to conduct services in both places. His visiting took him very far afield. He would undertake tours lasting two weeks, and when he arrived at a farm neighbours from a dozen miles around would gather for a service. From this it is evident that although the image of Aus-tralia as a penal colony was some way from being altogether lost, the country was beginning to assume the face of a more normal society.

He was noted for the understanding and encouragement he offered to others, but at the same time he did not shrink from the task of exer-cising discipline when circumstances dictated, and on one of his jour-neys to New Zealand certain missionaries had to be rebuked and one was expelled. Yet when missionaries from Tahiti arrived at his home utterly dispirited from their lack of success and the dangers to which they were subjected, instead of being berated and sent back to their posts directly, they were warmly received. The hospitality and sympathy shown them soon renewed their spirits and enabled them to take up the work again. Further good came from such incidents. Marsden thought of the benefit that would come from closer communication between the scattered missionaries, and so a ship was secured for sailing between the different islands and countries. It was paid for out of his own pocket.

Towards the end of 1814 he paid his first visit to New Zealand. The welcome he received from those who a short time previously had murdered some of his fellow countrymen was an indication of how his fame had gone before him. His skill as a peacemaker was immediately required as he interceded between two warring parties. Christmas Day 1814 was a memorable one, marking the occasion of the first act of public worship in New Zealand. The part played by Duaterra in these events cannot be valued too highly, and it appears that his divinely appointed task had been accomplished, for hardly had Marsden set out to return to Australia in March than the chieftain died. The missionary felt the loss keenly, not only from the perspective of personal friendship, but also from that of the great good the native had done and might have been expected to do. The Englishman was soon made aware of the distance yet to be traversed into the territory of superstition when he learnt that the widow had hanged herself with the approval and applause of her parents and brothers. Such was the code of conduct that prevailed.

He was to go back to New Zealand on a further six occasions, during which he was very much involved in the educational and political welfare of the people, and although he was well-received he was never allowed to forget the presence of cannibalism among the tribes. In an attempt to reassure him on his second visit, he was told he need not worry about the safety of the missionaries he was leaving, since 'the flesh of a New Zealander was sweeter than that of an European, in consequence of the white people eating so much salt'. In such a bizarre fashion was he acquainted with the co-existence of the savage and the gentle among the natives. One of his letters reveals the love for them that dominated him at all times:

> What would I have given to have had the book of life opened, which was yet a sealed book to them, to have shown them that God who made them, and to have led them to Calvary's mount, that they may see the Redeemer who had shed his precious blood for the redemption of the world, and was

there set up as an ensign for the nations. But it was not in my power to take the veil froom their hearts, I could only pray for them, and entreat the Father of mercies to visit them with his salvation.

Twenty years were to pass before he saw the first conversion in New Zealand, but his enterprising spirit was never discouraged and was eventually rewarded. Not only did he see individuals changed, but also communities benefit from the influences of Christianity. He writes of sitting in a house behind which, on a previous visit, the natives had killed and eaten a young girl. One woman who spent much of her time preaching the gospel to other women confessed that before she was converted she had killed and eaten nineteen children. It is in these terms that we must evaluate the contribution of Samuel Marsden to missionary endeavour.

In 1837 at the age of 72 he paid his last visit to New Zealand, his wife having died two years previously. He was acclaimed, not to say revered, wherever he went. For all his travelling to and in the country he was disappointed to the end in one respect, and that was the failure to pacify the warring factions. The example set by Europeans certainly did nothing to help his cause, and often what the natives saw spurred them on to committing fresh crimes. Even at his advanced age he resolved to do all in his power to bring about an improvement in the situation. There was not much, however, for him to do, for his end was nearer than he thought. In May the following year he died, and was buried in the church at Parramatta.

It had been his unhappy lot throughout his time in Australia to be the victim of malicious and unfounded charges, none of which could be substantiated. While most of these seem to have been brought against him because of his attempt to fulfil the duties of magistrate, a task he had undertaken only for the sake of the gospel, at the same time his fearless denunciation of sin made him a number of enemies. A lover of his unusual and multifarious parishioners, an impartial upholder of justice, a diligent preacher of the gospel, he remained all his life a generous and humble Christian. The spirit in which he followed his Master is best expressed in his response on being told of what slanders were reported of him:

> Sir, these men don't know the worst. Why, sir, if I were to walk down the streets of Parramatta with my heart laid bare, the very boys would pelt me.

8
Henry Martyn
(1781-1812)

The two friends faced each other. Feelings were running high and
uncontrolled temper had gained the upper hand in the case of one of
them. A knife appeared in his hand and flashed across the room. Happily it failed to find its mark and buried itself in the wall opposite.
Had the aim been more accurate the course of the man destined to be
one of the Church's great missionaries would have been vastly different. Not that he would have died as a result of this fit of passion. Far
from it. For the knife was thrown by—and not at—Henry Martyn.

The prospect of a long life does not seem to have been held out to
him. Born in Truro in February 1781, he was only two years old when

his mother died from tuberculosis. His sisters were to follow her to the grave from the same cause before he himself succumbed, and by the time he was twenty-eight he was the only one of the family still alive, surviving the others by a mere two years. Like all who would win heaven, the young Cornishman had many battles to fight with himself. The episode with the knife reveals how deadly were the inward foes with which he had to contend. It also indicates how powerful was the grace of God at work within him. His brief life further shows that the victory was no narrow one but displayed gloriously the complete triumph of the gospel.

His ability to learn was soon evident, as was his lack of application. The ease with which he advanced in knowledge he took as a reason to exempt himself from hard study, and at school he acquired something of a reputation for idleness. He was not very popular, and his small physique meant that he was bullied by other boys. This turned to his advantage, for in order to meet this problem he was put under the protection of another boy, who was to prove an enduring Christian influence on his life. On another occasion a setback, which in time was similarly to benefit him, was his failure in 1795 to enter Oxford. Two years later he went to Cambridge. There he renewed acquaintance with his protector at school; there he came under the rich ministry of Charles Simeon; and there he became a Christian.

Nor was it only the agency of God's servants in Cambridge that proved critical in his life. At home he had a sister who was praying for him and who was constantly pressing upon him the urgency of being reconciled to God. This seemed to be of little avail at first, as he now appears to have become popular among other students, and to have been more and more governed by selfish ambition. The quick temper which provoked the episode of the knife drove him to use virulent language against his father and sister. His father's death at this time was the spur needed to goad him into taking up his Bible and reading it. What began as little more than a duty became in time a necessary and compulsive exercise. A sister's prayers, a friend's constancy, a vicar's preaching, and a father's death—the sum of all these was that he came to trust in Christ. Success in academic terms came to him, but significantly, in the light of his evangelical experience, he comments, 'I obtained my highest wishes, but was surprised to find that I had grasped a shadow.' Henry Martyn had come to himself.

His mind had been set on a legal career, chiefly because it offered a lucrative reward. Now he began to think more in terms of serving Christ by being ordained. William Chalmers Burns was to know an identical experience of the purging effect of grace. Friendship with Simeon acted as the catalyst in Martyn's case. There followed a period of serving as curate to Simeon in Trinity Church, and taking the oversight of a little church at Lolworth, nearby. Simeon's influence upon him was by no means exhausted, for it was an observation by him of the value of William Carey's work in India that brought home to Martyn the dire needs of unevangelized countries. It is remarkable how the names of other missionaries feature in a consideration of the life of Henry Martyn: the parallel with Burns, the example of Carey, and then the diary of Brainerd. Martyn was an avid reader and admirer of David Brainerd—indeed one is tempted to call him the English counterpart of the young American. It hardly comes as a surprise to find that as he left for India, the captain on the voyage was a pupil of the great German missionary to India, Christian Schwarz.

The brilliant young graduate by no means entered lightly on his life's work. Two factors must be borne in mind.

The first is that he was an academic with all the love of seclusion that goes along with it. The realm of books and thought, and especially languages, constantly beckoned and enticed him. It was a perpetual struggle to bring himself to confront people, at home and abroad, with their unending future and their need of the gospel of Christ. And although it was no cold sense of duty that obligated him, he did sometimes need to make an effort to remind himself of his priorities.

The second factor is that there was another, stronger love in his life. It was his devotion to Lydia Grenfell, a passion he felt compelled to describe as akin to idolatry. The root of the matter here was Martyn's failure adequately to resolve the question: did his calling require him to remain unmarried? His head seemed to say yes; his heart seems to have said no. In India, try as he would, he could not rid himself of thoughts of her, and although convinced of the rightness of his course, yearned and longed for a letter that would give her consent to join him. His friends were divided on the subject. Before he left England, Charles Simeon, who was unmarried, counselled him against taking her with him. They never saw each other after he sailed.

Such were the struggles fought on the battlefield he found his soul to be. However Henry Martyn is judged, what is evident in his life is that he overcame by the blood of the Lamb.

His way was not made any clearer to him by the fact that the powerful East India Company frowned on the work of missionaries in India. Those already out there found restrictions imposed upon them. As a result Martyn went out not under the auspices of a missionary society, but as a chaplain of the East India Company. Although this meant working mainly among Europeans, it appeared to give greater scope for working among Indians than did being a 'missionary'.

The farewell from England was a protracted affair, but it afforded Martyn the privilege of fellowship in London with John Newton. When at last he sailed from Falmouth in August 1805 it was as part of a fleet carrying five thousand troops who were to fight at the Cape of Good Hope to recover it from the Dutch. The voyage was not a particularly pleasant one; his physical weakness was aggravated by thoughts of the happiness and ease he was leaving behind. Even so he found the antidote in prayer and 'soon launched sweetly into eternity'. The route took them to Brazil, and before they reached the Cape, he was found engaged in counselling and comforting victims of dysentery on board the ship. He saw the Cape recaptured before continuing the voyage to India. The response he met on the remainder of the journey was indifference, opposition, and ridicule—a great affliction to his sensitive spirit.

Arrived in Calcutta in May 1806 he was warmly received at nearby Aldeen by a clergyman in charge of an orphanage, David Brown. This was an immense relief to the new arrival, and he entered fully into fellowship with his friend. Sixteen miles from Calcutta was the small Danish colony of Serampore, centre of the missionary work initiated by Carey. The welcome was by no means universal, even among his clerical colleagues. There was a new church in Calcutta, St John's. When he was invited to preach there Martyn's first sermon aroused considerable antagonism. It seemed no different from being on board ship again. Worse, he was attacked from the very pulpit, and his proclamation of basic gospel doctrines extravagantly undermined. This did nothing to mollify his feelings at the coarse sights and sounds of heathen outrages being committed around him. Respecting these, his attitude was unequivocal, 'If I had words I would preach to the multitudes all the day, if I lost my life for it.'

His stay here was brief, and in October he set out for the military camp at Dinapore, near Patna. Here he had been appointed, some 350 miles inland from Calcutta. The long journey up-river was spent in reading, learning other languages, translating the Book of Acts into Hindustani, conversing and disputing. He came to Dinapore with a threefold purpose: to establish schools, to preach in Hindustani, and to translate the Scriptures and prepare tracts. On acquiring a bunga-low, he devoted one room to being the church of Dinapore. The sol-diers who came had little time for him and his message, although there were some exceptions. It was at the hospital that he was most appreciated. Perhaps this was to be expected, where, far from home, people would be more open to his kindness and his ministry. There was also a work among the Indian women, camp-followers who showed some interest, but whose response largely was discouraging.

If he had taken to heart what opinions were voiced concerning him, it is doubtful if he would have achieved anything. The Europeans thought it degrading that he should be troubled about Indians. The Indians hated him because he was an Englishman. Nevertheless he was encouraged. By the early months of 1807 he had established five schools for Indian children in and around Dinapore. Fears that he would compel the children to become Christians were dispelled. By February he had translated the Book of Common Prayer into Hindu-stani, and in March had concluded a commentary on the parables. There was also a service each Sunday at seven in the morning for Europeans, another at two in the afternoon for Hindus, together with hospital visitation.

His appetite for languages was voracious. When David Brown sug-gested a translation of the Bible into Persian, he could hardly wait to begin. While this gave him great opportunity of learning new truth from God's Word he was not unmindful of the danger to which he was exposed, that of 'preferring even a work professedly done for Him, to communion with Him'. Before the year which began so aus-piciously came to an end, two items of news from England plunged him into sadness—the death of his elder sister, and Lydia's refusal to join him.

His two principal helpers in the work of translation were a Hindu and an Arab. The second of these professed to be a Christian, but was sometimes an encouragement to Martyn, and at other times a burden.

61

Assisted by them, in March 1808 he had completed a translation of the New Testament into Hindustani. The remainder of the year was spent in revising this, and also in superintending the translation into Persian. This he accomplished while suffering severe pains in his chest, and in a temperature that was rarely below and sometimes above a hundred degrees. Response to the gospel seems always to have been contempt.

By the beginning of January 1809 he was drawn by the fascination of yet another language—this time Hebrew. It was also at this time that he was appointed chaplain at Cawnpore, some three hundred miles further up the Ganges. The journey at the height of the Indian summer almost robbed him of his life. When he arrived it was an immense relief to find fellowship with a Christian family. For want of a church building he preached to a thousand soldiers in an open square, the heat carrying off some of his hearers. His letters at this time reveal the effect upon him of the news of the approaching death of that sister used by God in his conversion. The year was also marked by his first attempts to preach the gospel publicly to the heathen, a company composed of about five hundred beggars who gathered to receive food and money from him. Encouragement in this came from Sabat, his Arab helper. The result of his preaching, unknown to Martyn, was that an influential sheikh who had come to observe, was won over by the gospel. He proved to be a very useful and influential Christian.

Meanwhile he found his health an increasing handicap, and was compelled to give up some of his responsibilities. The arrival of his friend Mr Corrie from Calcutta provided him with some relief, but Mr Corrie was on his way elsewhere and so the relief was only partial and temporary. There were other factors that conspired to indicate that perhaps the time had come for Martyn to leave India, if only for a while. Obviously he needed respite: why not a voyage, or a return to England? The prospect of seeing Lydia once more could not be exaggerated. However, guidance was finally given in another manner. Martyn found preaching physically demanding—'it is speaking that kills me'. Studying was his delight, and this seemed to provide the direction in which he was to go.

The Persian New Testament was complete, and the Arabic was almost finished. This was with the help of Sabat. A proud man, he was incensed by the criticisms of the translations, but Martyn could never allow them to be distributed in an unworthy state. So, with the

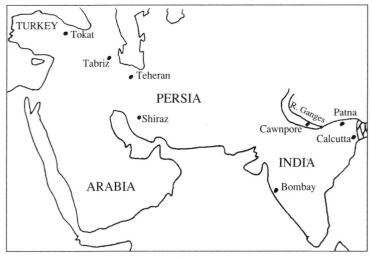

Places associated with Henry Martyn

confirmation of Mr Brown, it was decided that he should go to Persia to improve this translation and later to Arabia to complete his Arabic translation. The Hindustani version had been a success. It had been translated in India. What could be more obvious than the need to go to Persia and Arabia to complete versions of a similar calibre in those languages? In October 1810 he left Cawnpore for Calcutta. Conversation with friends served to rouse again the symptoms of the weakness that were apparent in Cawnpore. Even so he preached every Sunday in Calcutta but for one. In the first month of the following year he sailed for Persia.

During the voyage he celebrated his thirtieth birthday at Bombay. There, he reminded himself that this was the age at which Jesus began his ministry, and when John preached repentance. There was the inevitable reference to the death of David Brainerd at the same age. By this time Martyn knew that his life was to be curtailed. With all the energy he had already spent in service his journal records, 'Hitherto I have made my youth and insignificance an excuse for sloth and imbecility.'

A week after landing in Persia in May he set out for Shiraz. On the first day of the journey the temperature in the tent rose to 126 degrees. Later, all the party was shivering with cold. Safely arrived, and being assured that his Persian New Testament was of inferior quality he set about another translation. In this he had the assistance of an influential Persian who provided him with hospitality, and more particularly that of his brother-in-law, who spoke the purest form of Persian. From June to the following February, Martyn's time was spent most happily. Apart from involving himself in private and public arguments, in controverting and refuting the claims of Islam, and making the gospel a talking point amongst the highest authorities, he prosecuted the work of translation with great diligence. At the end of that period the New Testament was completed, fit to be presented to the Shah himself. For this was now the intention. If it met with imperial approval the way would be open for popular acceptance.

He left Shiraz a year after setting foot in Persia. His first object was to see the British ambassador without whom he could not hope to see the Shah. This involved a journey to Tabriz, in the far north-west of Persia, but finding that the Shah was at Teheran, Martyn thought to attempt to gain an audience there. This almost proved to be his undoing, when, challenged with the ultimatum of declaring that 'Muhammad is the prophet of God', he affirmed that Jesus was the Son of God. Enraged by this his opponents threatened to have his tongue torn out for blasphemy. His precious book he feared would be trampled underfoot. The alarms came to nothing, but it was evident that he must pursue his journey to Tabriz. Here he was doomed to disappointment, for he was again struck by fever, and thus thwarted in his ambition. However, the ambassador, Sir Gore Ousley, and his wife nursed him back to health. Sir Gore himself presented the Scripture to the Shah. It was greeted with much gratitude and favour.

His illness meant that travelling to Arabia was now out of the question. That left England. He set out for Constantinople. The journey, his last, proved too much for him. Nonetheless, it was not without its reward, and he treasured the sight of Mount Ararat where 'the whole church was once contained . . . Here the blessed saint landed in a new world; so may I, safe in Christ, outride the storm of life, and land at last on one of the everlasting hills!'

He had not long to wait. It was an impossible journey through dangerous terrain with uncongenial companions. The man ravaged by fever entered Tokat, in north-east Turkey, a town raging with plague. The result was inevitable. Like his hero Brainerd, his longing to go to God was satisfied. On 16 October 1812, he attained the summit of his everlasting hill. The student they called 'the man who had never lost an hour' had gained eternity.

9
Robert Morrison
(1782—1834)

Slum areas in major cities for a long time carried the unenviable record of being a breeding ground for the worst kind of human behaviour. The privations associated with these neighbourhoods have always been a significant factor in accounting for the vice and crime that are an unhappy feature of society. Newcastle-upon-Tyne, in the North of England, had such a district, which was able to lay claim to an altogether different distinction, for it produced two men, friends from boyhood, who were to make outstanding contributions in their particular fields. If the name of the one is better known even to Christians than the other, it is because in the scale of the world's values industrial progress is far more important than the advance of the kingdom of God. One of the pair was George Stephenson, builder of the Rocket and herald of the Railway Age; the other was Robert Morrison, first Protestant missionary to China.

Morrison's father was a Scot, and originally was a farm-labourer, but later found employment manufacturing shoemaking implements. Robert joined his father in this trade, but became dissatisfied in it. He left it for other work, only to return eventually. Although his father was a member of the Presbyterian Church this did not appear to inhibit the youth from falling a victim of drunkenness more than once. During the period away from working with his father he travelled the country with a company of strolling players. It seems to have been a shiftless kind of existence and hardly suited to his serious, rather humourless character. By the time he was fifteen he had become a Christian.

If his early pathway led in no certain direction, he later discovered where his real passion lay. It was among books. He came to love the Bible so much and to spend so much time reading it that he began to speak in biblical language. The long hours that he spent at work always found him with the Bible or some other books at hand, and he began to teach himself Latin, Greek, and Hebrew. This love of books so consumed him that he slept at the workshop in order that he might read into the small hours of the morning, and significantly, among the literature that he read were missionary magazines telling of William Carey. So fired was he by what he read that he determined to be a missionary, and to hope that God would send him to the most difficult part of the unevangelized world. His career is evidence of the degree to which God heard and answered his prayer. There could be no doubt about his motive and intention. Fifteen years after arriving in China he wrote that his aim had been 'to preach the Gospel to the heathen and convert [them] from Satan to God'.

In 1803 he moved to Hoxton Academy in London to prepare for the ministry, and the following year he attended the famous Missionary Academy of Dr David Bogue at Gosport. He made a great impression on Bogue who, along with the London Missionary Society, urged upon him the need to translate the Bible into Chinese. To this he agreed without any hesitation, requesting only that he be allowed to pursue medical studies in London. There he studied not only medicine but astronomy as well. From a young mandarin who came to live with him he learnt Chinese, and with this friend, Yong Sam-tek, he made the acquaintance of John Dyer, secretary to the Royal Hospital for Seamen, paying frequent visits to his home. Dyer's son, Samuel, developed a keen interest in China, so keen that he was to follow Morrison to the east, and his daughter Maria was one day to marry Hudson Taylor. In 1807 Morrison was ordained and received into the LMS. All the time he was intent on his goal, he was aware of pressure from his family not to go, but he was undeterred.

When the time came for sailing he found what many other missionaries discovered—the unwillingness of the East India Company to provide passage for those in the service of the gospel. Henry Martyn had landed at Calcutta in 1806 as a chaplain with the Company, but after this it had banned new missionaries from India. The Company, with its virtual control of India, and its increasing power in China, considered that the wholesome influence of Christianity would have an adverse effect as far as its more doubtful trading ventures were concerned. Adoniram Judson was another who suffered the hostility of the East India Company. The only course open to Morrison was to sail to America, and from there to India. The owner of the ship which was to take him on the final leg of the journey made no attempt to conceal his scornful attitude. 'And so, Mr Morrison,' he asked, 'you really expect that you will make an impression on the idolatry of the great Chinese Empire?' Unabashed, the pioneer replied, 'No, sir, I expect God will.' How far his expectations were realized in his own experience may be judged from the following figures. It was seven years before he saw one convert. Concerning him Morrison wrote in his journal, 'May he be the firstfruits of a great harvest; one of millions who shall believe and be saved.' During the next twenty years in fact he was to see only nine more converted, and when he died there were only three known native Christians in China. However, if God's purpose for China began with Robert Morrison, it did not end with him.

In September 1807, Canton greeted him with a grim presentation of the dangers, difficulties, and restrictions that awaited him. 'Barbarians,' 'foreign devils,' 'devil ships' were designations often on the lips of the Chinese. Foreign women were not allowed in Canton. There was a ban on the Chinese teaching their language to foreigners, death being the penalty for ignoring the prohibition. As far as any evangelization was concerned Morrison found himself constantly looking over his shoulder for the Chinese, the East India Company, and the Roman Catholic priests. Unfortunately, his burden was increased rather than lightened by the shameful attitude of the Christians he had left at home in Britain. Often he looked for the ships to bring him mail, but in vain. It seemed to him that whereas others received letters few cared to write to him. In response to one correspondent he wrote regarding 'your very welcome letter . . . but the second that I have received, after having written at least two hundred'. People would expect him to write long letters to them but would excuse themselves by saying they had little time to write. From such irresponsibility Hudson Taylor was to suffer later, and no doubt many others since. Nevertheless, although his activities had to be conducted in strict secrecy, he was far from inactive. In 1808 residents of the trading post or 'factory' in Canton moved for the summer to Macao, and he moved with them. There he succeeded in completing work on a dictionary of over a thousand pages.

His sense of loneliness was relieved when he married Mary Morton, the daughter of a doctor. Even this blessing could not be enjoyed to the full because of the attitude of the Cantonese to women, which meant that the couple had to spend much of their time apart, being together only in Macao. On the same day on which they were married the East India Company offered him employment as Chinese Secretary and Translator. This was a tribute to his proficiency in the language. Although such secular work was distasteful to him, he saw it as the provision of God. His salary would relieve the LMS of the expense of paying him, and his position with the Company would remove some of the uncertainty of the duration of his stay in China. The element of secrecy had still to be preserved, for if the British or Chinese discovered the nature of his covert activity he would have been sent back to Britain immediately. The nature of the war in which he was engaged was once more brought home to him when he was refused a portion of ground in which to bury his first child, who died on the day it was born. Only after long negotiation was he finally given permission.

Pioneer missionaries are almost by definition men and women of vision. Robert Morrison was no exception. He was interested in what was going on elsewhere, and his letters to England contained requests for information concerning the work of the gospel in the rest of the world. He encouraged and exhorted the LMS to recruit workers from America if none were forthcoming in the home country. He raised money in Macao for the work of the Bible Society in Calcutta. He envisaged an 'Anglo-Chinese College' for the training of European and Asian missionaries. He emphasised the need to make use of the printing press. All his thinking was directed to the one end of the more effective propagation of the good news of Jesus Christ. High on the list of his own priorities in this matter was the translation of the Bible. He corresponded with Carey, Ward, and Marshman regarding their efforts and was aggrieved to discover an unbecoming sense of rivalry, Marshman apparently wanting to be remembered as the first to translate the Bible into Chinese. As it happened he was successful in realizing his ambition, but the winning of the prize was a hollow victory, as was acknowledged by his own son, for the translation was of an inferior character. Once more the keynote for Morrison was secrecy, the translation and distribution of Christian literature by him and his helpers being a capital offence.

In Britain, Thomas Coke, now in his sixties, had been the means of stirring interest in the mission field. His death in 1814 on the way to India increased the interest. One of those caught up in this excitement was William Milne. A year before Coke's death Robert and Mary Morrison were holding a simple communion service in Macao when into the room came William and Rachel Milne, the colleagues for whom Morrison had longed. The joy of the four missionaries was soon tempered when Milne was required to leave Macao by the Portuguese authorities, his wife being allowed to remain because she was pregnant. His baptism of suffering came when he was unable to visit his wife when the baby was born in October. The enforced separation resulted in the further spread of the gospel, for Milne used the time to acquire some knowledge of Chinese, and travelled further afield than he would otherwise have done. After Morrison had completed his New Testament translation, Milne took copies of this along with him with tracts and catechisms for distribution. Slowly but surely the foundations were being laid and the work extended.

Mary Morrison's ill health was the occasion of a six-year period of separation when she took their two children with her to Britain. With William and Rachel Milne away in Malacca, Robert Morrison was on his own once more. He applied himself industriously as ever to translating the Old Testament, to further work on his English-Chinese Dictionary, and to a Chinese Grammar. Eventually the East India Company discovered the extent of his involvement in Christian activity and decided to dismiss him, a decision which they did not put into immediate effect because they realized that he was virtually impossible to replace. So much was this the case that when an embassy was sent to Peking, he was invited along as interpreter, an excursion that contributed greatly to refreshing his wearied spirits.

His return to Macao and Canton introduced him to fresh difficulties. The Chinese had broken into the press that was dealing with his productions; Milne was unwell; and the work that he was doing was being publicized in England, in spite of his request that his supporters should pray and keep quiet. However, if he was restricted in one direction he turned in another, and opened a dispensary. This was to develop beyond recognition in years to come. After ten years in China his achievements were considerable. To what has already been noted may be added the establishing of an Anglo-Chinese college at Malacca. In 1819 he was able to record his prize accomplishment, the completion of the Old Testament to add to that of the New, and the following year saw Mary and the children restored to him. Yet the waves of sorrow were soon to roll over him again. She had to remain in Macao while the Company demanded his presence in Canton. Worse was to come. The all-too-frequent visitor to the homes of so many of these dauntless early missionaries appeared. In 1821 she and a baby to whom she had just given birth both died. Once more he had to face the distress of fighting for a place where they could be buried. The two children had to be sent back to England, and almost a year to the day of Mary's death he lost his friend William Milne. A fire in Canton meant that the pressure of his work for the Company was eased, and he took the opportunity to travel to Malacca, where there was a congregation, never more than ten, meeting regularly; then to Penang and to Singapore. There he was encouraged by none other than the renowned founder of modern Singapore, Sir Stamford Raffles, a fine Christian.

He took his only furlough in 1823, leaving China in December on a Company ship for the voyage of fourteen weeks. The two years he spent in Britain were a time of unrelenting labour. Naturally the interests of China were uppermost in his mind. He travelled, cajoled, lectured, wrote, all to bring the need of his adopted country to the attention of his native land. He urged unmarried women to consider serving God as missionaries and trained a class of them at his home. He saw the expediency of a society to co-ordinate the study of the various languages of mankind, a vision that was to be fulfilled in the work of Cameron Townsend and the Wycliffe Bible Translators. Honours came his way during this time when he was introduced to the King, George IV, and was elected Fellow of the Royal Society, to add to the honorary doctorate he had been awarded by the University of Glasgow in 1817. At the end of the furlough, in April 1826, he returned with his new wife and two children. The matter of correspondence still weighed heavily upon his heart, and he told his friends that unless they wrote to him while he was still on ship it could be that they would not have a reply for two years.

His disillusionment with the attitude of Christians at home continued. At his death there were about eight men working in East Asia, including Charles Gutzlaff who was, according to Hudson Taylor, 'the grandfather of the China Inland Mission'. There were times when he wondered what would become of the work after his days, which he began to think were numbered. Still he laboured on in the most trying of circumstances, serving the East India Company and at the same time concealing his evangelical activities from it, seeking the good of a nation that simply would not be helped. Amid all the perils he derived great satisfaction and comfort from the energy that his son, John Robert, expended in the work. Although not a member of the mission, his heart, like that of his father, was in the welfare of the people of China. The strain of maintaining his integrity in an unusual situation, and the constant harassment from all sides were bound to take their toll. When it terminated his 27 years of employment, the East India Company did so without offering him any form of pension, although it had benefitted from his service. His health declined, as did that of his wife, and it became evident that once more separation from his cherished family was to be the order of the day. It was agreed that his wife and the younger children by his second marriage should return to England. This final chapter in his life ended perhaps as sadly as any that had gone before, for he died before hearing of their safe arrival. William Carey had gone to glory just two months before him in June 1834.

If multitudes of converts is the measure of the value of the life of a missionary, then Robert Morrison scarcely deserves mention. Thankfully it is not so, and heaven employs other criteria to judge a man's contribution. When asked, 'What do the Chinese with all their ancient civilization and wisdom require from Europe?' he replied, 'The knowledge of Christ.' It was in that spirit that he served his God, and strove to bring that knowledge to them. And if, as sometimes happens, the usefulness of missionaries to their native land is called into question, it will be sufficient to answer in the case of Robert Morrison, that when his name was mentioned in Parliament, 'the House broke into cheers'.

10
Adoniram Judson
(1788-1850)

From the moment Adoniram Judson learnt to read in a week at the age of three it was evident that he was destined for eminence. His gifts and character were such that had he not become a missionary they would have ensured for him a place of distinction in whatever role he would have chosen. Achievements were always within his grasp; the question was in which direction those achievements lay. His life was so eventful that if it was presented as a fictional account it would probably be dismissed as being improbable. Adventure, excitement, imprisonment, torture, success, despair, romance—all this and much more followed this larger-than-life figure in his endeavours to unseat the mighty Buddha from his throne in Burma.

If ambition can be instilled into a child, then Adoniram's father (after whom he was named) was responsible for the presence of the trait in his son. An obstinate, austere, Congregational minister, perhaps frustrated, he was determined that his precocious child would be accorded the place in men's esteem that he himself had been denied. Never in his wildest imaginations could he have guessed how his hopes and intentions would be realized. As Adoniram grew, always a little fearful of the image his father presented, he became aware of the burden his father had imposed upon him. Consequently, even into manhood, there seems to have been a combination, not to say confusion, of motives behind his actions.

Malden in Massachusetts provided Adoniram with the first of a number of boyhood homes. The duties of religion were impressed upon him early, and the desire to please (or fear of displeasing) his father meant much to him. When he entered Brown University on Rhode Island, however, other influences carried him along and soon he slipped his moorings. Deism and unbelief beckoned and the charmed student succumbed. On leaving college he found teaching and writing did not satisfy him, and he determined on another course.

Adoniram Judson

So far he had kept his persuasions secret from his parents. The effect the news had on them is better imagined than described. He saw that home was becoming a prison to his restless spirit, and freedom would have to be sought outside its walls. He set out for New York, intending to 'write for the stage'.

This expedition, so exciting in prospect, soon ended in disillusion, and after five weeks he was back at home. One incident during this period had shaken the fortress of rationalism that he had built around himself. He had spent one night in an inn, sleeping in a room next to a dying man. During the night the man had died. On inquiring as to who the man was, Judson was shocked to discover that he was one of his closest companions at college—a convinced antagonist of Christianity. Adoniram Judson knew that Jacob Eames was lost; he also knew that the same was true of himself. It was a very sober man who returned to his parents.

A new theological seminary had been established at Andover, and here Judson was admitted, although not yet converted. It was recognized that if he became a Christian he could be a minister without his equal. On these unorthodox grounds he was welcomed in the hope that the facilities available to him at the seminary would enable him to embrace the gospel. These designs were of God; it was here in November 1808 that Adoniram Judson was born again.

If to some men becoming a Christian was an end, to someone like Judson it could never be just that. Immediately it was a case of, 'Lord, what wilt thou have me to do?' Reading a book on the 'Kingdom of Ava' turned his mind to Burma. Even now he had not been purged of his ambition for he began to think in terms of being the first American missionary overseas. Overcoming family coolness (from his father) and opposition (from his mother and sister) he was prepared to encounter more of the same from his associates at college. To his surprise, however, he discovered that there were others who had been entertaining similar thoughts. One obstacle confronted them all—who was to send them? The Americans seemed to be dragging their feet. The answer was to consult David Bogue and the London Missionary Society. Adoniram Judson was chosen to go to London to see what could be done.

The voyage was not without incident, the British vessel being captured by the French and Judson ending up in a French prison. From this he effected his escape with the aid of a mysterious stranger. Returning home eight months after he had left, he lost no time in making further preparations. After his marriage to Ann Hasseltine, and his ordination, they set sail with another married couple, Samuel and Harriet Newell, in February 1812.

Their excitement on arriving in India was tempered by the counsel and warnings they received regarding Burma. Everything they heard dismayed them. It was ruled by an absolute dictator for whose whim there was no accounting, and for this reason prudence demanded that they give the country the widest possible berth. At that time there was only one missionary there, William Carey's son Felix, and he was allowed to remain for the probable reason that his wife was Burmese. The prospects of remaining in India were no brighter—the powerful East India Company was hostile to the propagation of any Western ideas that might be introduced by the missionaries. The Americans decided to accept the invitation of Dr Carey and his colleagues to remain at Calcutta and Serampore until they received further light concerning their future. In the meanwhile Judson, who had been exercised about the question of baptism by immersion, together with his wife, was baptized by William Ward.

After exploring various avenues and experiencing various trials, the couple came to Madras looking for a ship for Penang, but finding one for Rangoon. It appeared that in spite of all the cautions and alarms that had rung in their ears that the door was at last opening to 'the living hell of Burma'. Their happiness was clouded when their first child was still-born during the voyage. In July 1813 they reached Rangoon. Their hearts sank at the sight—and the smell—of the place. But it was the same place on which those same hearts had been set for so long. Their apprenticeship was short-lived. Felix Carey wrote of them with enthusiasm to his father, but the following year he entered government service. To all appearances the spiritual welfare of Burma rested in the hands of a novice missionary who had been a Christian for five years, and his young wife.

Judson was clear about where his priorities lay. His work was to prepare a foundation for any who would come after him. This meant providing a grammar of the language, constructing a dictionary, and giving the Burmese people the Bible in their own tongue. To these tasks he gave most of his time. He and Ann, who had a greater facility in the new language than her husband, were also making the acquaintance of their neighbours. At the same time as they faced obvious difficulties they were being encouraged. News reached them of the formation of a new missionary society at home to support them and also of the appointment of a printer, George Hough, who would join them in due course. Their joy at the birth of a baby boy turned to sadness at his death before he had attained his first year.

An attempt to reach Chittagong to the north proved almost disastrous. The combined effect of contrary weather and an incompetent captain was to drive the vessel carrying Judson across the Bay of Bengal to a beach north of Madras. On the voyage he had been struck by fever which left him as much dead as alive. This was the first of numerous encounters he had with death. On reaching land he made the three-hundred-mile journey to Madras where he spent three months with friends before he found a ship returning to Rangoon. An excursion that should have taken three months had turned into a nightmare that lasted more than seven. Ann's stay in Rangoon was not without event either. She and Hough and his family had been subjected to severe harrassments and had withstood a devastating plague of cholera which had swept through the city, carrying off a great number of its inhabitants. Along with this, rumours of war between Britain and Burma were rife. Hough considered that it was not right that his family's safety should be put in jeopardy, and left for Calcutta. In the meantime other missionaries had arrived.

One of the attempts to reach the Burmese was through the *zayat*. This was little more than a shelter used by the Buddhists where those who passed by might rest or talk and the teachers impart their knowledge and wisdom. Many of these lined the streets and Judson decided to adapt the system for evangelical purposes. It was at this *zayat* that in June 1819 Maung Nau became the first of the Burmese to profess conversion. He was soon followed by others.

A visit to 'the Golden Feet', that is the Emperor's presence, proved completely unavailing. It was an immense risk, and was literally to take one's life in one's hands. The missionaries thought that if they were given imperial approval then people might be less fearful of becoming Christians. They were heard politely but received a peremptory dismissal. So discouraged were they that they made up their minds to leave Burma. However the pleas of the native converts prevailed and Adoniram and Ann decided to remain in Rangoon. Her health gave cause for concern and they both sailed to Calcutta. On their return there was little improvement and it was resolved that she must go to America to recover. During her absence he was encouraged once more to move to the capital, Ava. When Ann returned they moved to their new home there. She had brought back with her another missionary couple and these, with the now restored Houghs, were to remain in Rangoon.

War broke out in 1824. For Adoniram Judson it was to mean unimagined suffering which he shared with others unfortunate enough to fall foul of the Burmese authorities. His friendship with an English merchant named Gouger meant that he was branded a spy. He was taken to 'Death Prison'. The next eighteen months were to be spent here and in another infamous prison. Until now his acquaintance with Burmese cruelty was second-hand; now it was to become intimate. Confined with fifty other men and women in the most atrocious conditions, they spent their time in filth and squalor. Vermin were their inseparable companions. The temperature outside was well over a hundred degrees. At night their feet were tied to a bamboo pole which was raised above their heads so that they were forced to sleep, if at all, with only their heads and shoulders on the ground. When Ann Judson visited her husband the sight of this normally fastidious man, so neat and presentable in appearance, crawling towards her in a condition that beggars description proved too much for her. When he was transferred to Oung-Pen-La it was only the fact that he was fettered to another prisoner that prevented him from ending his own life. To such a state had he been reduced. In all this his concern for the translation of the Scriptures was so great that Ann smuggled them into the prison in a pillow so that he could sleep on them every night!

On his release they moved to Amherst and then Moulmein, always considering where they could best serve the gospel. For a while he acted in negotiations with the Burmese government but only on the understanding that this might help to procure religious freedom for the people of Burma. While he was thus engaged in Ava the most distressing news reached him—Ann had died. One wonders whether he could have persevered as he did without her. Six months later their two-year-old daughter Maria was laid by her mother's side. It seemed that no sooner was he rising out of one trough than he was swamped by another of God's billows. Even so, suffering was not yet a matter of history for Adoniram Judson.

A period of extreme depression followed in which he seemed to plumb the depths of self-loathing. He felt he somehow had to punish himself. He went so far as to dig a grave beside which he would sit reminding himself of the worthlessness of the body, and by such means hope to come to know God better. For a time the work of the gospel came to a halt.

This gave way to better times. New missionaries seemed to be arriving constantly; there were conversions; eager enquiries were made about the Saviour; and churches were beginning to appear throughout Burma. In one year two hundred converts were baptized. In 1832 his translation of the New Testament was completed, followed in 1834 by that of the Old. His happiness was complete when his proposal of marriage to Sarah Boardman, widow of a colleague, was accepted. Their work went on with Sarah involved with the women and translating, as well as caring for the children who were born to them. Adoniram was revising his translation of the Bible along with instructing native preachers and evangelists. When his work on the Bible was finally done he turned his attention to the dictionary. This did not give him as much delight as more specifically Christian responsibilities, such as preaching, but it occupied him profitably at a time when his throat and voice were giving him trouble.

Sarah's health was also deteriorating and necessitated a period of rest in the United States. He was to accompany her with some of the children while the others were cared for in Burma. The great question was whether she would survive the journey. As the voyage progressed the answer became increasingly obvious. She was buried on the island of St Helena in August 1845. It was typical of the afflictions that regularly met him that it was not until November that news reached him in Boston of the death of their son Charles, aged one and a half. He had died a month before his mother.

If he was expecting a quiet stay in America he could not have been more mistaken. He was acclaimed wherever he went. Crowds gathered to hear him speak although he could barely whisper. Far from being forgotten as he thought, he was a legend.

He took with him on his return his third wife, Emily Chubbock. This fact, and the object of his choice, must have ruffled a few feathers. For one thing she was just over half as old as he was: for another she was a writer of popular stories: and for a third she did not write under her real name! Nonetheless she was a true Christian and loved Adoniram as deeply and devotedly as the others had done. They set up home in Rangoon since there were so many missionaries in Moulmein. Their efforts there were owned of God, but soon difficulties including serious illnesses indicated that they themselves should move to Moulmein. In 1849 the English-Burmese portion of the dictionary had been completed.

It was evident that the years and the hardships were catching up on him. A life which included encounters with the 'Red Rat', the 'Spotted Face', and a stay in 'Bat Castle' was bound to take its toll. He was spending more time in prayer as if in preparation for the final great journey. The suggested remedy was the inevitable sea voyage. For this he was ready. When Emily intimated that he might be entertaining doubts or fears his reply was characteristic: 'When Christ calls me home, I shall go with the gladness of a boy bounding away from his school.' As he embarked on this voyage there was a probable under-standing that it was to be his last, and one from which he would not return. So it proved, for during its course Adoniram Judson reached his desired haven.

11
John Williams
(1796-1839)

Perhaps *The Oxford Dictionary of the Christian Church* is a little misleading in its verdict that John Williams 'is chiefly notable for the burst of missionary enthusiasm that the news of his death aroused in England'. What he accomplished in his life and by his labour cannot be so easily dismissed. On the other hand there is no denying the impact made by the news of the violent way in which he met his end on the beach at Erromanga. It gave rise to a desire to perpetuate his memory by the launching of a ship dedicated to gospel work in the South Seas, a desire which has continued over a hundred years and which has begotten a succession of such vessels. Each one has borne the same name—John Williams.

If his death is associated with missionary ships it is not without significance that his birth occurred in the same year as the sailing of another, the *Duff*, bearing the first group of London Missionary Society missionaries to leave Britain. Of equal significance is the fact that the *Duff* was bound for the South Seas. Three years earlier William Carey had sailed for India. The missionary movement that was to flower in the following century was just getting under way, and to that movement Williams was to make a unique contribution.

In London his grandfather was one of the philanthropists of the eighteenth century, a businessman who cared for the spiritual and material needs of his workers, and in seeing to the interests of the souls of his employees and household he enlisted the aid of one of the outstanding Christian leaders of that day, William Romaine. Williams's mother remembered fidgeting when the godly clergyman would come along to conduct religious services each week at the request of the grandfather, but when she moved to Oxford on her marriage it was to someone with Romaine's evangelical convictions and fervour that she turned. Failing to find such a preacher among the Anglicans she turned to the Dissenters, who appear to have retained their hold upon her when she and her husband returned to London. Mr Williams did not share her love for the kingdom of God and spent many evenings a week in the tavern. Mrs Williams, for her part, was diligent in the attention she paid to the spiritual welfare of John and his three sisters.

At the home in the Tottenham district of the metropolis, the child soon showed in which direction his gifts and abilities lay. These were practical rather than intellectual, and John was happier with a hammer in his hand than a pen. The qualities that God would use among the natives were already in evidence to those who had eyes to see. When he was fourteen he went to work in an ironmonger's, and although his province was intended to be at the counter dealing with customers, he soon found his way into the workshop where he took every opportunity to practise his skills. His master was quick to appreciate what a treasure he had in the boy. Sadly, what spiritual interest he might have had through his mother's teaching was on the wane, and although he went to Moorfields Tabernacle, so closely associated with George White-field, it was with increasing reluctance. Like his father he preferred other society.

One Sunday evening in January 1814 he waited in the street for his friends, intending to spend the evening at the tavern. They were late, and his employer's wife persuaded him after much effort to go with her to church. At last he yielded. The pastor was not preaching that night, and his replacement was Timothy East from Birmingham. His text was, 'What is a man profited if he shall gain the whole world and lose his own soul? Or what shall a man give in exchange for his soul?' That night John Williams realized what a bad bargain he was making, and a woman's persistence gained reward beyond measure.

Some Christians wait many years before God sets them in their appointed place. With others events move rapidly. So it was in the case of John Williams. In the year of his conversion he became a member of the Tabernacle. A class for young people provided him with the opportunity of growing in knowledge of the Bible and of developing gifts of writing and speaking. The following year at a meeting of the London Missionary Society addressed by Matthew Wilks, pastor of the Tabernacle, Williams felt his soul stirred as he heard of the need in the South Sea islands, and of the heroism of the passengers of the *Duff*. In another year he had offered himself to the London Missionary Society, and without any formal training he was ordained alongside another great missionary of the cross, Robert Moffat, whose sights were set on Africa. In November the newly married young missionary sailed with his bride and the remainder of the party down the Thames, bound for the other side of the world. The voyage took a whole year before they arrived at their destination. In 1814 he was a careless apprentice on City Road in London, seeking entertainment; in 1817 he was a missionary in Tahiti seeking God's glory.

Thirty years previously a house had been built on the island for the notorious Captain Bligh. It was to these premises that Williams and his companions were escorted. Here he met those who had already been at work for twenty years, and from their lips he learned of the various encouragements that greeted him. The Tahitian language had been reduced to writing, and in its written form was being spread among the other islands. Work on the Gospel of Luke was already well under way. By 1815 King Pomare of Tahiti had been baptized. On the neighbouring island of Eimeo a chapel had been built. The new missionary lost no time in visiting the island and recorded his feelings:

> On the Sabbath morning after my arrival, we went and stood outside this place of worship, and heard one of the natives engaged in prayer. He began by addressing God as the God of Abraham, Isaac and Jacob, and thanking Him for hearing their prayers and sending them missionaries. He next prayed that we might soon attain their language, so that we might be able to teach them the Word of God.

Williams made his intentions clear from the beginning, and they did not involve spending his time confined to one island. As soon as he could he determined to take the gospel to as many of the scores of islands as possible. This obviously required a ship. On Eimeo he came across a half-built vessel. The missionaries had started work on it but had found the task beyond them. Here was an immediate opportunity for him to use his practical gifts to good effect. Aided by his colleagues he completed the project within eight days, and although the first attempt at launching her was a disaster, in another two days she was afloat. He was ready for his journeys among the islands. The long time spent on board between the northern and southern hemispheres had certainly not been wasted, and Williams had improved his opportunity. With his practical turn of mind he was often found exploring the ship, observing what took place, talking with the sailors. He was, unknown to himself, being prepared with skills of seamanship which were to prove invaluable to him in his ministry. Now he was about to prove those skills.

Among the surrounding islands there was one that especially attracted his attention. It was Raiatea, in the Society Isles. Its king was eager to have missionaries in his province, and so it was that Williams made his home there. With this as his base, he worked at building and constructing, he worked at acquiring the language, he worked at teaching, and he worked at preaching. The emphasis that he and other missionaries laid on literacy as well as evangelism was a very firm foundation for the way in which the progress of the islanders was secured. Dr Frank Laubach, whose name is synonymous with Christian literacy campaigns, said that these scattered communities 'have been lifted from centuries of savage cannibalism to a high place among the literate peoples almost wholly by missionary education.'

The elevation of the standards of the natives was also furthered by persuading them to recognize human rights and rights of property, to submit to an elementary legal system (including trial by jury), and to forswear certain unsavoury habits such as drunkenness. Housing and living conditions were transformed so that living quarters were divided into separate rooms instead of consisting of one communal room. Almost inevitably these improvements brought criticism in their wake, that foreign standards were imposed upon unwilling communities living in blissful, primitive circumstances. Missionaries seem always to be easy prey to such allegations. The charge might well be muted if it were remembered that these same communities once were societies where laziness and promiscuity abounded, where human sacrifice was common, and where the burial of infants while still alive was practised.

Restlessness may well be a prime quality in a missionary. If so, John Williams possessed it to an unusual degree. No sooner had he seen the good news take root and begin to bear fruit on one island than he was eager to be off to plant it on another. Not only so, for he seems to have infected the natives with his own evangelistic spirit, and they formed their own missionary society to take the gospel to other islands. So it was that when a canoe bearing natives from an island 350 miles away came to Raiatea, their request for someone to accompany them back to Rurutu with the gospel was answered by two of the inhabitants of Raiatea. A passing ship took the little company on their expedition. This fired Williams's vision. The islands which had been evangelized were the very ones to send missionaries to others. Stephen Neill comments on this aspect of the work in the South Seas:

Few marvels in Christian history can equal the faithfulness of these men and women [the natives] . . . Many watered the seed with their own blood, but the Churches grew, and far more widely than if reliance had been placed first and foremost on the European missionary.

This concept in turn inspired him with another idea—he needed a missionary ship of his own. He was convinced that this was the key to his scheme, and he wrote to London with his plan. It was hardly with enthusiasm that his idea was greeted, and so when he was on a visit to Sydney he used the money he had received by legacy from his mother to buy his own vessel. The return to Raiatea (via Rurutu) aboard the *Endeavour* was with a sense of anticipated triumph. With the arrival of the ship a new stage in the evangelistic enterprise began. Great dangers were faced, severe disappointments were endured, but glorious victories were won. New islands were visited as the *Endeavour* sailed further and further from its island base. 'Wiliamu' was becoming something of a celebrity.

John Williams's thirst was unquenchable, and his patience with the directors of the LMS was wearing thin. There were so many islands which had not heard the gospel, and the directors were so slow to respond to his challenge and example. He wrote home to them:

A missionary was never designed by Jesus Christ to gather a congregation of a hundred or two natives, and sit down at his ease, as contented as if every sinner was converted, while thousands around him . . . are eating each other's flesh and drinking each other's blood, living and dying without the Gospel. For my own part I cannot content myself within the narrow limits of a single reef; and if means are not afforded, a continent would to me be infinitely preferable; for there, if you cannot ride, you can walk; but to these isolated islands a ship must carry you.

To his dismay his plans received a temporary setback when the *Endeavour* had to be sold. He had been using her to trade among the islands, but for this there were certain regulations to be observed, and duties to be paid. These left him with no option, and it was with a heavy heart that she was taken back to Sydney. He chafed under the restrictions that were now imposed upon him, and eventually his frustration drove him to adopt the only solution he could see. He had visited the island of Rarotonga aboard a ship chartered by the LMS. Having spent some time there he was anxious to be back in Raiatea and to resume the work among other communities. However, no ship appeared to take him. Unable to endure what he regarded as passing, and perhaps wasted, time he resolved to build his own boat, and there on the beach at Rarotonga he constructed and launched the *Messenger of Peace*, a vessel of seventy or eighty tons. Only a man of amazing resource would have conceived such a plan, and it required even greater resources to carry it through successfully. The ship took him eastwards back to Raiatea, but already his eye was fixed even further west on Samoa and the New Hebrides. His first visit to Samoa in 1830 saw many of its inhabitants enter the kingdom of heaven, and he left behind eight Tahitian teachers. Among all the treasures gathered by him in the South Pacific, Samoa probably shines brightest.

In 1834 he came home to England with his wife and three children, seven others having died in infancy. Two months before they made their way up the English Channel, another ship sailed down, bound for Australia. On board were George Loveless and the Tolpuddle Martyrs, sentenced to transportation for forming a Labourers' Union, forerunner of the Trades Union movement. It was a busy furlough for Williams, for as well as addressing large meetings to stir interest in his work, he was anxious to have in print a record of the situation in the islands. As a result of his concern his impressions were published in a book called *Missionary Enterprises*. It appeared in 1837, the year in which Victoria ascended the throne, and she was chief among those of influence and authority who were sent a copy.

On his return south he was confirmed in his persuasion that although primarily he was a bringer of the gospel, he was also charged with introducing a new civilization. This was not because of any grand colonial or imperial arrogance, but because he saw it as a natural development and accompaniment of the new religion. In this he was pursuing the course set by an older man, Samuel Marsden, missionary to Australia and New Zealand. Williams's biographer records:

It has been very fortunate for the Pacific and Africa that the first white men to settle in them and to identify themselves with their people were missionaries like Williams who came to give rather than acquire and whose message and practices, however faulty and sometimes misguided, were drawn from a profound belief in Jesus Christ as the Saviour of men.

The LMS looked kindly on his campaign to purchase a new ship, and in 1838 the *Camden* set sail for the exotic islands of the South Seas, anchoring in November of that year at Pago Pago in Samoa. Anyone who thought he had come there to stay obviously did not know his man. He made his home on Upolu, but he had no intention of permanently settling there. Already he was planning an excursion to the New Hebrides. In January 1739 he sailed to Rarotonga, Raiatea, and Tahiti for the last time. Discouragements as well as encouragements met him there, but the communities never lost the place they had won in his heart. In April he was back in Samoa. There was a strange sense of foreboding about these last few months. One of his colleagues drowned. Williams wondered whether he would be the next. His wife was opposed to his going to the New Hebrides with their reputation for savagery. Nothing, however, could deter him, and while the west beckoned him he felt powerless to resist.

In November the little group of missionaries reached the New Hebrides. They visited Fotuna and Tanna, from where John Paton was later to escape for his life, and finally came to Erromanga. Their reception by the natives was cautious. Williams and his companions made their way ashore, and walked some distance up the beach. Suddenly the uneasy calm was broken. The missionaries ran back towards the ship but were overtaken. The end was violent and savage, and Williams fell under the clubs of his assailants. At a later date when his remains were recovered all that was left was a collection of bones. John Williams was a victim of cannibals.

Two questions remain unanswered regarding the death. It had been Williams's custom to send natives ashore first when visiting new islands. Why did he not do so on this occasion? And why did he not sense danger when he saw that there were no women among the party on the beach? Strange when his knowledge of native habits is recalled, and yet perhaps not so strange when his boldness and impatience are remembered. Ruth Tucker suggests that perhaps 'for a fleeting moment he lost himself in fanciful visions of his own invincibility'.

Death of John Williams on Erromanga

As far as the natives were concerned, their reason for the act is clear. The man who killed the missionary confessed later that his motive was revenge, since a party of traders had previously killed his only son. All these are points of debate. What is not open to question is what he achieved by way of translation of portions of the Bible, evangelism, education, and social improvements.

Among Mary Williams's last words to her husband were, 'Don't land on Erromanga, John!' But John was of that breed of men who hazard their lives for Jesus Christ. And in losing his life he had found it.

12
Allen Gardiner
(1794-1851)

Captain Allen Gardiner, R.N.

The note read: 'The success of the Tierra del Fuego mission is most wonderful, and shames me, as I always prophesied utter failure.' It was sent along with the annual subscription to the work of the missionary society. What made the pairing of those two features even more surprising was the fact that the letter was signed by none other than Charles Darwin. Many years previously the famous voyage of the *Beagle* had taken him to those same shores at the tip of South America, and as a result of his investigations there he had arrived at the unshakeable conclusion, often expressed, that it was 'utterly useless to send missionaries to such a set of savages as the Fuegians, who probably are the very lowest of the human race.'

Thus the wisdom of the world was confounded (not for the first nor for the last time) by the foolishness of God. Darwin's change of opinion was due largely to the resolute faith of a missionary of the cross whose eyes fell on the same scenes of degradation as did his. The evolutionist said, 'Nothing can be done.' The Christian said, 'God can.'

The truth of God meant a great deal to the parents of Allen Francis Gardiner, and when he was born in Basildon in the county of Berkshire they were eager to introduce him to that truth. Accordingly it featured significantly in his early education and much of their praying was focused upon him. Their hearts must have grown faint on occasions when they saw little fruit for their endeavours and prayers, witnessing in him a restlessness and love of adventure that might well have given rise to some misgivings on their part. There was no question as to which way his mind was inclined. His determination was to join the Navy. So entirely had this intention possessed him that while he was still very young his mother came upon him late one night, and found him devising a scheme for surprising and taking some of the enemy fleet in the harbour of La Rochelle on the west coast of France. Another time, thinking that he might one day find himself in West Africa he began to compile a vocabulary of the language of that area, and sought diligently to harden himself in preparation for the demands that such a life would make on him. He had barely entered his teens before taking the first steps towards realizing his ambition. He left home for the naval college at Portsmouth, and in 1810 he went to sea.

The toughening process to which he had subjected himself was not in vain. Rather it stood him in good stead and he soon showed his mettle in an engagement with an American warship. He proved himself to be a brave sailor and was promoted to the rank of lieutenant, a distinction that was to lead on to his becoming a commander. There was something portentous about his sailing later aboard another vessel; for she was *HMS Dauntless,* and if Allen Gardiner was to reveal any strength of character in the course which God had already appointed for him, his ship's name expressed it perfectly.

The kind of life he had chosen for himself naturally brought him many encounters with death. He himself escaped it while he saw another drown. Such experiences were used to make him think of his condition, and his readiness—or rather want of it—to appear before his Judge. The death of his mother reminded him even more forcefully of the state of his soul, but still he remained a stranger to that peace which she now enjoyed in its fullness, and perversely the gospel in which she had instructed him so faithfully became an object of scorn. Its influence upon him was not entirely lost, however, and one day in Portsmouth he determined to buy a Bible. He had to battle against a sense of shame, and the fear of man contested the claims of God on his soul as he sought to muster enough courage to purchase a copy. Valour in facing enemy action was one thing; bravery in countering scorn was another. At last he bought and began to read the Word of God and the truth instilled in his infancy began to burn.

While he was passing through this crisis his duties took him as far as India and China, and eventually South America. The ritualistic Roman churches of Santiago and Lima disgusted him, but in the South Pacific the sight of converted Tahitian natives left a deep impression. The precise hour when he became a Christian is not known, but when the *Dauntless* arrived in Sydney he was obliged by illness to return home, and the entry in his journal when he reached Cape Town shows that his heart had been changed. He was soon aware of the call of God to be a missionary and he sought the help of the London Missionary Society to work in South America. When this was not forthcoming he prepared himself for the Christian ministry, but this, too, came to nothing.

His marriage in 1823 was short-lived, and when his wife died ten years later his missionary desires were rekindled. He left England in September of 1834 and two months later reached Table Bay in South Africa. From here he travelled overland to Natal working among the Zulus in very precarious circumstances. In 1836, when he was forty-two, he returned to England to enlist helpers. That same year he married a second time and went back to Africa accompanied by his young wife and three children of his former marriage. Aided by a companion he succeeded in establishing a settlement and building schools in the area. It was Gardiner who gave the name Durban, after the Governor Sir Benjamin D'Urban, to the little group of huts that was to grow into an influential city. His efforts seemed doomed to failure with the arrival of the Boers, the Dutch farmers, which led to hostilities with the Zulus, but the results of those efforts were to be evident at a later date. This was not the only time that Gardiner was denied a sight of the fruit of his labours. Indeed it appears to have been his lot to sow where others were to reap. Meanwhile the irresistible call of South America was once more sounding in his ears, and the following year he made the voyage from Table Bay to Rio de Janeiro.

From there he sailed to Montevideo with the intention of reaching the Indians of the Pampas in Chile. Setting off with his family from Buenos Aires, he journeyed in a rough coach for nine hundred miles to Mendoza. Going south to Concepcion he left his family while he went to the places where the Indians were to be found. When he approached them and asked if he might instruct them in the ways of God, he discovered that their experience at the hand of the Jesuits meant that they refused to have anything to do with him or his gospel. This was but a confirmation of his impressions at Mendoza where he had not been permitted to sell Bibles. It seemed for the time being that South America was closed to him.

The restless spirit of the missionary impelled him to look elsewhere, and he determined to go to New Guinea. Sadly he found that the Dutch, who controlled the territory, were completely unappreciative of his good intentions, and adopted a cynical attitude. It was back to South America once more, this time to the island of Chiloe off the coast of Chile. Again the iniquitous influence of Romanism had closed the door firmly against the messenger of the saving grace of Jesus Christ. A lesser man might have concluded that there was nothing for it but to go back to England and labour in more comfortable and auspicious circumstances. Allen Gardiner was not of that breed. The entry in his journal at this time reads:

> We purpose to proceed to Berkeley Sound, in the Falkland Islands. Making this our place of residence, I intend to cross over in a sealer, and to spend the summer among the Patagonians. Who can tell but the Falkland Islands, so admirably suited for the purpose, may become the key to the aborigines both of Patagonia and of Tierra del Fuego?

It was in 1578 that Sir Francis Drake became the first Englishman Patagonians ever saw. They made a distinct impression upon him as they had upon the Portuguese explorer, Magellan. Back in 1821 it was a very different impression that they left on the mind of the young, newly converted naval officer of the *Dauntless* as he sailed along the coastline and gazed towards the land. For others they might be savages

who could not be tamed and civilized. For him they were people for whom Christ had died. As he and his companion Johnson anchored in Berkeley Sound in December 1841, the disappointments of the intervening years seemed to count for nothing. His hopes for the Indians burned as brightly as ever they had.

The opening exchanges were characterized by suspicion on both sides, and the missionaries certainly needed to exercise great care as to how far they could trust the Indians. Nevertheless their initial efforts appeared promising, and so Gardiner resolved to return to England in order to recruit more helpers for the work that he saw developing. Further disappointment lay in store for him however because his long absence from home meant that interest had declined. He presented his case to three missionary societies, none of which responded. His reaction was simple—to appeal to Christians directly instead of through the usual channels of the societies. His declaration of what had been done in Patagonia was followed by the exhortation:

> Let us remember Him who, though he was rich, yet for our sakes became poor, who willeth that all men should be saved and come to the knowledge of the truth, and who will not be satisfied until He has received the fulness of that harvest which the travail of His soul is still ripening.

The appeal was well received, with Christians moved to pray and to give. A group of men met in Brighton and committed themselves to the work that Gardiner had set before them. He was appointed secretary of this new society, named the Patagonian Mission, and when the others decided to send a man to Patagonia, Gardiner volunteered to go with him at his own expense. The two men left in December 1844, on the brig *Rosalie*, to renew attempts to plant and propagate the gospel in Patagonia. They received early indications that their attentions were unwelcome. His previous acquaintance with Wissale, the native chief, had alerted him to the fact that he was not to be trusted. Now it was evident that their lives were in danger. When the officers of a passing ship visited them Wissale declared his affection for the missionaries, but as soon as the vessel sailed he resumed his threatening behaviour. Both men were convinced that it was unwise to remain among the natives, and when another ship provided them with the opportunity to leave, it was with a mixture of relief and reluctance that they grasped it. Their arrival in England with the news of the failure of their venture inevitably raised questions as to the future of the infant missionary society. Needless to say, Allen Gardiner was unwavering in his convictions, and unswerving in his love for the South American Indians.

In September 1845, accompanied by a Spanish Protestant, Gardiner returned to Montevideo. To the familiar opposition of the priests there was now added the difficulty posed by Britain's political differences with his host country. It was this problem also that prevented him from working at and through Valparaiso in Chile on the west coast. Still undeterred by these obstacles he turned his attention to the Indians of Bolivia. In spite of attacks of illness suffered by him and his companion, he was encouraged by the attitude of the President to anticipate some success for his endeavours. It was not to be, however, for when he went back to England to recruit more help, revolution in

Bolivia had reinstated the party who favoured the priests, with the inevitable result. The place to which he now turned his face was the southernmost area of land before the vastness of Antarctica: the 'land of fire'—Tierra del Fuego.

Early in January 1848, he sailed from Cardiff with five companions aboard a merchant ship, the *Clymene*. They learnt early that their location was extremely dangerous and were soon the victims of theft. The native savagery of the Fuegians was not directed at them; nevertheless to establish a mission station on the island in those circumstances was almost an impossibility. The alternative was to anchor a ship in the bay where their possessions could be safe, and to visit the shore from there. With this in mind Gardiner and his colleagues went once more to England to raise funds and to secure the needs of the little company. Finding no help there he travelled to Germany to see if the Moravians, who were indefatigable missionaries, would aid them. They could offer him none. A similar response met him from Scotland. At last he was presented with a gift of six thousand pounds by a lady in England, and he returned on the *Ocean Queen* with two launches, the *Pioneer* and the *Speedwell*. He took with him six companions, one of whom had been with him on his previous journey. The party left Liverpool in September 1850. He was long accustomed to parting from family and country; this, however, was to be the last time.

The missionaries did not know of the drama that was being played out at home. Although the Society had prepared provisions for them no ship could be found to carry them to such remote parts. When one was eventually found it was too late. Meanwhile the situation on the island had hardly improved. The missionaries were invaded on their arrival and their property stolen. The need to preserve their stock of provisions was of great importance, and so they had to resort to embarking on their launches and putting out to sea. This afforded little relief, for the *Pioneer* was driven aground by the storms for which Cape Horn is notorious. Attempts to refloat her were rendered extremely perilous by the close attention paid them by the islanders. Armed as they were, the missionaries dared not use their guns in order to defend themselves for that would be to bring untold reproach on the gospel. Instead they knelt on the shore and prayed while the wondering natives gazed at them. They gained relief, but it was a temporary deliverance. The end was not far off.

Apart from the dangers threatened by the natives and the wind and sea, they saw some of their possessions catch fire, and they were subjected to scurvy. They were reduced to eating garden seeds, a fox, and mice. Allen Gardiner was blessed in the companions God gave him as he and they faced their last ordeal. They consisted of a carpenter, a waiter, a surgeon, and three fishermen. Not many years before the doctor had been a scornful unbeliever with no time for God, and who counted the Bible, in his own words 'a mere lumber book'. The carpenter had wanted to go on the voyage because 'being with Captain Gardiner was like a heaven on earth'. Such men would have upheld each other in all possible ways while they waited for a death which became increasingly inevitable. Gradually their fears that their expected relief would not come were realized. They left written records of their state. Scrawled on a rock were the words, 'Dig below. Gone to Spaniard's Harbour, March, 1851.' Their last days and hours must be pieced together from the pathetic remains of the journals some kept.

The first to die was a Cornish sailor. He died singing:

> Arise, my soul, arise,
> Shake off thy guilty fears;

Six weeks later another died, then another. So the sad, triumphant procession continued, each hard on the heels of the other into the presence of Christ. Unable to move for sheer lack of strength, dying of starvation, the restless boy who became a restless missionary wrote:

Blessed be my heavenly Father for the many mercies I enjoy: a comfortable bed, no pain or even cravings for hunger, though excessively weak, scarcely able to turn in my bed, at least it is a very great exertion; but I am, by His abounding grace, kept in perfect peace, refreshed with a sense of my Saviour's love and an assurance that all is wisely and mercifully appointed.

Gardiner's last entry in his journal read: 'Great and marvellous are the lovingkindnesses of my gracious God.' The little company died of starvation, but filled with the righteousness for which they hungered and thirsted.

It would be too easy to dismiss the young adventurer as a missionary in search of a mission field, for that might lay the great apostle Paul open to the same charge, notwithstanding the obvious favour that attended his energies. Travelling to three continents, sailing to some half dozen countries, overcomimg a continuous stream of disappointments—these facts speak of an intense love for Christ and a passion to tell others of him. Gardiner's story is one of faithfulness rather than success, yet the confession of Darwin dares us to write failure against his name. Since its publication probably no book has done more harm to the cause of Christ than *Origin of Species*. Certainly no witness to Allen Gardiner could be clearer than that of its author.

Gardiner's death eventually led to the birth of the South American Missionary Society in 1867.

13
Robert Moffat
(1795-1883)

God called Robert Moffat to be a missionary through a meeting that he missed by a week. The young man was working as a gardener in Warrington in the North of England when one evening as he was walking to the town his eye was caught by a poster announcing a service. There were two names on the placard, one of them was the

London Missionary Society, the other the Reverend William Roby of Manchester. The meeting itself had already passed, but no matter; what he had seen, he said in later years, had 'made him another man'. That casual, apparently chance circumstance had kindled a spark, the fire was to burn for many years, and the blaze was to consume him thousands of miles away from his native shores.

Early in his life his family left his birthplace at Ormiston, near Edinburgh. A brief experience as a sailor persuaded him that his future did not lie in that direction, and he found the land literally more to his liking than the sea. He was apprenticed as a gardener and after spending some time in Scotland he moved to Cheshire where his course was finally settled. Behind the preparations of infancy, boyhood, and youth lay the prayerful influences of devout parents whose chief concern was that he should know the Son of God as his Saviour. It is not without significance that his mother filled his mind and heart with accounts of the exploits of the servants of God in other countries, particularly those of the Moravians in Greenland.

The impressions of that conviction on the streets of Warrington were given no opportunity to fade, for Moffat lost no time in making his way to Manchester to the home of Mr Roby. There he found a ready listener as he poured out what was on his heart. Roby recommended him to the London Missionary Society, but when he offered himself for service he was refused. Undismayed, the Scot determined that the matter would not end there, and the following year he was accepted. In October 1816 at Surrey Chapel in London, he and eight others were set apart for their work with the Society, one of the others being John Williams, destined to lose his life at the hands of savages in the South Seas. Later that same month he embarked for Africa, arriving at Cape Town in January, 1817.

The frustrations that seem frequently to be the lot of missionaries made no exception in the case of Robert Moffat. They came in the form of discouragement from the Dutch and British officials, who frowned on missionary activity as likely to provoke unrest among the natives of the interior. Much more disturbing and alarming was the conduct of those who had come to Africa ostensibly to preach the gospel. The standard of their behaviour was astonishingly low, descending to the level of the quarrelsome, and even immoral. The bright visions he entertained of the task might well have been tarnished by what he had already encountered; nevertheless the period of waiting was patiently endured until the opportunity finally came for him to make his way into the interior.

His goal was the tribes of the country about the Orange River. The difficulties of the journey were immense, and comforts were few. This was also largely true of his stay in the territory. He came near death on more than one occasion, from lions, drinking poisoned water, and starvation. One way in which he sought to keep hunger pangs at bay was to bind his stomach with a thong. At the end of this period, however, lay one of the greatest encouragements he was ever to know in his long ministry in the continent—the conversion of Africaner.

This was a name synonymous with terror. He was a killer who had murdered a farmer and his family, was hunted by the authorities, and for whose capture rewards were offered. Although he was feared throughout the territory, contact with him had been made by a missionary prior to Moffat, and it was as a result of this that Moffat made his excursion. When gospel light finally expelled the darkness from his mind and heart, there was no doubting the change that had taken place. It was evident in his hunger for the Word of God, the topic of his conversation, and the gentleness of his character. On Moffat's decision to return to Cape Town he took Africaner with him. Among the responses that greeted him on his journey and at his arrival was sheer disbelief that he had survived his encounter with the notorious savage, and naked incredulity when the author of such real and imagined atrocities was presented to an astounded public.

The visit to Cape Town was not merely to show off the incontestable benefits of Christianity in the form of Africaner. Mary Smith, whom Moffat had left behind in England, arrived in December 1819 to be married to him, and together they set off, not now to Namaqualand but to the Kuruman river in Bechuanaland, among the Bechuanas. After some time at Lithako they moved to Kuruman itself in 1824. The station here was destined to become a centre of missionary activity in Africa, and for almost fifty years it grew, under the influence of the couple, into a model for others to copy.

They were not the first Christians to attempt to reach the Bechuanas, but notwithstanding the efforts previously expended upon them the natives adhered to their gross and unpleasant practices. The prospects for the young missionary and his wife were bleak indeed and at first seemed to worsen. The success which attended the efforts of a pagan rain-maker after a period of drought was the occasion for ridicule to be poured on the gospel. When the success proved short-lived the blame was laid firmly at the door of the representatives of that gospel, and they were commanded, under severe threats, to leave. Moffat's resolution in standing his ground seems to have nonplussed the natives, who, unsure what to do in the face of such bravery, left him and his little family alone. The tide turned in favour of the missionaries when he acted as an intermediary and peacemaker between the Bechuanas and invading enemies.

The little headway they seemed to be making was naturally a cause of many misgivings. Mary Moffat's despondency was the greater of the two, but no doubt she spoke for both when she expressed her feelings:

> Could we but see the smallest fruit, we could rejoice midst the privations and toils which we bear; but as it is, our hands do often hang down.

Among a number of reasons for their failure, no doubt the most potent was that Moffat had made hardly any effort to learn the language. Accordingly he determined that fluency in Sechuana was essential and set out to acquire it. The benefits were not long in coming, and in 1828 light began to pierce the gloomy clouds that had threatened to drive them from Kuruman. Improvements in living standards appeared, eagerness to hear the gospel now showed itself, and help was cheerfully given by the natives in projects devised by the missionaries to their advantage. Although at first there were no evidences of conversions, soon the appearance of tears on the cheeks of men (previously a matter of scorn) betokened a transformation that was to astound and encourage husband and wife. In 1829 the first baptisms were performed and the church at Kuruman established. The stone building erected in 1838 still stands.

Armed with the language, Moffat was now prepared to begin an assault on translation. Previous efforts as with most other endeavours had not achieved anything worthy of comment, but now the attack began in earnest. A rendering of the Westminster Catechism and the composition of hymns (he was the author of the first hymn in Sechuana) did not disguise from him the most important need of all—the Bible in the natives' own tongue. After painstaking work on the Gospel of Luke he was obliged to travel to Cape Town to have the translation printed, but on his arrival there he found the printers unwilling to undertake the work because the likely result would be that the African way of life would be raised to a higher plane. Such undesirable consequences, apparently, could not be tolerated. The only alternative was to print it himself, and this he did on the government press. Being forced to do this was a blessing in disguise since the newly-acquired skill would be needed for a press which had been donated and which he took back with him.

The appearance of the Gospel of Luke was followed by further translations, and by 1840 all the New Testament was completed. The printing of this required his return to England where he was to remain until 1843. During this furlough he was introduced to David Livingstone, a meeting that was to result in Livingstone's decision to go out to Africa, taking the Scriptures with him. He was later to become the Moffats' son-in-law. By 1851 Moffat had finished a rough translation of the whole of the Old Testament. From start to finish, translating the Bible had taken him 29 years. The importance he attached to this project is reflected in what he wrote to a friend:

> I have felt, in short, as if I must die if I dropped it, or at least be miserable to the end of my days did I not enlist all the time, research, and perseverance at my command in its accomplishment. In fine, I have found it to be an awful work to translate the Book of God.

His written work also included *Missionary Labours and Scenes in South Africa*, and a version in Sechuana of *Pilgrim's Progress*.

Moffat did not confine his labours to Kuruman. The inquisitive visit of a neighbouring chief to see the white man resulted in his going to the village of the chief. Five hundred people welcomed him, and the first sound that greeted him on the following morning was the eager clamour of the natives who had gathered to hear him. Before he had breakfasted he preached to them, and as they dispersed he retired to wash. He returned to his tent for something to eat only to find that the people had gathered there for a second sermon! He requested half an hour for his breakfast, but hardly were the words out of his mouth before a woman rushed up to him with a bowl filled with food and the exhortation to eat its contents entirely so that he could preach for a long time. They listened attentively and discussed what they heard, and in the evening were back for another preaching service.

Another heartening source was the contact with Moselekatse, king of the Matabele. A vicious tyrant in his own country, whose people lived in mortal dread of him, he had nothing but respect for Moffat, and after their meeting, there began a friendship which lasted for thirty years. Although he never became a Christian, his association with the missionaries brought about an astounding change in his whole demeanour. The closeness of this relationship showed itself in a remarkable incident. When overwork seemed to be threatening Moffat's health the directors of the Missionary Society encouraged him to seek refreshment for his mind and body by revisiting England or spending some time at one of the ports in Africa. His response was to pay a visit to Moselekatse and regain his strength in the company of his old friend.

Encouraged by the favourable reception given to Moffat by Moselekatse, the London Missionary Society proposed to establish a mission among the Matabele. Moffat was asked to use his good offices with the king to expedite the project by staying with the new missionaries until they were settled there. This, of course, he was only too glad to do and secured a welcome for the newcomers. By a happy providence one of those sent out from England to this work in 1858 was his own son, John Moffat. The early months of this venture were characterized by distrust and misunderstanding, the chief attempting to use the missionaries by persuading them to enter into trading agreement with him, while they insisted that their trading was spiritual and not material. They had come to deal in the Word of God and not in ivory. Their faithfulness was rewarded, and Robert Moffat had the satisfaction of seeing his work at Kuruman reproduced some seven hundred miles away.

Increasingly Kuruman became a missionary centre. From here Moffat went on his journeys whenever he was called, and although it was not ideally situated in terms of the main routes in Africa, it seemed to attract a constant stream of visitors. This was not always a welcome fact to Moffat who begrudged the valuable translation and revising time that was forfeited in entertaining for what he considered no good reason. His early training and work in England lay behind his diligence in practical matters such as constructing a canal and supervising the cultivation of five hundred acres of land by the natives. His domestic circumstances were at the same time an encouragement and a tribute to him. Of the seven children born to him and his wife, five became actively involved in missionary activity. In 1862 Livingstone's wife died, and soon afterwards her brother Robert. Compensation for these tragedies came when John Moffat joined his father at Kuruman in 1866. It is hard to take in the vast improvements in the conduct and living standards of the people among whom he worked. On his return to England he could say that sixty thousand pounds worth of transactions were completed in a year among the natives in and around Kuruman. Education was obviously of great importance as in any missionary enterprise, his daughter being teacher in the local school.

'Our glory and joy' is how Paul described the Christians at Thessalonica. For some years it appeared as though there would be no such cause for rejoicing in the heart of Robert Moffat. He could point to not a single conversion, and for a period afterwards to just one. Undaunted and diligent he was to see a dramatic change in lives about him that was to send him from Africa a fulfilled man. He left the country in 1870, his 53 years of service interrupted by only one furlough—if furlough be the name to give to his tireless effort to ensure a Bible for his charges. The couple's return to Britain naturally involved an immense upheaval, and the question of adjusting was taken out of Mary Moffat's hands by her death a few months after arriving. This left her husband a lonely old man, but by no means an idle recluse. His closing thirteen years were devoted to the cause of Christ in Africa just as earnestly as those spent in the continent, travelling the length and breadth of the British Isles bringing its need to the attention of his hearers. Among the many deserved and hard-won tributes which he received was the degree of Doctor of Divinity from Edinburgh University. His death occurred on 9 August 1883.

His own estimate of his life is best expressed in his estimate of the noble work to which he was called: 'Oh! brethren, the work for which God became man—a man of sorrows and acquainted with grief, the first missionary in the world—what a glorious work in which to be found.' A more objective verdict is provided by Ruth A. Tucker, a writer on missionary work throughout the history of the church:

He was overshadowed by his famous son-in-law, often being referred to as the father-in-law of David Livingstone.' Moffat was nevertheless the greater missionary of the two. He was an evangelist, a translator, an educator, a diplomat, and an explorer, and he effectively combined those roles to become one of Africa's greatest missionaries of all time.

Her tribute would no doubt be disowned by its subject, but approved by his relative. It provides a deserved memorial to one whose length of days were spent in praise of the Good Shepherd whose goodness never failed.

14
Johann Gerhard Oncken
(1800-1884)

'How many missionaries have you?' asked Dr Thomas Guthrie on one of Johann Oncken's visits to Edinburgh.

'Seven thousand,' came the reply.

'Beg your pardon,' said the Doctor, thinking there had been a mistake in the understanding of the question or in the hearing of the answer, 'I asked the number of missionaries.'

Oncken showed there had been no misunderstanding on either side. 'I know, but we consider every member as a missionary.'

That was the outlook of the man Spurgeon called 'The Apostle Paul of Germany', and which moved him to say on hearing of his death, 'That country has lost in Oncken a much greater man than she will today believe.'

In pursuit of satisfaction Napoleon's ambition was gorging itself on the misery of its victims at the beginning of the nineteenth century. In the little town of Varel, near the shore of the North Sea a few miles from Bremen, one of the young men who sought to stand against the French onslaught was forced to flee to England for refuge. He remained there an exile for two years until his death in London. The sadness of this commonplace account is completed by the fact that not long after his escape his wife gave birth to a son in January 1800. One instance of the trail of wretchedness that the French tyrant left in his wake was that Johann Gerhard Oncken and his father never saw each other.

Brought up in the home of his grandmother, he was taken to church by a neighbour each Sunday. How much good this did for his soul is extremely doubtful, for Lutheranism had sunk to a pitiable state that bore little resemblance to its Reformation origin. Fundamental doctrines, including the deity of Christ, were regarded as of no real account as the authority of Reason displaced that of the Bible. The assault on the Word of God, for which Germany must bear a large share of responsibility, was already under way. In later years Oncken admitted that as far as salvation through Christ was concerned his teachers gave him no instruction at all.

Under the blight of such barrenness he would have remained had he not been taken at the age of fourteen to Scotland by a merchant of that country. There he was introduced to the Presbyterian Church where he heard the gospel for the first time. In 1819 he moved to London, living with a Christian family and with them attending a Congregational church. Here again the gospel was preached, but it was while attending a service in a Methodist chapel that he finally yielded to the claims of the Saviour. When he received assurance of his salvation he lost no time in sharing his faith, for on that same day he kept some of the money from his daily food allowance, bought some tracts, and began to distribute them. The unexpected answer Dr Guthrie was to receive many years later was not idle theorizing by a leader aloof from his followers, but the response of one who from his earliest Christian experience set a standard from which he did not deviate, and which he required others to copy.

He returned to his homeland at the end of 1823, having been appointed by the Continental Society as their missionary for Germany. There he took up residence in Hamburg, for ever afterwards associated with his name. It had not escaped the effects of rationalism in its pulpits, a pernicious presence which did nothing to improve the moral condition of the city. It was here that Oncken began his preaching ministry. God set his seal on the young man's work in a remarkable way, one January beginning with just ten persons attending but resulting in the conversion of one of his finest helpers. The next meeting had eighteen in attendance, and the following, thirty. February opened with 180 present and closed with a hundred being turned away for lack of room.

Little wonder that he attracted attention, and even less wonder that some of that attention was unpleasant and unwelcome. What was a cause of dismay was the fact that much of the opposition came from the clergy. The hostility became so severe that the meetings had to be suspended, but this proved counter-productive to the interests of his persecutors who succeeded only in driving him out to the streets and into the most unlikely places, as well as the homes of his sympathizers. In this way more rather than fewer people were coming under the influence of the gospel. Along with his preaching he was very much involved in the distribution of Bibles, becoming in 1828 the agent of the Edinburgh Bible Society until 1878. Within this period he distributed over two million Bibles. Sunday school work also captured his interest.

The city of London provided him with a wife whom he married in 1828. It was a happy relationship though not without its sorrows. In three weeks a cholera epidemic took three of his household, including a little daughter. Others of his children were later to die. His frequent absence from home, and his imprisonments by the Hamburg authorities due to his preaching, meant that often some of the family hardships had to be borne by his wife alone and in this and other respects she proved an invaluable companion.

The question of baptism played a very important role in Oncken's ministry. From his earliest days he had resolved to take no course for which he could find no support or endorsement in Scripture. This led

Oncken's house in which the first Baptist church in Hamburg was formed

in turn to his questioning the practice of infant baptism, his refusal to have his first child baptized, and eventually to his own baptism as a believer. He sought guidance from the famous Scottish Bible commentator, Robert Haldane, who did so much work on the continent. What was he to do since there was no one at hand who was able to administer the rite? In this instance, however, Oncken did not find Haldane very helpful, for the advice he received was that he should baptize himself, an act which did not lack precedent, but concerning which he was not persuaded. Consequently, he and some of his friends waited another five years before they were baptized in 1834 by an American professor who was visiting Germany. The day following the group were formed into a church, the first Baptist church in Germany, and Oncken was ordained to the ministry by the same Professor Sears.

One of the results of this step was the severance of ties and relationships that had been enjoyed until then. On another level persecution increased, culminating in the pastor's first term of imprisonment. On his release there were costs to be paid, and in this he was aided by the church. Vows, threats, and promises failed to dislodge Oncken from his path, while he was encouraged by the fact that petitions from Britain and America, were received by the authorities and effected a slight easing of the situation. Another factor that brought a relaxation in the persecution was a fire that broke out in Hamburg in 1842. The church was about to move to a large warehouse of four stories which would serve as a meeting place and a store for the Bibles which were being distributed. A large portion of these premises were offered to the city authorities to assist them in their relief efforts. The gesture was readily acknowledged, and for eight months the warehouse became a refuge for eighty people. Although the persecution was not as serious after this, the church still felt the weight of opposition and the anniversary of the fire saw Oncken back in prison. So was kindness rewarded.

In accordance with his convictions it is perhaps best to see Oncken's missionary work in terms of planting Baptist churches. He himself writes of requests 'to send brethren who can preach the Gospel and take the oversight of the little bands of believers who have seceded from the national churches'. This task was executed not only in Germany but also in other countries of Europe. Indeed it would not be wide of the mark to call him the father of Continental Baptists.

In order to secure his end he employed two primary means. Firstly, he travelled widely. Where he did not go his followers went. Countries that came under his influence in this way included Denmark, Switzerland, Holland, Sweden, Romania, Bulgaria, and Russia. German-speaking Baptist churches as far afield as South Africa were established by one who had been taught by him. He took a particular interest in Russia, and when the tsar visited England he made the journey to London to enlist the help of Dean Stanley in bringing to the attention of the emperor the difficulties under which the Baptists were labouring. Shortly after this incident in 1874 persecution ceased until the death of the tsar.

Secondly, he saw to the training of young men who had been called to the work. Originally, visitors who were converted in Hamburg and were discovered evangelizing in the city were banished. Oncken saw that they went away well supplied with tracts and evangelistic material. Later, systematic instruction was given and the missionary enterprise more soundly and efficiently organized. Eventually, the Hamburg Baptist College was founded in 1888. Reinforcing and undergirding this endeavour was the publishing work. Nor was what we normally associate with missionary work his only concern. He showed a keen interest in such agencies as the National Bible Society of Scotland, the Religious Tract Society, the Trinitarian Bible Society and the American Baptist Missionary Society, whose missionary he had been appointed since 1835, and his work, in turn, had their support. Organizations and charities bearing the names, 'The Chapel Building Loan Fund,' 'The Widows' Fund,' 'The Relief Fund for Persecuted Christians,' bear testimony to the broad front along which he conducted his campaign. And if extension of the work abroad was encouraging, it was no less so at home where the church in Hamburg received 73 members by baptism in 1846, bringing the membership to 326.

Although there were temporary respites from persecution such as occurred after the Hamburg fire, Oncken and his fellow Baptists were always required to be on their guard. Threats and dangers seemed to be an inevitable accompaniment of his travels. He was fined and imprisoned. In Denmark anyone found consorting with him rendered himself liable to the severest penalties. Of this period of his life in the forties he writes:

> Our baptisms all took place under cover of the night and on my missionary tours, which were frequently extensive, I was banished successively from almost every State in Germany. I could never travel as an honest man by daylight, but was compelled to journey on foot in the darkness, to hold services, examine candidates, administer the ordinances, and form churches in the dead of night, and take care to be across the frontiers before break of day for fear of my pursuers.

He also faced the dangers normally associated with travelling vast distances, and on a visit to the USA in 1853 escaped with his life from a train disaster which killed more than fifty passengers. The effects of injuries he sustained remained with him for the rest of his life, but they were never allowed to restrict his efforts.

His evangelistic spirit was indomitable. Even war was not permitted to hamper its expression. Germany in these years was involved in a number of conflicts, and each one was taken by Oncken as an opportunity for the gospel. During the war with France in 1870, prayer meetings were held each evening in the Hamburg church, and each letter sent to Christians in the army contained tracts, so that even amidst the fighting the Word of God was made known. Over a million and a quarter tracts were used in this way, besides Gospels, Testaments, and religious books.

Given the importance Oncken attached to baptism it was natural that he should have made the acquaintance of Spurgeon, who shared the pulpit with him on several occasions at New Park Street. The church in London sent an annual contribution to the German work, and Spurgeon preached at the opening service of the new Hamburg church in 1867. He also composed two hymns to celebrate the occasion. The tribute Spurgeon paid his brother pastor was clearly not based on hearsay.

He was still travelling in the cause of the gospel in his eightieth year, but in November 1879 he suffered a stroke, and in the following year retired to Zurich, in Switzerland. Decline in his health was slow, and he lived for a further four years. His death eventually occurred at the close of 1884. On the death of his first wife, when he was left with five children to care for, he had written, 'The streams may be dried up, but the fountain never ceases to flow.' His long, useful, and devout life showed how deeply he had drunk of that fountain.

In any attempt to evaluate his contribution to missionary expansion there may be the temptation to criticize him for a too robust emphasis on the practice of baptism. It must not be forgotten, however, that this went along with a healthy reaction against the deadly influence of the liberalism that was abroad in the Lutheran Church. Until Oncken's work there was, apart from the Mennonites, no real Baptist presence on the continent of Europe. When he died the Union of German Baptists numbered more than 150 churches and 31,000 members. Other churches had been formed throughout Europe, and there was even one in the neighbourhood of Mount Ararat! Statistics are notoriously poor narrators, but those that we find in association with Oncken's life and work give more than a passing indication that he has won his place among the great pioneer missionaries.

15
William Chalmers Burns
(1815-1868)

There are thousands of missionaries who receive their salary from church or society in their homeland; there are thousands who receive no regular salary but choose to depend on the giving of individuals in response to the prompting of God; there can be very few who send home a year's salary in order to further the work they represent. So convinced was William Chalmers Burns of the need for workers in the field that this was the course he adopted so that others might be sent out. If the term 'burden' has sometimes been too readily and easily accorded, it was never the case with Burns. His endeavours as a preacher were so remarkably blessed by God that a place among the outstanding men of the pulpit was virtually guaranteed him. His decision was 'to scorn delights, and live laborious days'. He refused the fame that was virtually his in his native Scotland, 'choosing rather to suffer affliction with the people of God' in China. The mark of Moses was on W. C. Burns.

Like so many outstanding servants of the gospel he was born to Christian parents. In his case he had the added advantage that his father was a minister of the Church of Scotland. He attended the parish school at Kilsyth, near Glasgow, from which he emerged with a good rather than spectacular record. Books do not appear to have been particularly his delight, with a few exceptions, one of these being *The Pilgrim's Progress*. At the age of twelve his uncle took him to Aberdeen to school where his intellectual gifts began to flourish. He entered university in the same town and on completing his course there announced his intention of becoming a lawyer like his uncle. His motive was far from being elevated: it was simply that the wealth and luxury enjoyed by members of the legal profession appealed to him.

Scarcely had he moved to Edinburgh to become an articled clerk when, in his own words, 'an arrow from the quiver of the King of

Zion' pierced his heart and Christ became a Saviour to him. The means employed by God were varied but it is encouraging and challenging to know that the influences of his family were significant: overhearing his father praying, and receiving a letter from his sisters in which they spoke openly of their confidence of heaven. At the moment of his conversion he was aware of a call to the ministry of the gospel and in pursuit of this call he returned to Aberdeen in 1832 before completing his training in divinity in Glasgow. While in Glasgow he helped in the formation of the Students' Missionary Society which in turn was to prove the agency through which came the summons to serve God in a foreign land. It was also while here that he came under the influence and ministry of the saintly 'Rabbi' Duncan. Although his contact with Robert Murray M'Cheyne still lay in the future he already shared with him the aching heart that drove both men, like their Master, to seek tirelessly the lost souls of men. In 1839, just before his twenty-fourth birthday, he was licensed to preach as a probationer for the ministry. But where was he to go?

He had previously made known his desire to go as a missionary to India. When obstacles arose preventing this wish from being granted he was not left idle nor were doubts allowed to trouble him. In the summer of the same year he was asked to go to the very country which seemed denied to him but now he was compelled to refuse the invitation. He had received another request which he had accepted, and which was to make his name revered throughout Scotland. More importantly it was a request that was to open the way to a field of amazing fruitfulness in his homeland. Missionary work was deferred —not for a moment forgotten—while he yielded to this new design of God. M'Cheyne, the young, godly minister of St Peter's, Dundee, about to sail for Palestine, had asked Burns to take his place while he was away. Little could either man have imagined what was to issue from their agreement. It would be nine years before his initial longing was realized but most certainly they were not wasted years.

When Burns came to Dundee in April that year he was under no illusions regarding the task that awaited him. M'Cheyne had already left his mark on the place and success had already attended his preaching. Undismayed, and barely a month after being licensed, he applied himself to the work. He won immediate popularity, which proved to be his first battlefield. 'Hungering after applause from man' was as much a temptation to him as to any other, but where other men might have yielded, prayer and diligence ensured that it was a snare which he avoided. Both he and his congregation were blessed as the Spirit of God moved among them. However, God's unmistakable seal was set upon his ministry not at Dundee but at his father's church at Kilsyth.

He had been invited to preach at the communion season in the little town. Having preached on Friday and Sunday with no unusual effects he proposed to address them for the last time on the Tuesday morning. It was the beginning of a harvest that was reaped not only in Kilsyth but in many other parts of the country. So powerfully did the Holy Spirit come upon the preacher that the service which began shortly after 10 o'clock lasted for five hours. The call to battle that he issued deeply impressed his father and his brother—'No cross, no crown.' During that period his pleadings with the people were so impassioned that many were struck to the ground as they sought God's mercy. The previous century the parish had known similar quickening, and when he went home at three o'clock the preacher's father thought that it had been 'awakened from a dream of a hundred years!' The revival continued in Kilsyth until October. When Burns returned to Dundee in August, his ministry was attended with similar scenes. M'Cheyne reported to the Presbytery of Aberdeen that when he came home from Palestine there were 39 prayer meetings held in connection with the church every week, five of them composed entirely of little children.

Released from his commitment at St Peter's, Burns devoted himself to evangelistic activity in various places. Perth and Aberdeen were among the chief towns and cities visited. Whether in church buildings or in the open-air meetings, the effects were the same. Men and women seemed to have but one concern and that was, how to be right with God. Nor were his efforts at this time confined to Scotland; he preached in Sunderland and Newcastle in the north of England, remarking of the latter that 'the sleep of death is on the city'. It was certainly a sleep that he disturbed. During one open-air meeting he was pelted with manure, only to preach the following Sunday in the same manner. So aware was he of the importance of the occasion that he 'could almost have torn the pulpit to pieces'. Having spent nearly four hours in the open-air service he went to the house where he was staying at about 9 o'clock, thinking his labours for the day were over. He was called from his respite by the news that the church was full, the congregation waiting for him since 7 o'clock. When for a while he took the pulpit of Alexander Moody Stuart at Edinburgh he did not spare himself, working among and visiting students, soldiers, orphans, prisoners and the insane. In 1843 he was involved in the Disruption controversy of the Church of Scotland, addressing a gathering on the eve of that occasion on the need for the Spirit of God to be poured out on them. He visited Dublin, with an eye to working among Roman Catholics, and in 1844, in response to an invitation, crossed the Atlantic to Canada where he spent two years.

On his return he felt concerned once more about missionary work. There was a marked lack of enthusiasm when he offered himself, the response being that no one would object to his going if he was so minded but there was no special opening for him. At the same time, however, an inquiry came from the English Presbyterian Church Missionary Committee as to whether there was anyone in Scotland who might be prepared to go as their first missionary to China. After some equivocating on the part of the committee and much seeking of God's will on the part of Burns, it was resolved that he should go. When asked how soon he could go his reply was instant: 'Tomorrow!' As he was about to enter a church in London on 8 June 1847 to conduct a service he received news that the ship that was to carry him was ready to leave Portsmouth. He lost no time in catching a train and the following evening he was on his way. Hong Kong was reached in November.

Thirteen years previously one of the pioneer missionaries to China had died. He was Robert Morrison of the London Missionary Society, and although conversions had been very few, his achievements in other directions were such as to put his successors in his debt. He had compiled a Dictionary of Chinese and, with the help of a colleague, translated the Bible into Chinese. When Burns arrived, there were fifty Protestant missionaries already in the country. After boarding with some of them in Hong Kong and acquainting himself with the language, he sought new lodgings so that he might be closer to the Chinese people. Here he engaged a Chinese teacher and together they opened a school. His first year was spent quietly in this way with the boys, encouraging them to worship, and developing a confidence in the new language, but his heart was set on preaching to the natives in their own tongue. With this in view the school was discontinued early in 1849 as he moved from place to place with his Chinese assistants. In this he was not restricted at all, but in a letter home he writes:

> In other days it has been my solemn privilege to enter into the labours of others, and it may be that here I am to labour where others are to reap.

He felt keenly an inclination to settle and work in Canton, where he worked for sixteen months, knowing much to dishearten him and being urged to go to Amoy. Difficulty in securing premises meant that he had to surrender what plans he had for Canton, and in June 1851 he moved to Amoy. This was a port about four hundred miles north-east of Hong Kong. Here he met new missionary colleagues and had to learn a new dialect. It gave him obvious pleasure at this time to complete a translation of the book that had meant much to him in those far-away boyhood days in Kilsyth, *The Pilgrim's Progress*.

In 1853 he was once more out in the field visiting the large city of Chang-chow. Large crowds gathered, who seemed prepared to listen for three or four hours at a time. Even more encouraging were the early months of the following year at Pechuia. There were conversions, and when he returned after a brief absence, the two natives he had left there had much in which to rejoice. Forty to sixty people each night were filling the preaching room, many of them won to Christ. It was not a year of unmixed delight, however. The death of the wife of a particularly close colleague, Dr James Young, occurred. The effect on the doctor was so severe that he had to return home and it was agreed that Burns should accompany him. While in Scotland a letter received from the church in Pechuia expressed their yearning for him to return to them. The sad death of Dr Young meant that Burns's stay was not extended and in March 1855 he was again on his way to China.

On his return an attempt to contact the Taiping rebels failed. But as he and his Chinese servant made their way back to Shanghai they were able to distribute literature. The eagerness to have the books was matched by an inability to understand them, and affected Burns deeply. The next six months were to see him sail from Shanghai along the rivers and canals giving out the Scriptures and preaching the gospel. In this he was aided by a native Christian, and later by an 'excellent young English missionary'. Not the least benefit gained by Burns from this friendship with Hudson Taylor was that he copied Taylor's practice of wearing Chinese clothing, a change that made him and his preaching more readily received by the crowd. As there was an over-concentration of missionaries in the Shanghai area the two decided in 1856 to make Swatow their new centre. The friendship ended all too soon when Taylor went back to Shanghai for his medical equipment. During his absence Burns fell foul of the authorities and was taken to Canton. On his release he planned to return to Swatow but was advised against this by the British representative, and so remained in Canton helping the English and American missionaries there. Not surprisingly in the confused circumstances, contact with Taylor was broken, and it was not until 1858 that Burns learnt of his friend's marriage in Ningpo. Burns waited no longer and made for Swatow. As far as he knew there had been no converts; but as he had intimated earlier, perhaps now his work was to be one of sowing.

The next few years were spent in Amoy, Swatow, and Fuh-chow. The demands made upon him were varied: churches needed organizing, members needed disciplining, the seed sown needed watering. He himself was encouraged when the Amoy church set apart two native evangelists and when fruit began to appear in Swatow. Along with this the clouds of persecution were growing darker. Christian Chinese had their property stolen and their fields plundered, while candidates for baptism came in for severe beatings at the hands of their families. To deal with this threat Burns went to make representations to the ambassador at Peking. He arrived in October 1863, and having completed his errand, he remained there for four years. During this time he compiled a hymn-book and turned his attention again to his beloved *Pilgrim's Progress,* rendering it in the Peking dialect. Immediately after this he began to translate the Psalms. Needless to say he preached whenever opportunity afforded itself.

The last stage of his own pilgrimage was about to be completed. Nieu-chwang beckoned and to it he set his face. The reason behind this was typical—'because there was no one labouring there'. Had not Robert Murray M'Cheyne written to him years before on his coming to Dundee, 'You will not find many companions'? If that was true of Scotland how much more of Manchuria! He encouraged others to follow him, for although there were Roman Catholics there, he was the

119

only Protestant representative. The end of his ministry was near, but its character had lost none of its earnestness.

A bare six months were left to him before the gates of the Celestial City opened to admit him. A letter to his mother at the opening of 1868 discloses that he was suffering illness, and that he realized something of its seriousness:

> Unless it should please God to rebuke the disease, it is evident what the end must soon be, and I write these lines beforehand to say that I am happy, and ready through the abounding grace of God either to live or to die. May the God of all consolation comfort you when the tidings of my decease shall reach you, and through the redeeming blood of Jesus may we meet with joy before the throne above!

In April 1868 William Chalmers Burns went to his reward. He had carried the cross; now for the crown.

16
David Livingstone
(1813-1873)

In the history of Christian missionaries no name is better known than that of David Livingstone. This is probably owing in large measure to the importance of his exploits as an explorer. Indeed the question has been mooted as to whether he was primarily a missionary or an explorer. For all the discussion that might provoke, there would be no doubt at all in the mind of Livingstone himself, and he would be surprised that the query had been raised at all. When a man is discovered dead upon his knees we need not delay long before concluding what are the springs of his actions.

The first 25 years of the nineteenth century saw the birth of a number of boys in Scotland who were to be distinguished by their effort to make known the gospel in distant countries. Among these infant missionaries was the child born to Neil and Agnes Livingstone in March 1813, in Blantyre, a village just above Glasgow. The home was poor, the parents godly, the atmosphere redolent of a deep appreciation of the meaning of the death of Christ. Industrious habits were soon instilled in David, and at the age of ten he was already at work in a linen factory, at the same time displaying an early thirst for knowledge. One of his first purchases from his first week's wages was a Latin grammar, but his range of interests was very broad. He delighted in books of travel and science, and the study of rocks, herbs and flowers occupied his time. It appears that the one subject that held no great pleasure for him was religion. However, on becoming a Christian he showed an immediate concern for missionary work.

Although at first he had no intention of serving God overseas, little time elapsed before he responded to an appeal to go to China. As well as devoting himself to theological training he resolved to study medicine. The wages he earned enabled him to do this at Glasgow. He identified himself with a Congregational church, finding the laxity of the Church of Scotland and of the Episcopalian Church an obstacle. This abhorrence of insincerity and falsehood was to manifest itself on the mission field where for two years he did not celebrate the Lord's Supper, deeming the people unworthy.

In 1838 he was accepted by the London Missionary Society, and was sent to prepare himself under the guidance of Richard Cecil in Essex. He showed no marked promise, lacking in fluency in prayer, and on one occasion having to fly out of the pulpit, being unable to remember his sermon. Further probation was required and granted. Meanwhile China was closed because of the opium war, but a meeting with Robert Moffat, visiting England after 23 years missionary service in Africa, redirected his steps. With the award of a medical diploma in 1840, David Livingstone was ordained a missionary. In December he sailed for Africa.

Moffat's station was in Kuruman, seven hundred miles north of Cape Town. He was still in England when his young helper arrived there, but the Scot was not one to idle his time away. Removing himself from the company of Europeans he learnt the language, ways, and customs of the Bakawains. His eager, restless spirit showed itself further in a desire to thrust more deeply inland. A few journeys were undertaken with a view to establishing a new station. One was opened at Mabotsa. Here Livingstone nearly met his death when he was attacked by a lion. He was rescued by his companions, but his arm was permanently maimed. The false joint in the arm was one of the means used to identify his body when it was brought back to England.

Marriage to Moffat's daughter, Mary, in 1845, was followed by a move from Mabotsa that took him eventually to Kolobeng. Such was his influence that the Bakawains with their chief, Sechele, went after him. Here he remained for five years, during which he drew enormous encouragement from the conversion of Sechele. There was much to discourage him, for the work was slow and his motives were suspected by the natives. He also had to contend with the effect of drought which afflicted them more after the gospel had been brought to them than before. The complaint was made that 'we never get rain, while these tribes who never pray as we do obtain abundance'.

The stay at Kolobeng was not unbroken. There were many journeys of hundreds of miles among the Makololo people. Kolobeng was becoming unsuitable, and Livingstone was concerned to establish some work further north. Two enemies were a persistent threat to him and his companions, the tsetse fly and fever, and three attempts were required before the village of the Makololo chief was reached, and even then it proved unfitted for a mission station. Even so, in 1849 during his first journey, he had discovered Lake N'gami, practically unknown and discounted when compared with his later discovery in 1851, that of the mighty Zambesi. But it was with a heavy heart that he went back to Kolobeng.

The Bakawains' need was becoming more urgent, and Livingstone was aching to open up more of the great continent. 'Providence', he said, 'seems to call me to the regions beyond.' For further journeys he dare not take his family. The only alternative was for them to return to England. It was no easy decision. In the call of the interior Livingstone discerned the call of God, and this must be obeyed even at the high cost of separation from his family.

After bidding them farewell at Cape Town he was delayed in returning. During his absence the Boers of Transvaal had shown their intense hostility. They resented Livingstone's influence on the natives, and feared for the effect on the ivory traffic, which they desired to keep in their own hands. When he came to Kolobeng once more he heard of a vicious attack made on the Bakawains, resulting in the death of sixty of the tribe, together with the destruction of his home and the loss of his possessions. It appears that the intention of the Boers was to kill him, and had he not been detained he would very likely have lost his life.

In his search for a healthy spot for a mission station among the Makololo, Livingstone continued to be disappointed. Response to the gospel was meagre. He was advised to settle down and devote himself to working in one area. However, his vision was not to be so limited. Far from being dismayed he wrote:

> Like voices crying in the wilderness we prepare the way for the glorious future in which missionaries telling the same tale of love will convert by every sermon.

He shared the holy ambition of the apostle Paul to be the first to preach the gospel where the name of Christ had never been heard.

David Livingstone now embarked on another project. To say it was one of astounding proportions appears almost commonplace in the life of one whose every exploit amazed. Seeing the need for another way from the coast to the interior, he set out to find one. Accompanied by a group of Makololo he travelled westward towards the coast. Encountering swamps, crossing rivers, walking and wading for so much of the journey, meeting dangers and hardships at every turn, in seven months he suffered 31 attacks of fever. His eventual arrival at the sea, at the Portuguese St Paul de Loanda, marked the end of the expedition—or so it seemed. For the end was not yet the end. He would have been perfectly justified in going directly to his family in England, but he had promised his companions that he would take them back. After a while the return journey was undertaken. Remarkably the 27 who went with him were brought safely home. Nor was this all. Despite contracting rheumatic fever, a few months rest sufficed before he set off once more.

This journey to the west coast had not provided a satisfactory route, so he sought one to the east coast. Again, ever present dangers were overcome, and the hardships faced compensated by discovering the Victoria Falls in 1855. Quilimane on the east coast, in present-day Mozambique, was reached in May 1856, making him the first European to have crossed the continent, from the South Atlantic to the Indian Ocean. During those momentous journeys two awards were made to him, a degree from Glasgow University in recognition of his services in the cause of science and Christian philanthropy, and also the gold medal of the Geographical Society. The accuracy with which he fixed geographical points won great praise.

At last he felt free to return to Britain. It was to be reunited with his family, to share in the sadness of the death of his father, and to receive the esteem and honour accorded to him wherever he went. Much of 1857 was spent in writing *Missionary Travels in South Africa,* and then in addressing various meetings throughout the country. After setting aside from the proceeds of the sale of his book what he regarded as sufficient for providing for his children, he invested the remainder in the work which had captured his heart and occupied his life.

When he returned to Africa the following year it was not in the name of the LMS. Believing it was his divine vocation to make accessible the remote vastness of the continent, and realizing that many would not consider this a valid object on which missionary finance should be spent, he accepted a post as consul at Quilimane. This carried with it responsibility for and command of an expedition to explore the interior. Any criticism that his affection for the natives and his love of God had grown cold was countered by the fact that he arranged for his brother-in-law to work among the Makololo, and paid his salary himself.

Accompanied by his wife and youngest son he also took with him a steam launch which it was hoped would be an immense advantage in travelling the rivers. It was a disappointment to him that almost as soon as they arrived at Cape Town, Mary became ill and was unable to accompany him. The launch proved to be an unrelieved handicap in terms of expense and speed, and was replaced by another, the *Lady Nyassa,* after the discovery by Livingstone of the lake of the same name. Her purpose was to be to sail the waters of her namesake. On this journey he was able to help establish the Universities Mission on a tributary of the Zambesi called the Shire. During his absence his wife's illness was prolonged, and he was crushed when death took her. The four years of separation since their arrival in Africa were lightened for three months at the start of 1862 before she was lost to him. To read the words he wrote at this time in his journal and his letters home is to feel intensely the devastation he experienced as he wept over her 'who well deserved many tears'.

All the while he was haunted by the odious spectre of the slave trade. In his effort to suppress this market in human beings he was promised the help of the Portuguese. In practice this help was scarcely given. He imagined that opening up the country would discourage slavery. In effect the traders followed him and turned his discoveries to their advantage. The degradation of the slave trade was sickening. Villages, tracks, and forests yielded up their grisly tale of skeletons. Corpses floated along the rivers. Extracts from Livingstone's writings reveal the nightmares of his sleep and of their existence in reality. The horrors of such commerce were a major motive in his labour for his adopted country.

The expedition did not turn out to be as successful as he had hoped, and in the event was prohibitively expensive. Consequently he was recalled. His hopes of putting the *Lady Nyassa* on the lake were dashed. On reaching the coast he had to dispose of the vessel, and rather than sell her to the Portuguese, who would have used her in the slave trade, he took her the 2,500 miles from Zanzibar to Bombay, in India, with a crew of three Europeans and seven natives, a voyage that took him 45 days. Livingstone knew what it was to pay a high price for his principles. From Bombay he returned to England, where his efforts were largely directed to alerting the public to the wickedness of the trade in which the Portuguese were involved.

He left England for the last time in 1865. He had been requested to discover the true sources of the Nile. Insisting that this did not mean abandoning the duty of a missionary, he agreed to undertake the engagement. Some of those who accompanied him were far from reliable, one of them returning to Zanzibar and disguising the fact of his desertion with reports that Dr Livingstone had been murdered at Lake Nyassa. Two other deserters took with them what was the doctor's most valuable possession, his medicine box. This proved to be a massive blow as far as his health was concerned and must have hastened his end. His journals recount a steady decline containing such entries as this in January 1867: 'In changing my dress this A.M. I was frightened at my own emaciation.' In April he records: 'I am excessively weak; can not walk without tottering, and have constant singing in the head, but the Highest will lead me farther.'

In 1869 he suffered from six weeks of pneumonia. Amazingly his explorations continued, and further discoveries of various lakes were made. Undaunted, he pursued the search for the Nile sources, not for personal glory but out of a sense of duty to the Royal Geographical Society, and above all the knowledge that it would increase his influence for good to Africa. The hardships he endured are almost beyond credibility. Disappointments and danger constantly accompanied him. Hundreds of miles were travelled to reach supplies that had been sent from the coast only to find that they had been ransacked and scattered and his letters lost.

For five years the search went on, and with the passing of each one the longing to go home deepened. The theft, treachery, massacres that he encountered were no isolated occurrences. Tremendous demands were made on his body and spirit, and he was adequate for them all. It would be nothing less than a fitting end to a heroic adventure if the river to which his steps brought him at last was the Nile. It was not. After this heart-breaking experience, there followed the five hundred mile journey to Ujiji, where he arrived 'a mere ruckle of bones', and there he found some relief.

This was in the famous meeting with H. M. Stanley. Sent out by the *New York Herald* the journalist found the missionary in November 1871. Conversation, meals, news, supplies, all served to revive Livingstone's spirit. Stanley was the only white man he had seen for six years. Stanley's pleadings that his new-found friend might return with him fell on deaf ears. The reason was transparent—the sources of the Nile were still to be discovered. Not only this, but there was the determination that all his efforts might somehow bring an end to slavery. 'To heal the open sore of the world' was an ever present goal. His journals reveal his mind, its vows, intentions, pleadings in the presence of God.

Having parted from Stanley he set out again with a band of followers. The sufferings were no lighter than previously. The driving force remained the same, 'I would forget all my cold, hunger, suffering and trials, if I could be the means of putting a stop to this cursed traffic.' On his last birthday, March 19, 1873 he wrote:

> Thanks to the Almighty Preserver of men for sparing me thus so far on the journey of life. Can I hope for ultimate success? So many obstacles have arisen. Let not Satan prevail over me, O my Lord Jesus.

When unable to walk because of weakness and pain he insisted on being carried lest the advance should be halted. At last even his indomitable spirit had to succumb. On 1 May 1873, in the village of Itala, his travelling came to an end. He had not found the source of the Nile, but he had come to the source of the river of God.

Another episode, and that by no means the least remarkable, was yet to be written. His companion, Jacob Wainwright, removed and buried his heart and internal organs in Africa. The body was carefully embalmed, carried by his faithful black attendants a thousand miles to the coast near Zanzibar, and the long journey to England was begun. Southampton was reached in April 1874. Almost a year after his death his remains were laid to rest in Westminster Abbey.

How is he to be described? An explorer who evangelized? Or a missionary who explored? Enough has been said in this chapter to indicate why there has been debate. The answer lies in the narrow, limited version of the gospel entertained by so many today, contrasted with the extensive, wide prospects entertained by Livingstone. His eyes were not on his generation alone but also on those to come. If he knew little success he also knew that by his labours the time would come when unlimited prosperity would accompany the proclamation of the sacrifice offered at Calvary. His vision was not that of a tribe, or a country, or a continent, but of a world for Christ.

His journeys in Africa took him 29,000 miles, every one of them in the name of the Lord Jesus. Traveller, astronomer, doctor, emancipator, evangelist, the list of his achievements goes on. His own words demonstrate what were his priorities, and there is no doubt his priorities were right: 'Viewed in relation to my calling, the end of the geographical feat is only the beginning of the enterprise.'

17
F. W. Baedeker
(1823-1906)

To the gourmet Egon Ronay is a name to be conjured with; if you buy second-hand cars you will swear by Glass; should learning foreign languages be your interest then Berlitz will be your password; for they are all the acknowledged authorities in their different fields. For his part the seasoned traveller will know that his Baedeker cannot be surpassed. The connection between the missionary and the compiler of the guidebooks is not as remote as might be supposed. They were cousins, and the one was a contributor to the productions of the other in helping people find their way around the continent. There can be no doubt that the exercise stood F. W. Baedeker in good stead, since he travelled so widely in Europe in God's service. His later work was still that of giving directions to those unfamiliar with the journey. What had changed was the destination.

His father had acquired some fame as an ornithologist, and so there were certain privileges and benefits which he would have enjoyed in his home in Germany. Even so it was austerity rather than luxury that characterized his upbringing, and although he came under the influence of strong moral principles they do not appear to have been evangelical. Indeed over half his long life had passed before he became a Christian. His early years were spent in business, the army, and in much travelling, his excursions taking him as far as Tasmania. During this period he was married, but sadly his wife died three months after the wedding.

His decision to end his unsettled way of life came during a visit to England, when, together with a friend, he decided to establish a school in Weston-super-Mare. In 1862 the widowed mother of one of his pupils became his second wife. They were a devoted and happy couple, and in the long periods of absence from home and separation from each other which were to come in the service of the gospel, she was to prove a tower of strength. Moving to England was to mark another even more significant change in his life. This was in 1866, when, in his early forties, he became a Christian while attending a series of meetings addressed by the renowned Lord Radstock. Along with the remarkable spiritual transformation went a corresponding improvememt in his health. People had been prophesying for him an early grave. Instead he was to undertake a strenuous course of journeying that would have taxed men much younger and apparently healthier. Such preparations as God had ordered for him were completed by studies in Bristol and in two German universities, from one of which he was awarded a doctorate in Philosophy. More importantly his stay in Bristol brought him into contact with his fellow countryman, George Müller, whose influence was to tell for many years. In 1892 Müller laid hands on him and 'separated him to the special ministry to the banished brethren'. Müller was 86, Baedeker a mere 68.

Eight years were to elapse after his conversion before Baedeker's vocation was recognized, and this seems less by design on his part than by the way circumstances conspired to indicate the path he should take. While on a visit to Berlin he was asked to interpret for an American preacher who was conducting evangelistic meetings in the city. Such was the effect left by the interpreter as much as by the preacher that he was urged to set out on his own account and exercise his evangelistic gifts. Thus it was that with fifty years of his life past, when most men are contemplating a life of retirement, he began to be a missionary. From this comparatively small beginning in Germany his concern grew out of all proportion. In 1877 he let his home in England for three years, and moved with his wife and adopted daughter to Russia. After this his sphere of activity included most of Europe and extended into Asia.

Although never boorish, he did not allow the niceties of etiquette and protocol to weigh too much with him. The extreme urgency with which he viewed his task seems to have provoked him to interpret our Lord's instructions in Luke 10 about saluting no one by the way with a rare seriousness. Thus, the preparations for his first meeting in Russia set a pattern which he was frequently to adopt. They began with the following request to the governor of the city:

> I am staying in your city for a few days. See, here is my passport. I am from England. I am an evangelist, and should like to hold a meeting here.

If you will arrange for a meeting in your drawing-room, I am willing to conduct it, and deliver an address.

This novel approach was greeted by the official with positive eagerness, and was not the last time that such directness paid dividend. Nor did he allow obstacles to remain where, with a little application, they might be removed. Forbidden on one occasion to preach because it was an illegal activity, he asked if he might lecture instead and was given immediate permission. The bills that were being issued advertizing his preaching service were changed to announce that a lecture would be given. The subject was 'Sin and Salvation'! It was repeated more than once and was heard by thousands. People who, like Baedeker, come to faith in Christ in later years often act with a dispatch and earnestness that indicates a deep yearning to compensate for lost time and wasted opportunity.

His name will for ever be associated with Russia. Until recently the country and the vast areas of the USSR held a bleak and sinister fascination for many. The persecution of Christians associated with the communist regime, however, did not begin with the revolution of 1917. The nineteenth century had been one of disturbance and turmoil. The tsar who ruled when Baedeker was beginning his work was, in fact, the victim of terrorist bombs. The Russian Orthodox Church was firmly in the grip of the state, and the changing policies of the tsars gave no ground for lasting confidence to anyone. Evangelicals such as Baptists and a group known as Stundists certainly felt the lash of opposition in an attempt to stamp them out. Banishment to Siberia for religious beliefs is no twentieth century innovation. It was to this situation that Baedeker felt an irresistible call, seemingly oblivious of every comfort his abilities could have afforded him, possessed of a desire to strengthen his oppressed brothers and to lead others to the life that is found only in Jesus Christ.

To recite statistics of life in the prison camps is easy; to perceive the horror that lay behind them, impossible. The sufferings of the prisoners was compounded by the fact that many of them were accompanied by their wives and children. On visiting a prison in Moscow, Baedeker found a party of exiles about to set off for Siberia, some carrying infants in arms. This journey they were to accomplish on foot. The number of men and women thus punished must remain a guess, but Baedeker reckoned there were about 50,000 escaped prisoners in Siberia. The thought of reaching these people would have been dismissed by most men as soon as it was entertained. For him, however, challenges were not presented in order to be shunned, but to be faced. The awareness that he was, like Paul, a debtor to all men, lay behind his determination to set out in 1890 on his first journey across Asia. As far as the gospel was concerned some of this was virgin territory.

His mammoth journey began at St Petersburg, the one-time Leningrad, at the tip of the Gulf of Finland. Tracing its course on a map gives an impression of the burden he felt for the poor victims of oppression. It took him to Moscow and then east to Perm. From there he crossed the Ural mountains to Tobolsk, and then by steamer down the river Ob to Tomsk. The route continued overland to Lake Baikal and along the Chinese border. Two more rivers assisted him until the second, the Amur, brought him to the eastern ocean. Even then he was not finished. From this Land's End of the continent he crossed to the island of Sakhalin which harboured 'the most hardened cut-throats of the most remorseless penal settlement' of them all.

His itinerary of some 7,000 miles had taken him four months. At its end he had distributed 12,000 copies of the Scriptures and had preached to some 40,000 prisoners. The demands it made on him provoked him to write at the time, 'This is a journey I shall certainly never make a second time.' That was a vow his quickened conscience and sympathetic heart did not allow him to keep. Such was his diligence that it is hard to imagine that he overlooked one prison camp in this time, always preaching the gospel, distributing Bibles, and bringing gifts to the inmates. Any injustice he encountered was brought to the notice of the prison governor, and more than one sufferer had cause to thank God for his attention. His keen eye seems to have been swift to search out instances of unduly harsh treatment. From Japan he made his way home visiting Shanghai, Saigon, Singapore, Colombo, and Port Said. The beginning of December saw him safely arrived in England.

Nothing could be further from the truth than to think that Baedeker's work was exclusively among the unfortunates of Siberia. He moved very freely among the higher ranks of society, discovering that although 'not many mighty, not many noble' were called, God was very much at work among the aristocracy. And after all, did not he himself owe his experience of Christ to the faithfulness of one of their number? He was certainly no stranger to the drawing-rooms and palaces of the rich and privileged, one of the most godly being the Princess Lieven in St Petersburg, who appears to have been a Russian Countess of Huntingdon. One meeting in the home of a Count Brobinsky caused a raising of the eyebrows of Dr and Mrs Baedeker when, upon the conclusion of the address, the gentle ladies lit up their cigarettes before discussing what they had just heard! His journal is liberally sprinkled with references to barons and counts, and while he was in Sweden the Queen sent for him. The temptation to idleness which these associations afforded him were resisted steadfastly, and the impression is given that he would much prefer to be among the prisoners than among the lords and ladies. In Finland he was able to combine both aspects of his work since his introduction to the prisons there was effected by a Baroness von Wrede, a most committed worker among the prisoners.

One other name from among the ranks of the famous must be mentioned in any account of Baedeker's life, and that is Count Leo Tolstoy. The two met and exchanged opinions on religion, on which subject the differences were irreconcilable. The novelist had accepted pacifism, vegetarianism and poverty in order to attain his goal in life and to arrive at some moral ideal. He exerted a wide influence on his followers, some of whom for faithfulness to his teachings were sent to Siberia, perhaps to the very camps visited by the missionary. For his part Baedeker spelt out clearly those evangelical principles he always maintained before high and low. It is more than likely that some of the characters that feature in the writings are based upon Baedeker's life and ministry, and although Tolstoy's treatment of the evangelist and what he represented is decidedly unsympathetic, this fact in itself shows the significance the Count attached to him.

From the importance he gave to the distribution of the Scriptures in his travels it will be no surprise to learn that he supported wholeheartedly the work of the British and Foreign Bible Society. Other organizations in which he expressed a great interest were the Evangelical Alliance, and the Protestant Alliance. As befits a man with the name Baedeker he never stopped travelling, and in the last year of his life, at the age of seventy-three, he made four visits to the continent, esteeming the needs of his brothers and sisters there too great for him to ignore at the expense of what comforts he might have anticipated in his last days. Death came to him and for him while he was away from home at a conference in Bristol. According to the words on his headstone, he 'went in to see the King in his beauty'.

F. W. Baedeker is an example in many respects, perhaps in one thing above all. He had more reason than most to bemoan the fact that so many years were spent in ignorance of the one who died for him. Rather than compound the error by spending yet more time in regretting that loss, he determined that what remained to him of life should be spent in unswerving service to his Lord and Master. Even so, what reflections he did allow himself are typified in one of his letters, 'I find out now what a sorry missionary I really am.' If this is an unprofitable servant, every man has reason to examine himself scrupulously.

18
John Paton
(1824-1907)

The young Scot rose to his feet from where he had been kneeling in prayer and looked around for his bonnet. It was not to be seen. Eventually he found it on a branch on a nearby tree, not on the ground where he had put it. He puzzled as to how it could have moved from one place to the other, but there seemed no explanation. The following day the scene was repeated, the head gear placed on the ground but discovered in a tree. He stood there, bewildered, not noticing the enjoyment of the girl who was the cause of his perplexity. She had followed him and observed him at his devotions, crept up on him, and quietly amused herself at his expense. However, she little bargained for the outcome of her high spirits, and when on the next day he came to the same spot, he found this note pinned to the tree:

> She who stole away your bonnet is ashamed of what she did; she has a great respect for you, and asks you to pray for her, that she may become as good a Christian as you.

The relationship between the serious youth and the spirited girl who was so impressed by his religious exercises developed from this unconventional beginning to a marriage that was to issue in the birth of one of the finest missionaries to grace the pages of Christian history.

It will be already evident that the home to which John Gibson Paton was born on 24 May 1824 was uncommon. He and the other children early learnt where their father went, and what he was about, after meals. He retired to one of the rooms of the cottage, and 'we children got to understand by a sort of spiritual instinct . . . that prayers were being poured out there for us, as of old, by the High Priest within the veil in the Most Holy Place'. John's desire was to be like his father.

His early years were spent near Dumfries, in southern Scotland, where by the age of twelve he had left school and was learning his father's trade of stocking-maker. Beside the sixteen hours he worked each day, he was at his books, for he was resolved to be a minister or a missionary. Six weeks at the Dumfries Academy served only to whet still further his appetite for learning. This proved a stepping stone to his arrival at Glasgow where he combined the work of tract distributor and visitor, employed by one of the city churches, with that of a student at the Free Church Seminary. Illness interrupted his studies, and on more than one occasion lack of funds threatened to cut short his seminary career. A teaching post at a very rough school, where he was eminently successful, enabled him to continue. This period also saw him working in the Glasgow City Mission.

If John Paton had not become a missionary in the South Seas, his earlier work as a missionary in Glasgow would have called forth admiration. The area assigned to him was around Green Street in the Calton district, one of the worst. Almost bereft of Christian influences, its sinfulness walked hand in hand with shamelessness. He managed to secure premises for a Sunday evening service in a hay loft. After a year the number of people attending this meeting was six or seven, with a similar number in a house on a week night. The directors interpreted this as a sign that the Green Street district had had its opportunity, and could not be reached by these ordinary means. Paton begged to be allowed a further trial period. Remarkable results ensued. The congregation grew, meetings multiplied, activities increased, conversions were recorded. New premises were secured. Just as well—for the weekly attendance was now five to six hundred! Of this astonishing chapter in his life he writes:

> If I never attained the scholarship for which I thirsted . . . I yet had much of the blessed Master's presence in all my efforts, which many better scholars sorely lacked: and I was sustained by the lofty aim which burned all these years bright within my soul, namely,—to be qualified as a preacher of the Gospel of Christ, to be owned and used by Him for the salvation of perishing men.

Concern was being shown at this time in the Reformed Presbyterian Church of Scotland, where Paton had been nurtured, that a colleague be found for John Inglis, a missionary in the New Hebrides. The Synod's failure to find such a man produced two effects in John Paton. The first was to be blinded by tears of disappointment that there was no one to meet the need. The second response was the more practical one of offering himself to be that one. When he shared his decision with a fellow student, Joseph Copeland, the latter resolved to do the same. There were many who pleaded with Paton to remain at home to work, but he would not be deflected from his purpose, and he and his friend were both formally accepted for the exacting work. Three weeks after their ordination in March 1858 the two men, with Paton's young wife, sailed from Scotland, bound for the South Seas. At Melbourne, Australia, they boarded another vessel to take them to the island of Aneityum, the most southerly of the thirty islands comprising the New Hebrides. The heartlessness of the captain meant that disaster almost struck them before landing. Their safe arrival, however, was interpreted as an indication that God was with them. There they were greeted by other missionaries, including Dr Inglis, before undertaking the final leg of their long voyage, to Tanna, where a site was secured for them at Port Resolution.

John Paton's heart sank at the sight and sound of the inhabitants of the island. The grotesque appearance of their naked bodies, the wild shrieking as 'Harbour people' and 'Inland people' pursued their endless quarrels, the gunfire as the men fought while their women and children carried on as though nothing abnormal was happening—all this left him dismayed. The victims of one battle had been cooked and eaten the night they died. This did not disturb the boy who made tea for the missionaries. What did upset him was the fact that the blood of the unfortunates had polluted the water, and so he was unable to provide the tea! Perhaps most offensive of all was the news that the widow of one of those who had died was strangled, so that she could accompany her husband to the next world, there to continue serving him. What did encourage Paton was what he had seen of the change in the conduct of the natives on Aneityum as the result of the preaching of the missionaries.

With his work scarcely begun, he suffered the most dreadful loss imaginable, and by no means uncommon in missionary annals. Arrived in Tanna in November, he saw his wife buried four months later. This was three weeks after she had given birth to a son who survived his mother by seventeen days. Strangely, from the day of his marriage, he felt she would be taken from him shortly. That this did nothing to lessen the force of the blow is evident to anyone who reads his own reflections on the event. The willingness to trust where he cannot trace displays itself in this extract:

> I do not pretend to see through the mystery of such visitations,—wherein God calls away the young, the promising, and those sorely needed for His service here; but this I do know and feel, that in the light of such dispensations, it becomes us all to love and serve our blessed Lord Jesus so that we may be ready at His call for death and Eternity.

His first unfavourable impressions of Tanna were constantly reinforced, and it is clear that it was only his great love for the Saviour that sustained him. The horrifying extent of cannibalism became more apparent, as did the cheapness of human life, especially that of a woman. On one occasion three women were sacrificed in order to secure the recovery of the health of the chief. Regularly the blame for any tragedies or setbacks was laid at Paton's door. It seems that the only time anyone would take his side was when they could gain any benefit from doing so. His lot was not made any easier by the fact that he constantly succumbed to fever. Added to this was the inhuman cruelty of the occasional white traders who called at the island. Because they had the same fair complexion as the missionaries, their motives and attitudes were thought by the natives to be the same. One of the most malicious devices of a particular group of traders was that of spreading measles among the Tannese. Large numbers met their death, some of them by the extreme measures they took to find relief.

Encouragements were few, but there were some. A building was erected to serve as church and school. The price of the wood was fifty pairs of trousers for the natives, these articles of clothing being supplied by the Bible class he had left in Glasgow. Another gift from a friend in Glasgow was a printing press. After struggling tirelessly over the technique of printing, his joy was uncontained when the first pages of the Word of God in Tannese were printed. The natives from whom he took heart were the Aneityumese teachers who proved remarkably faithful among their unfriendly neighbours. Apart from these, some forty people attended the worship, although Paton travelled from the coast inland to preach to all the warring factions. For all this the number of Christians was a bare handful. His time on Tanna ended ingloriously in escape for his life. Previously he had

THE NEW HEBRIDES

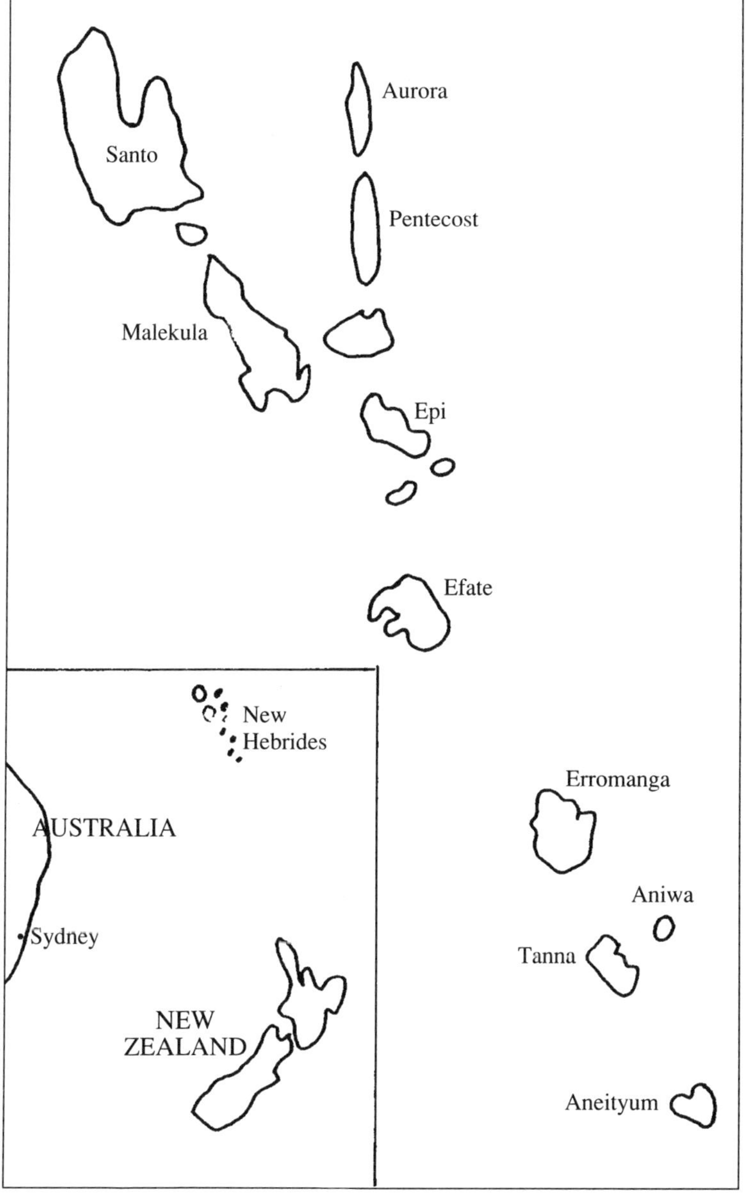

Aurora

Santo

Pentecost

Malekula

Epi

Efate

New
Hebrides

AUSTRALIA

Erromanga

Aniwa

Sydney

Tanna

NEW
ZEALAND

Aneityum

declined persuasions to leave. When he did leave he met criticism from some quarters, one 'dear friend' declaring to his face, 'You should not have left . . . It would have been to your honour, and better for the cause of our Mission, had you been killed at the post of duty.'

Paton's intention was to remain at Aneityum before returning to Tanna. He was urged, however, to visit Australia on a different commission. This was to arouse interest there among the Presbyterian churches in the New Hebrides Mission, and more especially to raise money there for the building of a new ship for the mission. Arriving in Australia in 1862, he was industrious in travelling through New South Wales, Victoria, Tasmania, and South Australia. Much of the support he enlisted came from children and Sunday schools. This was initiated by his scheme of giving them the responsibility of being shareholders. For sixpence a share the children knew the importance of their part in the great enterprise and that they owned a ship. Moreover, he was reminded of his natives on Tanna each time he saw the Aborigines of Australia. He remembered the words of Charles Kingsley concerning them, 'cannot take in the Gospel . . . Poor brutes in human shape . . . like brute beasts.' Kingsley's attitude would have been echoed in many quarters, but such dismay as Paton felt would only have stirred him to more intense efforts.

From Australia he was encouraged to return to Scotland, chiefly to recruit more missionaries. The voyage, during which the ship was struck by lightning in a ferocious storm, ended in August 1863. Neither was his visit to the north of his homeland without incident—he was frostbitten in the foot, and had to make part of the journey lashed to the mast of the ship because of violent weather. There was much to delight him in his year at home. There was the reunion with his devout parents and those of his wife; the children here, with as much enthusiasm as their fellows in Australia, became shareholders in the scheme for the *Dayspring*, the name of the new ship; his Church did him the honour of making him Moderator; four new missionaries volunteered; and he found a new wife. Thus heartened he returned to Australia.

Within an hour of landing at Sydney he faced a problem. The *Dayspring* had arrived, but he could not take possession of her because certain expenses had to be met. It appeared that no one was prepared to help. Some ministers actually suggested selling her, while others thought that since the Sunday schools had given them the ship, the missionaries should be able to maintain her out of their own pockets. This advice was given on Saturday; at the close of Sunday God had remarkably met the need.

A brief visit to the islands made it clear that it was necessary for him to go to Australia to make permanent arrangements regarding support for the ship. Again Sydney greeted him with a difficulty, this time ethical rather than financial. *HMS Curacoa* had visited the islands and had punished the natives for murdering certain traders. A publication in the city showed pictures of the Tannese being shelled and killed from offshore, where the *Dayspring* was seen astern of the *Curacao*. The inference drawn from this was extremely damaging. The story spread to Britain and America, no doubt augmented by further details. Paton felt himself to be the most detested man in Australia, until the Commodore cleared the missionaries from any blame whatsoever. The true version was consequently published by the newspapers, but the harm was done, and the flood of criticism took a while to subside.

It was considered unwise for him to go back to Tanna at that time, and so in 1866 he went to Aniwa, an island about twenty miles north-east of Tanna. Measuring a mere seven miles by two, it was to be home for him for fifteen years. After an initial, kind reception he found that similar dangers awaited him on this island as on the other. Often his only escape from a swinging club or a musket aimed at him was to rush into the arms of the native so that he could inflict no damage, and wait until his anger had abated. At other times it was a simple matter of standing still and praying. Typically, the Aniwans considered themselves better than the Tannese. One of the gruesome marks of this distinction was demonstrated when Paton asked one of the chiefs about two large baskets of human bones that he had gathered. 'How do these bones come to be here?' was the missionary's inquiry. Misunderstanding the point of the question, the chief expressed the superior culture of the Aniwans in his reply, 'Ah, we are not Tannamen! We don't eat the bones!'

In such circumstances where human life was so cheap, care of children was a priority. After the building of the mission house two orphanages were erected. Of these Paton was able to testify that some of their best Christians and teachers came from them.

The first convert on Aniwa was Chief Namakei. His brother, who had tried to shoot Paton, also became a Christian. Others followed. Some testimonies are astounding—murderers of their own children being born again, and one man being brought to Christ by his second wife, for whose sake he had murdered his first wife. Some are puzzling—the young boy whose regret on becoming a Christian was that he would now be denied the honour of being a murderer. Needless to say he was eventually better instructed.

It was the incident of the well that proved decisive as far as Paton's ministry on the island was concerned. When he informed the natives of his intention of providing a water supply by means of opening a well, their response was to think he had gone mad. Believing that God would meet the need, but fearing that the water would be salty, Paton went to work. Thirty feet down his hopes were realized. The following Sunday Namakei asked to preach, and gave glory to God. The consequences were amazing. The well and the sermon 'broke the back of Heathenism on Aniwa'. Some may question the motives of those who so readily exchanged one religion for another. The godly missionary entertained no suspicions. People flocked to hear the gospel; where there was no prayer to God in any house, it was considered heathen; and the Sabbath was observed with a zeal that would have brought a glow to the faces of his Scottish forebears.

The first communion on Aniwa had an incalculable effect on John Paton:

> At the moment when I put the bread and wine into those dark hands, once stained with the blood of cannibalism, but now stretched out to receive and partake the emblems and seals of the Redeemer's love, I had a foretaste of the joy of Glory that well nigh broke my heart to pieces. I shall never taste a deeper bliss, till I gaze on the glorified face of Jesus Himself.

Increasingly he was away from Aniwa, but always his travels were in the interests of his beloved natives. Journeys to Australia and New Zealand were chiefly concerned with fund-raising for a replacement for the original *Dayspring*. In 1884 he returned to Britain to stir interest in and gather contributions towards a third, steam-powered *Dayspring*. During this visit he met such worthies as F. B. Meyer, George Müller (who gave him fifty pounds to the cause), and C. H. Spurgeon (who saluted him as the 'King of the Cannibals'). He set out for Britain with a target of £6,000. He returned to Australia after eighteen months with £9,000. This money came from rich and poor, high and low.

His time from 1886 until 1892 was occupied with travelling in and between the Australasian colonies and the New Hebrides. Then came another distant journey, this time to Canada and the USA. The object now was to prevent the exploitation of his islanders at the hands of traders who corrupted them by the sale of drugs, intoxicating liquor, and armaments. It was also necessary to eliminate the Kanaka trade, the selling of slaves. His privilege this time extended to meeting two of the Presidents of the USA. His own conservative estimate is that on this visit he addressed on average two meetings every day and five on Sunday.

From New York he sailed to Britain, returning to Victoria in 1894. In all his travelling, he never lost sight of his goal. Raising money and fighting social wrongs did not usurp his dominating purpose. He knew that if he won sinners for Christ and furthered the consecration of Christians the money needed would be rapidly supplied. His primary aim was always 'the saving of souls by the story of the New Hebrides'.

His visit to Aniwa in 1898 was of particular significance, for he took with him his translation of the New Testament in the Aniwan tongue. In 1902 he took an Aniwan hymn-book, and a translation of the Shorter Catechism, both his own work. His last visit, aged eighty, in 1904 provided a demonstration of his spirit. He had to be prevented from rebuilding the house! Back in Australia, while travelling to a meeting he was to address, he met with an accident. Recovering from unconsciousness, he insisted on addressing the meeting. Full restoration was not to be expected, although he pleaded to be allowed to go back to Aniwa. On 27 January he went to his reward.

John Paton's forefathers were Covenanters, men who faced threatenings and perils, were tireless in their gospel endeavours, 'escaped the edge of the sword . . . waxed valiant in fight', knew how near an association there sometimes is between the shedding of blood and the maintaining of the truth. Their noble son was worthy of their line.

'Aniwa; an island entirely given to me by the Lord, the whole population of which, in course of time, became Christian.' What of Tanna? This chapter began with Paton's father; it ends with his son.

143

In 1896 another missionary went there. Just previously two women and a man had been killed and eaten. Thirty-four years before John Paton had fled for his life. Things had changed very little. The new missionary, arriving under no illusions, was to see Tanna won for Christ. His name was Frank Paton.

19
Hudson Taylor
(1832-1905)

During the latter half of the nineteenth century and into the first decade of this, China was passing through an immense upheaval. *The Times Atlas of World History* has a chapter headed 'The collapse of the Chinese Empire 1842 to 1911'. There were several major uprisings in the 1850s and 1860s, two of them resulting in 25 million dead. At least 10 million died in the years 1877 to 1879 during a famine in the north of the country. There were wars with the British, the French, the Russians, and the Japanese. Clearly it was not a period which would tempt foreigners to the land. However, it closely coincided with the span of Hudson Taylor's life—and he was no ordinary foreigner.

The Barnsley home where he grew up was a godly one. The spirit of patient suffering for Christ's sake, so evident in the missionary, had shown itself in his great-grandfather. He, who had had the inestimable privilege of entertaining John Wesley in his home, endured much during the course of the Methodist Revival, being stoned, facing death, and having powdered glass rubbed in his eyes. Of such a character were the forebears of Hudson Taylor. His father was a chemist, and his mother, with whom he shared a very warm relationship, a daughter of the Wesleyan manse. His delicate health meant that he was educated mostly at home. The intensity of his studies there may be gauged by the fact that at the age of four years he had learned the Hebrew alphabet. At about the same time, such was the conversation on the Taylor hearth, young Hudson would avow his intention of going as a missionary to China.

Attendance at school lasted from when he was eleven until he was thirteen. Then he began work in his father's shop, and the study of dispensing. There seems to have been a number of spiritual crises and commitments in his life, the first of these taking place when he was fourteen. His decision then to give his heart to God soon met an exacting test. He began working in a bank and although, because of eye trouble, this lasted only nine months, that was long enough for the attraction of riches to make its appeal, and for the influence of his associates to incline him to unbelief. Such siren-songs failed to capture him, and after stumbling, he soon regained his feet.

God's remarkable ways are seen in his conversion. Finding time on his hands, he came across some pamphlets and tracts belonging to his father. He began to look through one, intending to read the story with which it opened, and ignore the application of the gospel at its close. At the same time his mother, seventy or eighty miles away, was constrained by God to pray particularly for her son. This she did for a number of hours, until she was given assurance that her prayers were answered, upon which she praised God for the fact that he had been converted. Meanwhile Hudson had been struck by a phrase in the tract—'the finished work of Christ'. Meditation upon these words led him to trust the Saviour. Thus was God working in two hearts, separated by many miles, to the same end. On her return, she was greeted by an excited young man bursting to tell her the news. Before he could share his experience with her, she surprised him with the fact that she already knew!

Six months later came another significant occasion. Writing to his sister Amelia, another of the family to whom he was particularly close, he speaks of an intense longing for God. Hardly had he sealed the letter before his longing was met and an overwhelming sense of God's presence came upon him. The effect was as dramatic as the experience itself. 'From that time', he writes, 'the conviction never left me that I was called to China.'

Immediately he began to prepare himself. Apart from studying Chinese through a copy of Luke's Gospel in Mandarin, he denied himself certain comforts, and imposed certain disciplines on himself. He undertook work among the sick and poor. He acquainted himself with the work in China through reading magazines, and began to write to Mr George Pearse, secretary of the Chinese Evangelization Society. Along with all this, Latin, Greek, Theology, and Medicine occupied his time and energy. And an important principle was being shaped, from which he was never to depart, and according to which those who followed him were expected to live.

If there is one word more than any other which characterizes Hudson Taylor, it is the word 'faith'. For him, the outpouring of faith meant trusting only in God for all his needs. It meant not running to seek and enlist the help of men when God had appeared to fail. He began to practise this principle at home, before going to China. There is a beauty, a simplicity, a devotion, and a challenge in his expression, 'How important to learn before leaving England, to move man through God by prayer alone'.

At the age of nineteen he moved to Hull to further his study of Medicine. Now the principle was tested. Nor was it merely a matter of receiving from God. He loved to give to God, and so tithing was soon left far behind as he gave away two-thirds of his income. When his employer failed to pay him on time, a gentle reminder was out of the question. Faced with a case of extreme need, he left the hypocrisy of praying for God to help a little family while holding on to the last half-crown he possessed, so that was given. In these and similar cases, faith was proved, and God found to recompense more than adequately. All the while, concern for China grew, and Jesus's compassion for the multitude was reflected in his servant.

147

A visit to London to meet a German missionary to China proved to be a discouraging experience from one perspective, for the missionary told him that the Chinese would not receive him on account of his fair complexion. From another perspective the visit was beneficial, for not only did he meet George Pearse, but he was introduced to a circle of friends who were to be a great support to him during his time in China. This visit was followed by a move to the capital to pursue his medical studies yet further. A dilemma he encountered here was met in typical fashion. His father had promised to meet his expenses while there; so had the Chinese Evangelization Society. Whose help should he accept? Trusting in God he reasoned that the Society would assume his father was supporting him, and vice versa. His stay in London, where he almost died through poisoning his finger in the course of his work, was to last a year. In 1853 he was appointed assistant to a surgeon at a London hospital, but events were occurring to hasten his move to China. The Taiping rebellion had broken out, and as it spread it was rumoured by some that the rebels were Christians. The Chinese Evangelization Society thought the time was opportune for Hudson Taylor to sail. On 19 September, 1853 the *Dumfries* set out from Liverpool with just the one passenger on board. Her—and his—destination was China.

Hudson Taylor arrived in Shanghai amid scenes of chaos. The rebels held the city which was besieged by 50,000 imperial soldiers. Horrific sights and sounds greeted him. He found refuge in the compound of the London Missionary Society where he was kindly received and treated by Dr Lockhart. His problems multiplied, and he received a rude awakening when he found that his own Society had let him down badly. Their treatment of him was shameful, and he was driven back on the generosity of Dr Lockhart, whose paying guest he was forced to be. Worse, outside sources informed him that new workers, Dr and Mrs Parker were on their way, accompanied by three children. Concerning these and their arrival he had no word from the Society.

Embarrassed by his dependence on Dr Lockhart, he rented premises in an extremely dangerous locality—so much so that his house was struck by gunfire. Nonetheless he gave himself to the study of the language, evangelism, and to helping the victims of the war. When the house next door to his was destroyed, he decided the time had come to move. This was just in time for the arrival of Dr Parker and his family.

In spite of such fearsome circumstances he undertook new ventures. Either in the company of Dr Parker or workers from other societies he travelled to take the gospel to previously unevangelized areas. One of these was a two hundred mile journey up the Yangtse. The dangers he faced may be imagined—he was a frequent witness of men being beheaded, and himself came very near to being lynched on one occasion. The spiritual needs of the interior were impressed more and more upon his mind. It was with a view to this work that he now adopted Chinese dress. Among the encouragements of this time were his first convert's request for baptism, and also the interest taken in the work by Mr W. T. Berger. He was to prove a staunch friend at home and a most generous financial supporter.

A deep but sadly brief friendship developed at this time between Hudson Taylor and another great missionary, William Chalmers Burns. They were men of one mind and one heart. Their fellowship together was precious to both of them as they travelled together on the waterways. Their stay in Swatow, a centre of the opium trade and the most wicked place in which Hudson Taylor had been, came to an abrupt end when he went to Shanghai for some medical equipment. The war which had broken out between Britain and China took its toll and Burns was carried off a prisoner during his companion's absence. So a partnership that promised so much terminated, and the two men were never to see each other again.

However, God was preparing another gift for him. Prevented from returning to Swatow, he eventually settled in Ningpo. There he met and fell in love with Maria Dyer, the daughter of missionary parents. He encountered severe opposition from certain people, and his case was not helped by the fact that he had resigned from the Chinese Evangelization Society, an association that had become increasingly intolerable. Having made plain to her the precarious position, humanly speaking, in which she placed herself if she married him, he found her love for him as deep as his for her. On 20 January 1858 Hudson Taylor and Maria Dyer became husband and wife.

The following two years were to prove eventful. Within twelve months there was a church at Ningpo. As well as this Maria nearly died, but was delivered after much prayer, Their home and their lives were frequently in danger, and their first child, Grace, was born with tumult raging outside. And there was another test of faith. Dr Parker who had opened a hospital at Ningpo was compelled to return to Scotland upon the death of his wife. Hudson Taylor, with no idea where funds were to originate, was convinced that the hospital must be kept open. With supplies rapidly decreasing a cheque from Mr Berger arrived. Nor was this all. He had been left an inheritance and wrote to the missionary asking how the money could be spent.

The constant strain was telling. In 1860 Taylor's health was suffering and he had to make the painful decision to close the hospital and return to England. Here he was to remain for six years. This temporary retreat was the precursor of great advance.

The burden for inland China was growing, and the only relief he could find was in prayer and the Word of God. 'First,' he wrote:

> earnest prayer to God to thrust forth labourers, and second, the deepening of the spiritual life of the Church, so that men should be unable to stay at home, were what was needed.

Autumn 1865 saw the publication of *China's Spiritual Needs and Claims*. Similar to Carey's *Enquiry* it obviously concentrates on the one country. The short title says all. Within its 120 pages, facts are marshalled, responsibilities presented, challenges issued. It took Hudson Taylor almost a year to write and during that period a titanic struggle was taking place in the soul of the author. He was evidently moving toward a crisis from which he instinctively drew back. He had asked for five devoted workers for China, but realized that far more were obviously needed. He had no doubt that if he asked God for them, they would be supplied, and opportunities for service abounded. But could he endure the awful responsibility of inviting men to face such a massive task, and then bear the reproach if these men failed or were disillusioned? He could hardly sleep as he pondered and wrestled. During his stay in England he sought the advice of George Müller, and did not find him wanting. Müller encouraged him to pursue the same path of faith that he himself was walking.

The unlikely venue where the matter was resolved was the beach at Brighton. There he willingly surrendered, but told God with great boldness that the consequences of such obedience must lie in his own divine province. He prayed for 24 workers, two for each of the eleven provinces not provided with a missionary, and two for Mongolia. The margin of his Bible reads, 'Prayed for twenty-four willing, skilful workers at Brighton June 25, 1865.' Two days later he deposited ten pounds in an account he had opened in the name of a new society. The birth-pangs were over. The China Inland Mission was born.

When the *Lammermuir* weighed anchor on 26 May 1866, Hudson Taylor was accompanied by his wife and (by now) four children, and sixteen workers, eight having gone before. The 24 requested had been provided. His qualities of leadership were soon in demand as he sought to create and maintain a spiritual, family relationship among his companions. God's blessing was soon evident, twenty of the crew professing faith in Christ during the voyage. The party settled initially at Hangchow, but by the end of 1867 they were working in eight important cities. In all, the infant Mission now had 34 workers in the field.

Hard times now awaited him, but these never stifled his hunger for advance. In 1867, his daughter Grace died, a very heavy blow to her parents. The following year they moved to Yangchow. Opposition to their arrival mounted to fury, and the Mission premises were attacked, ultimately being set on fire. For two days this continued before the situation eased. Undismayed by these events he broke new ground to the north. recognizing the hand of God in all that befell him. September 1869 brought another spiritual crisis in his experience. It was as well that it occurred then, for it prepared him for severe trials in 1870. As he and Maria arranged to send their four eldest children home, keeping the youngest with them, the shadows were already gathering. Never again on earth were they to meet as a complete family. Samuel, one of the children, died just before he was to sail with his brothers and sister. Their fifth son, Noel, died two weeks after being born, a matter of days before the mother herself. The rain had descended, the floods had come, the winds had blown. But Hudson Taylor's house was founded on a rock—it did not fall.

A visit to England in 1871 saw him remarried, and the next year he and his new wife returned to China. An accident left him with a damaged spine, but lying on his back was no excuse for idleness. Praying and planning was to result in great expansion of the work. The devotion the couple showed to the work is indicated by their gift to the Mission of several thousand pounds from a legacy, their frequent separations, and their tireless journeyings. His vision was constantly enlarged, his appeals for workers were always met, from eighteen, to seventy, to a hundred, and at the Missionary Conference in Shanghai, in 1890, he launched an appeal for a thousand new evangelists. The year 1885 saw the sailing of the famous Cambridge Seven.

The amazing growth of the work, the fact that it was becoming international in character, and his advancing years were leading him not to retirement, but to another form of service. In 1888 he responded to invitations from men such as D. L. Moody to visit America. When he left North America for China four months later he was accompanied by fourteen new workers. Through his visits or his writings, people from Norway, Sweden, Germany, Australia were all desirous to be involved in the work. The China Inland Mission by now had associates from over twenty different countries.

Signs of breakdown in his health appeared in the spring of 1900 while on a visit to America. On his return to England in June of that year his condition was so serious that he was taken immediately to Switzerland for rest and possible recovery. It was here that Mrs Taylor died in 1904. Her husband had one unfulfilled desire—a longing for another sight of his beloved China. The following year he was able to sail there.

What a welcome greeted him! Indications of the triumph of the gospel were everywhere. How the sight gladdened his heart as he thought of the conditions that prevailed on his first arrival! The transformation was beyond description. As for himself, the unknown stranger of over half a century previously was met with great esteem. During his journey he stood where his dear Maria and four children were buried. Soon he was to find his resting place with them. On 1 June in Chansha, having spoken to Christians in the chapel in the morning, in the evening he was taken to be with the Lord.

Common sense, largeness of heart, cheerfulness of spirit, and a sense of humour were all characteristic of him. There was an urgency in all that he did. He claimed that the sun had never risen upon him in China without finding him at prayer. His influence was vast, four thousand people following him and serving under his direction in China. Above all he was a man of faith who stated that his life was based on three facts:

There is a Living God.
He has spoken in the Bible.
He means what He says and will do all He has promised.

The following words from a letter to his cherished mother express perfectly his own judgment on his life and his dependence on God:

Envied of some, despised by many, hated perhaps by others; often blamed for things I never heard of, or had nothing to do with; an innovator on what have become established rules of missionary practice; an opponent of mighty systems of heathen error and superstitions; working without precedent in many respects, and with few experienced helpers; often sick in body, as well as perplexed in mind and embarrassed by circumstances; had not the Lord been specially gracious to me, had not my mind been sustained by the conviction that the work is His, and that He is with me in what it is no empty figure to call 'the thick of the conflict', I must have fainted and broken down. But the battle is the Lord's: and He will conquer. We may fail, do fail continually; but He never fails.

20
Griffith John
(1831-1912)

The deacons of Allt-wen in South Wales, made no attempt to hide their dismay. Surely there had been some mistake. The boy before them had made the short journey up the Swansea Valley to preach at their evening service, but they could not possibly allow him to do so. Young, short, strangely dressed, he did not even look like a preacher. What were they to do? They left him alone while they decided which course to take.

At that moment it seemed that the answer to their problem literally appeared on the scene. A well-known preacher entered the building, and they fell upon him with earnest gratitude. He had been preaching in a neighbouring church, and on his way home had decided to attend their meeting. To the harassed officers there could be no more obvious solution to their dilemma. He must take the pulpit. Instantly the man declined, saying that he wished to hear the young man in the corner. The deacons would have none of it. What could be more absurd than to have such an experienced man sitting in the congregation while a mere novice undertook the task of preaching? For his part the youth, who must by then have been very disconsolate, was prepared to comply with whatever decision was reached. Eventually the older visitor surrendered to the persuasions of the deacons. The other was to take the devotions. So they proceeded. The unwanted preacher read the Scriptures, announced a hymn and began to pray. Let him continue the story in his own words:

> Long before the close of prayer, all hearts were greatly moved, and the place had become a veritable Bethel. At the close, some of the deacons rushed up the stairs and begged me to go on. I refused, and said that I had done the work which they had given me to do. Then my friend . . . besought me to go on, as he could not face the congregation if I declined to preach.
>
> I felt I must comply with the wishes of one who had shown so much kindness to me, so I turned back, gave out another hymn, and preached from Romans viii. 18. My soul was deeply moved, the vast audience caught the fire, and before the close of the sermon the whole congregation was on its feet shouting 'glory' and 'amen.'

We may surmise that this was not the last time Griffith John occupied the pulpit of Allt-wen chapel.

His childhood circumstances were less happy than they might have been, for he was left motherless when a year old. This meant that he came very much under the influence of his father, a man for whom religion was the mainspring of life. The boy's infancy was spent in the company of older men whose chief subject of discussion was the cause of religion. Coupled with this was the custom of Sunday school attendance, where Scripture verses were learnt, religious themes inculcated, and the Bible's truths revered. Habits of seriousness were thus ingrained in him from his earliest days.

A memorable occasion in his life was when his older sister was received into membership at Ebenezer Congregationalist Chapel in

Swansea. She was twelve years old, and Griffith watched the proceedings with deep interest. The question posed itself to him—why should not he become a member? People were divided in their response to his intense query, and the division was represented by two of the deacons. The gentler of the two saw no objection at all: the other counselled caution. Eventually both arrived at the same conclusion, that the child was a true Christian. There was nothing that stood in the way of his taking this step, and they would be wrong to detain him. He was accordingly given the privileges of a member when he was eight years of age. Against those who doubted the wisdom of all this, the boy's conviction was as firm as it was genuine, 'I knew I was a sinner, and that Jesus was my Saviour . . . I knew enough to be saved.'

As he grew into manhood he began to arouse a great deal of attention. His first sermon he preached when he was fourteen. The measure of popularity he was accorded did not affect him adversely: indeed he displayed a maturity beyond his years, for he considered himself too young for the high honour of the pulpit, and for this reason did not preach for two years. After he resumed the responsibility a further two years elapsed before he was convinced of a call to the ministry, and so entered the denominational college at Brecon.

During his student days he distinguished himself by his ability and industry. If he was not tempted in the direction of laziness his remarkable gifts meant that temptation came from another source. He was conscious of the alluring voice of ambition and its empty insinuations—could he not take his place alongside the great giants who had graced the Welsh pulpit in the past? However, he was enabled to deliver his soul from such a pitfall when God inclined his heart to the mission field. Missionaries did not run the risk of falling victim to popular applause. One of the men who influenced his thinking in this manner was David Griffiths, a pioneer missionary in Madagascar on a visit to the college.

From Brecon Griffith John moved to Bedford for further training with the London Missionary Society. There the desire to go to Madagascar grew, but his course was unexpectedly changed when within a year he was invited to go to China. On completing his preparation in Bedford he was ordained in April 1855, a few days prior to his marriage to the daughter of the man who had fired him in Brecon with the prospect of Madagascar. Shortly afterwards Griffith and Margaret John left their homeland and arrived in Woosung, near Shanghai, on 24 September. At Shanghai they joined the missionary settlement under Dr W. H. Medhurst.

Within six months he was able to converse in Chinese and immediately set about working among the people of the city. Soon he was making journeys into the surrounding areas, often in the company of Hudson Taylor. A little later he and his wife and son made their headquarters at Bing-wu, between Shanghai and Hangchow. While he was fully occupied around these districts of the east coast of China his eyes were turned westward. The flame of the pioneer missionary burned unquenchably in his spirit—'it is the desire of my heart to labour in the regions beyond'. The fulfilment of that desire, however, had to be postponed, chiefly on account of the Taiping rebellion. This was only one, albeit the most serious, of a number of revolts against the government of the Manchus. Meanwhile he explored every avenue possible in order to extend the influence of the gospel.

The danger to which he and his companions exposed themselves at this time may be adjudged from their attempt to enter Soochow to escape possible attacks from the warring factions. This feat they accomplished with great difficulty, their boat having to force its way into the city through rivers choked with corpses. Enforced absence from Shanghai meant that he lost the opportunity of travelling with a British expedition up the Yangtse to Hankow, a city of critical importance in the plans he envisaged. One of his colleagues had gone on the journey and returned full of enthusiasm for the possibilities presented. Griffith John did not lose another opportunity, and in June 1861, with a fellow missionary called Wilson, he arrived in the city always to be associated with his name.

The strategic position of Hankow as a commercial centre provided its obvious appeal to God's servants for their own purposes. The first premises they acquired were by no means the most sanitary, yet by the end of the summmer their families had joined them. They were soon rewarded by the baptism of the first convert after just nine months there. During their second year the church in Hankow numbered seven. There were other British residents in the city, and English services that were much appreciated were instituted for their benefit. The delight of the little group was not allowed to go undisturbed, however, for in August 1863 Wilson died.

The neighbouring city of Wuchang was next to be occupied, and the encouragement continued with the building of new residences and chapels. After five years the membership rose to 57, while the following year saw another 51 added. These were riches indeed compared with the meagre returns that many other missionaries had to show for their endeavours. Other missionaries joined them and the quality of discipleship shown by some of the converts was exceptional. Medical work was not forgotten, and included a hospital in Hankow and a dispensary in Wuchang.

Although he is not remembered for his travels as a missionary nevertheless one expedition is worth recording. With his companion James Wylie he made a journey of three thousand miles through Chungking to Chen-tu the capital of Szechwan province, returning through Shen-si province. They were the first Protestant missionaries to attempt successfully such an exploit. Nor was it a pointless or fruitless exercise for he reckoned that by the journey 'the valleys of the Yangtse and the Han have been taken possession of in the name of Christ.'

Furlough in 1870 provided him with opportunities of inspiring Christians at home with the need of China. It was also an opportunity of showing his unquestioned optimism. In his mind there was no doubt as to the eventual triumph of the work he represented. It would not be accomplished overnight, but the possibility of failure was not to be entertained. That his preaching gifts had not suffered by his absence from the pulpit was evidenced by the response of the congregations he addressed at the time. These included an out-door meeting attended by five thousand people at Machynlleth in Mid Wales, and the gathering that listened to him preaching the Annual Missionary Sermon for the London Missionary Society. The joy with which he anticipated his return was marred by the death on the voyage of his wife.

The years between 1873 and 1881 were as eventful as any in his life. They saw him show his ability as a missionary statesman. The Hankow Tract Society was established at this time. At Hsiao-kan, near Hankow, the seeds of what became an important work among lepers were sown. He took a very active part in the setting up of the first Missionary Conference held in China. He came within an inch of losing his life at the hands of violent persecutors, being caught on a bridge, with a thousand people baying for his blood. His pursuers stood on one bank of the river, while he was met by threats of what fate awaited him if he dared to set foot on the other! The end of this period saw him absent once more from China. He had remarried and his wife's ill health required his presence with her in America. In 1882 both were back in China after a brief visit to England.

The blessing of God upon the work led him to express his frustration at the lack of helpers. In a letter to the L.M.S. he writes of the hundreds waiting for baptism, but bewails the inadequacy of resources. Because of this he and his colleagues were unable to follow where God was advancing. Against this may be set the heart-warming awareness of the band of Chinese preachers and workers who were gathering about him. Meanwhile another district was beckoning to him. This promised to be the hardest of all and in many respects fulfilled the promise; for it was the boast of the province of Hunan that when its people growled foreigners ran. Griffith John, however, was not a man to run away. Rather the blood of Nehemiah ran freely through his veins. Though separated by centuries the challenge of enemies was flung back by both these servants of God: 'Should such a man as I flee?'

He had made his first attempt in 1879, but had been driven away. The second effort was in 1882, and this endeavour again had to be abandoned. The passage of time did not remove the dangers, and riots in Central China were traced to their source in the capital of Hunan. It was in 1897 that a third attempt was ventured. This proved more encouraging although it ended in withdrawal. Two years later the missionary was accompanied by an official escort and was peacefully received. His persistence had brought its reward. He had opened the doors, and thereafter Societies and missionaries entered them without hindrance.

His first love never left him. Preaching was of primary importance to him, and if he surrendered the fame held out to him by the Welsh pulpit, he found great delight and profit in the Chinese. He arranged a preaching festival on the lines of those to which he was accustomed in his homeland. This was held in the open air and drew a huge gathering of hearers. Apart from this there were his more regular appointments on Sundays and weekdays. As the character of his congregations varied so did his methods of reaching them. This readiness and ability to adapt was evident in another of his contributions, that of translation. He was responsible for two renderings of the New Testament, one in the Mandarin literary style and another in the popular. From the Old Testament he translated the books of Psalms and Proverbs. A catechism, hymn-book and many tracts also came from his hand. The many facets of his work were recognized in 1899 when the University of Edinburgh conferred upon him the degree of Doctor of Divinity.

At the turn of the century his steadfastness during the notorious Boxer Rebellion brought him much applause. His stay in Hankow when he was urged to go down the river was an example of his courage and his faith. He played no small part in education in that city, taking a leading role in the founding of the Anglo-Chinese College, later known as the Griffith John College. The Margaret Hospital for Chinese women again owed its existence in large measure to him.

Failing strength necessitated a respite in 1906. For this he went to his sons in New York. Disdaining the invitations to spend time in Britain, he lost no time in returning to his adopted home. With obvious increased limitations he sought to engage himself once again in his work in Hankow. Not surprisingly his strength was not equal to his spirit, and another, this time final, absence from China was forced upon him. Fifty years after arriving at Hankow he bade it farewell, not now for America, but for Wales. His death took place in Swansea on 25 July 1912.

Not all preachers are missionaries; neither are all missionaries preachers. In this we discern the wisdom and the sovereignty of the Spirit, 'dividing to every man severally as he will'. Like the apostles Griffith John was both. Their privilege was his; their vocation was his; their message was his; their zeal was his; their faithfulness was his; now their reward was his.

21
Mary Slessor
(1848-1915)

Mary Slessor was an example of that kind of Christian that men, in their wisdom, say is never to be found. She was frightened into the kingdom. When she was a child an old widow warned her and her friends of the dangers of hell-fire, and that unless they turned to Christ that would be their fate. Horror seized her and sleep was driven away. There was only one thing for it—that was to repent and believe. If the manner of her conversion was unconventional it is scarcely surprising that some of her missionary endeavours were less than orthodox. This is not to say that she terrified people in the way she had been, but certain approved canons of missionary behaviour were not observed as strictly as might have been expected.

It was a poor and not very happy home into which Mary was born in Aberdeen. Although her mother was a woman of a deeply religious disposition, her father's inclinations were otherwise and his drinking habits brought the family to poverty. A move to Dundee to make a new beginning did nothing to relieve circumstances. Death had already taken her older brother, and Mary was now the oldest child. She and her mother came to dread Saturday nights when the miserable violence to which drink had reduced Mr Slessor was spent on his wife and daughter. Mary became a somewhat frequent visitor to the pawnbroker. Her father's death may have provided her with some relief but it also meant that now the burden of supporting the family fell upon her young shoulders.

Her mother's influence on the direction Mary's life was to take was evident from the beginning. It was she who saw to it that Mary and the others went to church on Sundays. Mary had the happy facility of being able to gather friends around her, and this she used to good effect in bringing others with her to Sunday school where she early became a teacher. A tireless worker, she gave herself completely to working in a mission in the slums around the church that she attended. Not the least of the qualities required there was great courage, a feature she exhibited to an astonishing degree. Calabar, a town and province near the coast in the south-east corner of Nigeria, where she was to spend most of her life, was a name with which she became familiar from her earliest years owing to her mother's consuming interest in that particular field. Her older brother who had died had often spoken of becoming a missionary. She had another brother whom her mother longed to dedicate to the work at Calabar, but sadly he also died. Mary began to wonder: was it possible that she could take her brother's place? News of the death of David Livingstone in 1874 seemed to settle the matter for her. Assured of her mother's willingness—and probably delight—she left Dundee in March 1876 for preparation in Edinburgh. This was to last for all of three months. However, the real training had been taking place from her earliest years when she was infected with Mrs Slessor's enthusiasm.

In August that same year, having been appointed as missionary teacher by the United Presbyterian Church, she left Liverpool to arrive the following month in Africa. There had been a mission station in Calabar for thirty years and Mary soon settled to the routine of teaching in the day school and visiting. She aquainted herself with the beliefs and practices of the natives. Naturally impatient and high-spirited, she found the work progressing rather too slowly for her. One of the means by which she relieved her feelings was to climb trees, claiming that between two of the communities which she served there was no tree worthy of the name that she had not climbed. The tasks she was assigned would have satisfied many another but she ached for something more demanding. She was frequently ill and one attack of fever left her all but dead. In her weakened state her mind turned more and more to home, and when the time of her first furlough came in 1879 she returned without delay to Scotland.

On arriving back at Calabar she was delighted to know that she was to be in charge of a station at Old Town on the east bank of the Calabar river. The people here were utterly degraded but she applied herself to her task with energy and devotion. With no other white person to help her, the burden laid upon her was enormous. Constantly an object of curiosity, she used this as well as every other opportunity to speak of the Saviour. Sunday proved to be anything but a day of

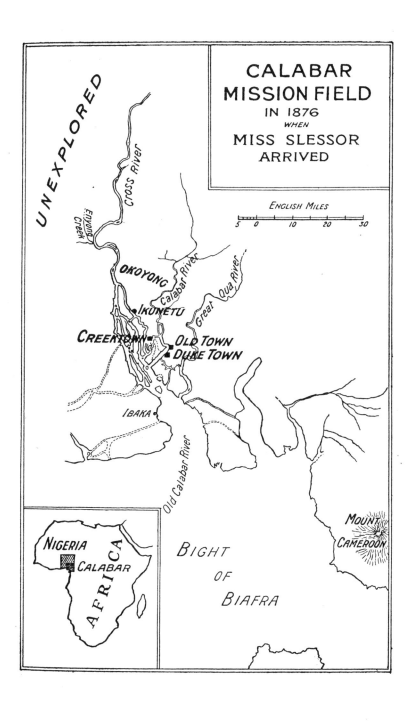

UNEXPLORED

CALABAR
MISSION FIELD
IN 1876
WHEN
MISS SLESSOR
ARRIVED

ENGLISH MILES
5 0   10   20   30

Cross River

Edyong Creek

OKOYONG

Calabar River

Great Qua River

IKUNETU

CREEKTOWN   OLD TOWN
             DUKE TOWN

IBAKA

Old Calabar River

Nigeria
CALABAR
AFRICA

BIGHT

OF

BIAFRA

MOUNT
CAMEROON

rest:from early morning she was travelling, visiting, holding services in her own and surrounding districts. Her ceaseless labours soon showed their value as standards of behaviour were raised. There were some customs that proved very difficult to uproot and never seemed to have been completely destroyed. One of these was the infamy of twin murder:

> A woman who gave birth to twins was regarded with horror. The belief was that the father of one of the infants was an evil spirit, and that the mother had been guilty of a great sin; one at least of the children was believed to be a monster, and as they were never seen by outsiders or allowed to live, no one could disprove the fact. They were seized, their backs were broken, and they were crushed into a calabash or water-pot and taken out—not by the doorway, but by a hole broken in the back wall, which was at once built up—and thrown into the bush, where they were left to be eaten by insects and wild beasts.

Little wonder that Mary's fierce passion raged against such a massacre of innocents.

The state of her health in 1883 meant that she was ordered home to rest. She took with her a twin named Janie whom she had rescued and who was to be a great help to her in after years. Her return from this furlough was to be delayed because of circumstances in her family. Owing to ill health her mother and one of her sisters moved to Devon. Unexpectedly another sister in Scotland died. On Mary's return to the mission field she received news of her mother's death, soon to be followed by that of her sister in Devon. They were hard and difficult days for Mary Slessor. 'Home' now belonged to the past. Faithfulness in God's service did not exempt her any more than others from the common, sharp afflictions of life.

She had now moved to another district called Creek Town where she gathered another family about her. This consisted of five children who lived with her permanently, but she was always caring for abandoned children, of whom there was no shortage. The attention she devoted to these was constantly interrupted by people who came to her for help of one kind and another. Sickness needed treatment; hunger had to be satisfied; disputes required to be resolved. She wrote:

> If I told you what I have seen and known of human sorrow during the past months you would weep till your heart ached.

As she dealt with these and many other problems she was always careful to remind men and women and boys and girls of the love of God for them and the great sacrifice he had made for them.

Not even the duties in which she was now engaged could slake her thirst. News of the vile grip that superstition exercised on the minds of Africans in inland districts continued to stir her. These regions called endlessly to her with a cry that would not be stifled. The district of Okoyong was to feel in its midst what power there is in a life wholly given to God. For her part she was under no illusions—a few visits in preparation had left her with the conviction, 'Man can do nothing with such a people.' Later her opinion was confirmed as she wrote of some of the young people, 'It is almost impossible to love them.'

The setting up of schools at Ekenge and Ifako (before the erection of buildings) soon made an impact. When eventually the natives roused themselves a church and schoolhouse were built, the designing and much of the manual work being done by the missionary herself. The task of educating and evangelizing went on against the background—and opposition—of witchcraft, drunkenness, and immorality. One of her most important achievements was the establishing of some form of trade relations with the people of Calabar. The appearance of an account of her building exploits in the *Missionary Herald* moved a young Scots carpenter, Charles Ovens, to come out to Africa to help her in the work. His arrival was a great encouragement to her. An even greater encouragement was the gratitude certain people were expressing to her for the improvement which was slowly but surely appearing amongst them.

About the time of her furlough in 1891 came news that provoked no small degree of surprise. It seemed that Mary had fallen in love. However, her engagement to Charles Morrison progressed no further. To have pursued the matter would have meant her leaving Okoyong, and that was a step she would never contemplate.

There was no question about the trust she inspired among the natives. The moment anyone became aware of danger, or of practices of which they knew she would disapprove, the cry was raised, 'Run, Ma! run!' And whatever task she was doing was abandoned for the emergency, to be continued later. Recognition of her worth came from an unexpected source—the British Government. When new laws and the civilizing influences they would bring were proposed, she pointed out the problems this would introduce in Okoyong: the people would not take kindly to any imposition from an outside authority. Power therefore was given to her to introduce any changes necessary. The public affairs of the tribe were conducted through her, and at court cases, she presided. She was virtually a 'consular agent'. Her method of dispensing justice would not have met with universal approval by any means—she never seems to have let mere facts cloud the real issues and did not allow legal technicalities get in the way of fairness. Thus one plaintiff, while having his suit upheld against another, was punished for, among other things, not treating his mother properly, neglecting his farm, and washing only rarely! (Later she was to be elevated to the even more prestigious post of permanent Vice-President of Itu Native Court, this, unlike the other, being an official appointment).

She was never free from ill health, and this obviously did not lighten her burden. When the population moved she moved with them. Sometimes she would think of 'retirement'. For her this meant building her own house near one of the mission stations and settling down there with her children—the thought of being parted from them was unbearable to her. Progress in the work was very slow and the lack of conversions troubled her. Nevertheless there were encouragements: conditions were improving, new and younger missionaries were coming out to the field, and best of all in 1903 that which crowned all her endeavours. Seven young Christians were baptized and the first communion service was held—truly a time to be remembered.

Shortly afterwards she was on the move once more, this time to Itu and its neighbourhood, notorious in the past as a market place for slavery and where cannibalism was still practised. It was not very long before a congregation was gathering at Itu composed of 'three hundred intelligent and well-dressed people', and on a visit to nearby Amasu she found 68 pupils in the school she had started there, 38 of whom were already able to read. In all this she was assisted by her oldest adopted daughter and other helpers, but the hard graft of pioneering was all hers.

In May 1907 she visited Scotland for the last time. Her return in the autumn of the same year meant that the furlough had been all too short, and therefore proved of very little benefit. She came back to hard work and busy days. One visitor, tired after officiating at one meeting on the Sunday, found that she had been out conducting ten— and that was not one of her more demanding days. The next day people were gathering at six o'clock in the morning in order to consult her. Frailty and tiredness were constant experiences, yet on she drove herself.

Las Palmas in the Canary Islands is today a popular and exotic holiday resort. It probably never entertained a less likely and more deserving guest than Mary Slessor. For it was here in 1912 that she took her first holiday—and that with gratitude to those who had provided it, but also with struggles with her conscience regarding those she considered more deserving and more needy. Respite did not come easily to her and after this vacation it was, incredibly, back to the building, cementing, teaching, and every other kind of work. Although she did not look for reward and could never understand why she should be considered worthy of any recognition, in 1913 she was dignified with the royal award bearing the cumbrous title, 'Honorary Associate of the Order of the Hospital of St. John of Jerusalem in England'.

Meanwhile there was always the ceaseless journeying, for it seemed that Mary Slessor did not know what it was to stand still. Expansion of the work went on to the end. And the end did come as her people knew and feared it would. Her weak and spent body appeared unwilling to surrender to the indomitable spirit it contained. Fever and sickness constantly dogged her until in February 1915, at the age of sixty-six, she died.

She never took the care for herself that others would have exhorted her to do. Simple precautions like wearing a hat were ignored by her. The task in hand always took precedence over everything else. Yet who would deny that she had her priorities right? There was an occasion—there were many—when her spare frame cried out for rest but she had committed herself to helping a group of people. From this she dared not excuse herself. As she went to keep her promise it was in the spirit of the words that she was later to write, and which with massive irony may best sum up her life: 'No more idleness for me.' Death did not mark the end of Mary's service. It merely marked her entrance to another field.

22
David Baron
(1855-1926)

One of the effects of the great evangelical revival of the eighteenth
century was the tremendous missionary expansion of the following
century. The fruits of the one were seen in the other. Although the
Puritan emigrants to the New World in the first half of the seventeenth century considered themselves to be missionaries as well as
exiles and refugees, a further hundred and fifty years elapsed before
an explosion of world-wide missionary interest and endeavour
occurred. It was then that the Christian church took seriously its
obligation to carry the gospel to men and women of every country

and sought to fulfil that obligation. No land was regarded as unworthy to receive the good news. There was one group of people, however, unique in the history of God's dealings with the human race, and the sad truth concerning them was that they had no land. But God had not forgotten his ancient people.

Prominent in the renewed interest in evangelism among the Jews was the Church of Scotland. In 1839 four of its ministers, including Robert Murray M'Cheyne, had visited Palestine on a Mission of Inquiry into the state of the Jews. On their return a work was established in Budapest, Hungary, where John Duncan was sent with four others. The blessing that attended their labour there is indicated by the following report of Duncan:

> Our hands now became so full of work that frequently we had not time so much as to eat bread; from early morning till late at night we were occupied in guiding, counselling and instructing those who were inquiring earnestly what they must do to be saved . . . For a time the whole Jewish community was deeply moved, wondering whereunto these things would grow.

Among those won to Christ in Budapest were such noted Hebrew Christians as Adolph Saphir and Alfred Edersheim. From there the work spread to Amsterdam, Constantinople, Breslau, and Prague before missionaries were eventually settled in Palestine. Horatius and Andrew Bonar were keen supporters of this exciting venture.

Interest was not confined to Scotland, however, and in 1876 John Wilkinson founded the Mildmay Mission to the Jews. Mildmay was something of a centre for evangelicalism at the time, and a large hall had been erected for the purpose of holding the conventions which were then becoming fashionable. The common concern for the conversion of the Jews meant that close relationships were established between the Scottish work and that of Mildmay, and Andrew Bonar acknowledged the indebtedness of the Scots to the Mildmay Mission. Such enthusiasm for the spiritual welfare of his own people provided the foundation on which David Baron was to build.

He was born to Jewish parents in Russia, and spent his early years in the Polish town of Suwalki, two hundred miles north-east of Warsaw. For as long as he could remember he sought to please God in the classic way taught by his religion, which meant keeping diligently all the laws and observing all the ceremonies. While he gave himself to the task he was aware of the failure of all his industrious efforts to bring him peace with God. In spite of the sincere commendation and admiration of his acquaintances, the approval he most coveted escaped him, and the sinful condition of his heart was something that always condemned his most earnest attempts: 'I felt that there was a great difference between *being holy* and merely *doing* what men call holy acts.'

While still a boy a serious accident drove home to him more deeply the seriousness of his situation, and when his mother sought to reassure him concerning his hope of heaven he replied that if his hope depended on his own goodness then all was lost. Strangely, at the same time he was able to comfort her by telling her that God would restore him to health. In his education much emphasis was laid upon his religious heritage, and at the age of ten he entered a Rabbinical College where he distinguished himself. The scrupulous attention given to the minutiae of the law is seen in the choice of subject for his discourse at his Bar Mitzvah, 'The necessity of putting away leaven'. In this way was his youth spent, searching for an answer to his need, knowing the Scriptures that pointed to that answer, and yet for many years not having heard mention of the name of the Saviour who was that answer.

The outworking of God's decrees very often appears to men to be the result of chance happenings. So it was in the case of David Baron. One of his brothers-in-law had decided to emigrate to America, and he was to accompany him. While they were in Berlin the brother-in-law was robbed, and so David forfeited his fare to enable his companion to complete the journey, intending to follow him as circumstances permitted. Eventually he made his way over to England, arriving in Hull wondering as to the next step he should take. It was here in 1877 that it became apparent to him that God was meeting him, and that the purpose of the strange events of recent months became evident. In Hull he met Arthur Koenig, a Hebrew Christian, who first spoke to him of his need of Christ. Baron knew Jesus only by the name 'Tooleh' meaning 'Crucified', and had been instructed that he taught his followers to serve idols and to persecute the Jews. He was bitter in his attitude to Koenig whom he regarded as a renegade for turning Christian. His arguments against Koenig were useless for he could not escape the impression that the man was far happier than he was, and that the reason for this happiness was his relationship with God through Jesus Christ. Koenig introduced him to John Wilkinson and gave him a copy of the New Testament. Diligent inquiry into this led him to the one conclusion—that the release from condemnation that he sought could be found only in the Saviour. His own verdict was that 'there is actually nothing in modern Judaism to meet the cravings of an awakened soul', and after moving to London and renewing acquaintance with Wilkinson he knew his sins forgiven by faith in the blood of Christ.

Eighteen months after first hearing the gospel in Hull he was baptized in London. By this time his father had heard the news of what he considered his son's apostasy, and addressed a letter to 'My lost son David'. The immense heartache caused to parent and child can be well imagined, and when he knew of the effect his conversion had on his father, David was subjected to an agony of temptation. Grace was given to him and he was able to comfort his father in his correspondence, in the course of which he wrote the whole of the Gospel of Matthew and the Epistle to the Hebrews. There was a happy outcome to this, for although his father refused at first to let anyone see the letters, as his sight grew weaker another son was allowed to read them, with the result that the brother professed himself to be a Christian. Father and son did meet once more and were reconciled, while still differing regarding their convictions.

Following a period of training he joined the Mildmay Mission to the Jews in 1881. He was immediately sent to Edinburgh, Glasgow, and Dundee on evangelistic work among the Jews, thus reinforcing the Scots connection. Blessing attended his endeavours there, and Andrew Bonar was to write thanking the Mission for sending them 'such a labourer as Mr Baron'. He was later to settle in Glasgow for two years before returning to London. His association with the Mission continued for twelve years during which time he worked in the capital and the Midlands. Visits were also made further afield to Germany, Poland, Austria, and Hungary. In 1891 John Wilkinson felt that more needed to be done for the Jews in Palestine. Thus David Baron found himself representing the Mission in the important port of Jaffa. He was accompanied there by his wife, an English lady from Dover whom he had met when he went to the town in response to a request that someone be sent to preach the gospel to the Jews there. The request had come from the lady he was to marry.

Towards the end of his time with the Mildmay Mission he received two invitations from Scotland. One was from the Free Church, asking him to consider working on their behalf in Prague, and the other from certain Christians in Glasgow asking him to take charge of a proposed work in that city called 'The Bonar Memorial Mission to the Jews'. He declined both offers, and it seems clear that he was entertaining thoughts of a new venture. He was confirmed in these new ideas through his friendship with Charles Andrew Schönberger, brother-in-law of Adolph Saphir, and a worker with the Free Church of Scotland Mission to Jews and also with the British Jews Society. Both men were led to adopt similar principles in their work, and without any ill feeling towards their former colleagues, sought to be released from their commitments. Together they formed the Hebrew Christian Testimony to Israel. They were to receive no fixed income, make no appeals for funds, but to seek all their wants and requirements by prayer directly to God. Above all, their chief principle was to work as Jews among Jews. The new mission was founded in 1893.

For the first two years of its existence they had no home nor centre for the work. From their first efforts in the Soho district of London they extended their interest and concern over a wider area, travelling and witnessing wherever the opportunity presented itself. Obviously they found that they needed premises where they could preach and meet with Jews for discussion and debate, and after hiring a very unsuitable property, were eventually able to acquire a house in 1901. The provision of God for the premises was remarkable. There was an outstanding amount of two thousand pounds which had to be found in a week. On the Monday Baron and some friends prayed particularly for this sum, and on the Friday he received a letter containing a cheque for the exact amount. A similar incident over a matter of five hundred pounds occurred later, this time the sum being contributed from three sources, one in Australia, another in Wales, and the third in the Midlands. His attitude to financial affairs was always one of scrupulous honesty. He received on one occasion a cheque for a sum of money to be used for the relief of Russian Jews. The money was to be distributed by one of his colleagues on the Continent. When the cheque was received by Baron the colleague was no longer associated with the Mission, and so the cheque was returned to the donor.

Much work was done in the Mission House each day. Every day, except the Jewish Sabbath and the Lord's Day, services of a particular character were conducted there. One visitor records his impressions of what must have been a normal scene:

> On the day of my visit, in the large upper room sixty Jews were assembled . . . The attendance rises sometimes to seventy, eighty, ninety, and even a hundred. During three hours, from 4 to 7 o'clock, questions are put by the audience. During the time I was present there was no pause; man after man, Bible in hand, rose and put his question. Every man had a Bible before him. The answer was distinctly and emphatically given by Mr Schönberger, who in turn with Mr Baron and two other able colleagues shares in this special form of service, and gives immediate replies to eager questions.

This was followed by a Bible Reading which itself lasted for another hour.

The extensive travelling in which he was engaged while with the Mildmay Mission was continued after he had separated from them. This involved him in journeys in Europe and Asia, and between 1890 and 1912 he made seven visits to Palestine, but there was a growing conviction of the need for a settled representation of the work in that land. His persuasion of the rightness of this development deepened, and far from being discouraged by societies and missions already working there, he was warmly welcomed, and was able to send missionaries to Haifa to co-operate with the British Society for the Propagation of the Gospel among the Jews. These were very significant years for the Jews, for 1897 saw the first World Zionist Congress. David Baron took a keen interest in this nationalist movement and was encouraged by the good will of its leader, Theodore Herzl. Twenty years later Zionism succeeded in obtaining from Britain the Balfour Declaration which resulted in the formation of the state of Israel in 1948. Naturally he was excited by such epoch-making events as these, not from the political standpoint but rather the spiritual. Although the number of Jews returning was not as large as he had hoped, yet their calibre encouraged him, and he was excited by the observation that 'they are from all accounts very accessible with the Gospel, especially when brought to them by Hebrew Christians, and are eagerly reading the New Testament'.

He left many written works to posterity, many chapters in his books having first appeared as articles in the HCTI magazine *The Scattered Nation*. Much of what he wrote was expository, and all was directed to making known to the Jews that the prophecies contained in their Scriptures were fulfilled in the coming of the Messiah. His acquaintance with the Old Testament and the Talmudic writings was hardly surpassed and gave substance to his literary efforts. An indication of the emphasis he laid may be gathered from the titles he published, such as *Rays of Messiah's Glory, Israel's Inalienable Possessions,* and *The Ancient Scriptures for the Modern Jew*. He was persuaded that one of the causes of the weakness of Christianity was 'the ignoring of the position of Israel in relation to the purpose of God, as revealed in the Scriptures', and to correct such failure he devoted himself in his preaching and in his writing.

He did not enjoy good health during the last few years of his life, and this affected the performance of his work. His heart was in the work of his beloved Hebrew Christian Testimony to the end, and he defied the counsel of his doctor when he advised him to rest more. If he was unable to attend the Mission House with his accustomed frequency, his absence was enforced. A week after his last visit there to see the children and to attend the open-air meeting he contracted pneumonia. Within another week he had died. To the end he endured with Paul that 'great heaviness and continual sorrow' for his nation, and constantly betrayed an intense yearning for the salvation of his privileged people. Now the sadness was forgotten, swallowed up in the presence of him 'of whom Moses in the law, and the prophets, did write'.

23
Jonathan Goforth
(1859-1936)

Mention Jonathan Goforth in any conversation about missionaries and the almost inevitable response will be, 'What a splendid name for a missionary!' The pioneering instincts with which he was endowed meant that he was perfectly fitted to bear the name. On a visit to England in 1910 he discovered that the first of his forebears to bear the name was given it when he left home and family rather than compromise his conscience.

His birth took place on a farm in Ontario, Canada, where he was early initiated into the hardships that life was to hold for him. All the members of his family were diligent and industrious, and Jonathan came behind in none of those virtues. By the time he was fifteen he was put in charge of another farm that the family owned. His father's confidence in giving him this responsibility was not unfounded and was soon amply rewarded. Nor was it only in physical toil that the young man excelled. He had a powerful urge to improve himself intellectually, with the aim eventually of becoming a lawyer and politician.

This remained his ambition when he became a Christian. Although his mother had taught him to read the Bible and pray from his earliest years, he had not come to trust the Saviour as a child. He was converted at eighteen under the ministry of his faithful pastor, and immediately set about serving his new Master. He began to distribute tracts, he commenced a Sunday service close to where he lived, he introduced family worship at home, and he withstood the godless arguments of his teacher who had been bewitched by the writings of the infidel Tom Paine—ultimately succeeding in rescuing class and teacher from the snare. Jonathan Goforth was not a man to let the grass grow under his feet.

His political ambition received its mortal wound a year following his experience of salvation. From the moment he opened the pages of

The Memoirs of Robert Murray M'Cheyne while driving his horse and buggy homeward, he was captured. The drive home had to be discontinued. Such a book demanded his complete attention. Hours passed as he lay by the wayside reading, and when the journey was once more undertaken God had replaced the old desire with a new, unmistakable vocation to spend his life in leading the lost to Christ.

As he prepared to enter Knox College in Toronto his intention was to be a minister in Canada. Once more his course was dramatically changed, this time while listening to a missionary from Formosa (present-day Taiwan). Dr George Mackay told his congregation how he had spent the previous two years seeking to persuade some young man to come out to help him, but all to no avail. He was returning alone. The remark stung the young Goforth as he thought of how he had taken into his own hands a decision that properly belonged to God. He had made up his own mind as to how and where he would serve God. 'From that moment', he records, 'I became a foreign missionary.'

The artlessness of his manner and zeal made him the butt of the jokes and pranks of his fellow students, but so marked was the impression he made upon them that it was the students of Knox who undertook to raise funds to send him to China. Undeterred by their initial response, he persisted in his custom of visiting the prison and in his work in the slum district. Not for him the more sophisticated and refined approach as he went from house to house. He preferred rather the direct method of putting his foot in the door, thus ensuring some hearing for his message. At the beginning of an autumn term in Knox College he was asked by the Principal how many families in Toronto he had visited during that summer. Back came the astonishing answer, 'Nine hundred and sixty.' Such amazing passion could not fail to affect others, and it is little wonder that although at first the Presbyterian Church was reluctant to open a new field in China because of existing demands elsewhere, Goforth so fired imaginations that when his student days ended he was appointed by that same church to serve as a missionary in China. He was married in 1887, and in February the following year he and his wife Rosalind set sail from Vancouver, eager to begin the work to which God had called them. On board, the sound of the captain being carried drunk to his cabin did nothing to quell his enthusiasm.

176

The first nine months of their stay (during which they lost their possessions in a house fire) were spent in language study at Chefoo, prior to their making their way to their ultimate destination which was the province of Honan. The problems that awaited them were indicated in a letter they received from Hudson Taylor:

> We as a Mission have sought for ten years to enter the Province of Honan from the south and have only just succeeded . . . Brother, if you would enter that Province, you must go forward on your knees.

The journey to Honan was accomplished with the generous help of other missionaries. Their excitement was not unmarred, for their little daughter Gertrude died of dysentery when she was still less than a year old. Such distress—and they were to meet with similar circumstances on many more occasions—did not stand in their way. Encouragement came with the arrival of eight recruits from Canada in December 1889, and on the evening of that same day the first Presbytery of North Honan was formed, although no real work had yet begun there. From their headquarters just outside Honan excursions were made into the province which put their lives in great danger on many occasions. It was a day to be remembered when they made their first home in Chuwang inside Honan with their son Paul, five months old. Meanwhile the burial of their second child, Donald, was a further reminder of the terrible cost at which such gains were made.

Although Goforth and his companions, who included Chinese converts, were usually received in the villages with politeness, they were not unaware of the rising tide of feeling against foreigners—along the Yangtse some missionaries were murdered. He was also struck down with an attack of typhoid fever. As well as this the little company had to contend with the circulation of the most dreadful reports of their activities. It was rumoured that the reason for the success of the remedies they dispensed was that they contained very precious ingredients, such as the eyes and hearts of children. It was against such odds that he struggled until, after a short furlough, the little family joined him in what his wife called 'the greatest and most important step forward Goforth had yet taken'. This was the long anticipated move to the city of Changte. There in the autumn of 1895 they made their permanent home.

The evident blessing of God was on the work from the beginning. The building work had to be continued while crowds came to the mission compound, and it was not simply out of curiosity that they attended. Besides doing construction work, in a letter he writes of 'constant preaching on an average of eight hours a day'. Even with the help of a converted opium smoker, and with the encouragement of the astonishing response to the gospel, the demands that were made upon him and his wife were bound to tax them. In the first five months of their time at Changte he calculated that more than 25,000 had come to the mission station and had listened to the good news of Christ. When they moved to a new bungalow they held an 'open house' when visitors were shown around their home. Numerous articles were inevitably stolen in spite of all the precautions taken but they were undismayed by the losses they sustained. On one day in 1899 1,835 men passed through the house, and Rosalind Goforth entertained 500 women!

Feeling against foreigners erupted with frightening violence once again during 1900 in the infamous Boxer Rebellion. This outbreak overtook the Goforth family along with many other missionaries, but not before they had laid two more children in their infant graves. They were prevailed upon to make good their escape although they were reluctant to take such advice. It was as well they did so. Deliverance finally came but only after the little company had suffered harrowing indignities, encountered near disaster, and Goforth himself had come within an inch of his life. Mobs threatened them frequently in their flight, and it was with immense gratitude that they arrived at Hankow and then Shanghai. The relief afforded by a return to their homeland was sadly tempered by the inroads into the Church which they detected were being made by two separate but related enemies. These were the attacks on the Bible made by the advocates of Higher Criticism, and the almost inevitable accompaniment of a spirit of worldliness which sapped the energies of Christians grown careless.

Jonathan Goforth could not have been an easy man to live with, and his wife's heart must have sunk on many occasions when she heard of some fresh plan that he suggested. On returning to China he proposed a course of action which she felt she could not wholeheartedly support because of the problems and dangers to which it would expose the children. He pleaded with her, and told her that he feared for the children if she did not go along with him. He seems to have taken it as a divine warning against Mrs Goforth's reticence when one of the children was taken dangerously ill, and as a divine confirmation of the rightness of his intention when yet another succumbed to illness and failed to recover. Whatever the rights and wrongs of such an argument the two were eventually agreed and embarked on a course which meant constant moving from place to place in their pioneering endeavour.

Inspiration for further development of his work came from reading reports of the Welsh Revival of 1904. He devoted himself, without neglecting his routine, to reading and studying the Bible with earnest prayer that a similar demonstration of the power of the Spirit might attend his ministry. Before long his request was granted. One evening while preaching he was conscious of something he had never experienced before affecting his congregation. As he turned to his helpers, they seemed themselves to be under some deep impression. One of them said to him, 'Brother, he for whom we have prayed so long, was here in very deed tonight.' Another dimension had been added to Goforth's ministry. A three-week tour in Korea was followed by the journey back through Manchuria. So greatly was his preaching owned during this return that he was invited to go back to Manchuria to conduct further meetings. What occurred there and in his own station of Changte can be described only in terms of an outpouring of the Holy Spirit. Hundreds attended the meetings, which lasted for hours, and often the problem was how to bring them to a close. Reports of his activities were accorded a mixed reception in Canada, and his furlough in 1910 proved to be a disappointment to him. A visit to England included a week at the Keswick Convention, known for the dismay rather than favour with which it greeted news of such excitement as Goforth represented. He was welcomed on the platform and as a result was invited to become a Keswick missioner. Before he could do so, however, he was directed back to China.

It was a sad occasion for the missionary when matters came to such a head that he felt resignation was the only course left open to him. The issue which provoked this action was the modernist-fundamentalist controversy. As a result he had to leave Changte and for some time led a nomadic existence, hardly ever staying in the same place more than five days. Needless to say his work continued to be owned of God. In 1927, in his sixty-eighth year he went back to Manchuria, this time to undertake the kind of task that appeared nearest his heart—pioneering. The work here was just as fruitful as anywhere else he had been. Oubreak of plague there meant that they were compelled to take refuge in Korea. This provided another opportunity for God to manifest his protecting hand, for in their journey they were delivered not only from the plague but also from fire and a train wreck. Modern day Vietnam was also visited.

By now the willing spirit was having to contend with the weak flesh. Jonathan Goforth was struck with blindness. Pneumonia and haemorrhages were further indications that the end was approaching. Rest did not come easily to him and a measure of recovery found him again at his post within the limits imposed by his condition. At the same time requests came from Canada that he come to stir up the church at home. This appeared the wisest course in the circumstances, but it did not result in any slackening of effort on his part, and he was soon accepting engagements eight or sometimes ten times a week. Less than a month before he died, in seventeen days he had delivered 22 addresses.

When at last the end came it was on the morning of 6 October 1936. He had given his last address the previous night. What more fitting than that its title should have been, 'How the Spirit's fire swept Korea'? It was that very fire that blazed in his heart with a ferocity that could not be quenched, and consumed anything in its path that rendered him unworthy of Christ. One of the tributes paid him at his funeral service was this:

He resembled Paul more than he resembled any other man in the Bible. In missionary zeal, for example, I never met a man so like Paul. I have read about such men, Livingstone, Judson, Taylor, and such like.

Jonathan Goforth would have been happy and proud to be among the 'such like'.

24
C. T. Studd
(1860-1931)

'Privileged' is as good a word as any, and better than most, to describe the environment in which C. T. Studd was reared. His father had spent some years in India as a planter and there made a fortune. He came home to England where he developed and expressed his sporting instincts in a number of directions. With a love of fox-hunting he combined a keen interest in horse-racing, owning a string of horses, and on one occasion winning the Grand National. At Tedworth House in Wiltshire he used some of his land as a cricket ground where his sons displayed their outstanding abilities, which were to bring them unique achievements. All these activities were accompanied by the usual round of 'society' amusements such as the theatre and balls and visits to Town. Mr Studd and his family passed their days in the lap of luxury. C. T. with his older brothers, J. E. K. and G. B., received the most exclusive education in the country, when they attended Eton. There they excelled at cricket, creating a record when each captained the cricket eleven in successive years. Life was very pleasant, comfortable, promising for the boys, with no disturbing prospect to cast its shadow over their hopes and ambitions. Until their father, Edward Studd, heard D. L. Moody.

Nothing was the same after Edward Studd became a Christian. He gave up his questionable pursuits, particularly those involving gambling, and the whole direction of his life was changed. Now his concern was to win others for Christ, and his wealth and influence were used to this end. The large hall in the house was furnished with chairs so that it became a room for holding meetings to which his friends and neighbours were invited, and influential people from London were asked to preach the gospel.

At the time of their father's conversion the Studd brothers were at Eton, but they did not entirely escape the effects of his zeal. C. T.'s comment was: 'It did make one's hair stand on end. Everyone in the house had a dog's life of it until they were converted.' One of the visitors their father had invited was not at all popular with the high-spirited boys, because of his seriousness. However, he spoke of Christ to each one of them in turn on the same day, and each one became a Christian without the other two knowing. It was only when they were back at Eton and received a letter from their father that they were made aware of what had happened.

The splendour of cricket at Eton gave way to the glory of cricket at Cambridge. While here C. T. Studd carved out for himself a career that was as memorable as it was brief. A member of the University team that defeated the Australians, he was also selected to play for England in a team that included the famous W. G. Grace. It was the team that lost to Australia for the first time ever, but he was included in the party that went to Australia to regain the coveted 'Ashes'. His intense dedication to his batting, which was to be reflected later in his approach to missionary work, won him universal renown. Wisden's, the cricketing 'Bible', regarded him twice as the best all-round player in England, and commented that 'some years have elapsed since the post has been filled by a player so excellent in all the three departments of the game.' W. G. Grace thought that from 1881 to 1884 he 'had few superiors as an all-round player'. With such early adulation the young Studd had the world at his feet, until his course was altered. In a remarkable way, as with his father, one of the instruments God used to turn him was the indefatigable D. L. Moody.

J. E. K., the oldest brother, became known in cricketing circles as the 'Austere Man' as a result of his glowing testimony. By contrast, C. T. was to regard the first six years of his Christian experience as being spent in a backslidden condition. This was hardly surprising perhaps when one considers the success that had attended him. Then a number of seemingly unrelated factors began to have an effect on his life. Two old ladies had been praying for him while he was in Australia; his brother George contracted a dangerous illness, bringing him near to death, and this had a sobering effect on Charlie; and in one of Moody's meetings God met him once more. From then on his life was never the same, and he was possessed by that consuming passion to lead people to Christ that was to be characteristic of him for the rest of his days.

The yearning to be absolute in his service of God was answered by the call to be a missionary in China. In this desire he met with strong opposition from his own family, but God enabled him to overcome in this domestic conflict. He had an interview with Hudson Taylor and was accepted by the China Inland Mission. In this venture he was accompanied by six other Cambridge students. The impact they made on the secular and religious world was truly impressive, while the influence they had on the student world was immense. Everyone was talking and reading about the 'Cambridge Seven'.

It was February 1885 when they sailed for China. This was to be the first period of Studd's work abroad in various countries, and lasted for ten years. They were eventful and full of hardship. If his letters home at this time are written in a racy style, that certainly does not reflect a breezy, cavalier approach to his labour. Rather they are the product of a joy that carried him through great discomfort and difficulty. Three years later he married an Irish Salvation Army lass, Priscilla Stewart. He was never a person given to convention, and his attitude to courtship, love, his bride-to-be, marriage, as to so many other matters in his life, was far from what might be considered normal. Nevertheless theirs was a true and happy union as they worked in strange and trying circumstances for the advancement of the kingdom. From the outset persecution was their lot, and he remarks that for five years every time they stepped out of doors they were greeted with curses. The blame for every misfortune fell upon them. In spite of this they saw people converted, and he was able to open an Opium Refuge, much as modern Christians work among drug addicts. Already his attitude of total dedication to and utter dependence on God was being shaped, and when he inherited a fortune of about £30,000 (amounting to hundreds of thousands of pounds by today's standards) he gave away every penny to gospel work, Moody, George Müller, and General Booth being among the recipients.

In spite of his prowess as an athlete Studd did not enjoy good health, and in 1893 he almost died. The following year he and his wife and daughters came home to England, but this was far from being a period of rest. He travelled round the country stirring up interest in the mission field. In 1896 he was invited to the United States and became involved in the infant Student Volunteer Missionary Union, out of which grew the Student Christian Movement. He was there for eighteen months, sometimes addressing as many as six meetings a day. Thousands

C. T. Studd

attended these meetings, with hundreds offering themselves for missionary service.

He felt a particular sense of indebtedness to India, arising naturally out of the time his father had spent there. Consequently, he was from 1900 to 1906 pastor of the church at Ootacamund, South India. The evangelistic drive was as strong as ever, and he joined a cricket tour in order to have opportunities to speak to the soldiers. While in India he had the privilege of baptizing his four daughters, one of those present being Amy Carmichael. Two more years in England saw his unrelenting zeal directed as ever to making known the gospel of Jesus Christ. His standing in the world of sport still enabled him to draw crowds, whom he addressed in his usual forthright manner. He spoke of the difference between his former religion and that which he now owned:

> I once had another religion, mincing, lisping, bated breath, proper, hunting the Bible for hidden truths, but no obedience, no sacrifice. Then came the change. The real thing came before me. Soft speech became crude salt. The parlour game with the nurses became real cricket on the public ground. Words became deeds. The commands of Christ became not merely Sunday recitations, but battle calls to be obeyed, unless one would lose one's self-respect and manhood. Assent to creed was born again into decisive action of obedience.

The call to Africa came in a most unusual way and appealed greatly to his sense of fun. While in Liverpool in 1908 a notice caught his eye and his immediate interest. It read, 'Cannibals want missionaries'. 'For more reasons than one,' he thought. In the meeting so ambiguously publicized, he was stung into action. The speaker had travelled across Africa, and said that there were parts where traders, scientists, officials and so on had been on their business, but no Christians on theirs. C. T. Studd determined to take up the challenge. His doctors were against it; his financial circumstances were against it; his wife was against it. But he was convinced that God was for it— and that was enough. In December 1910, alone, and at an age when most men do not think of pioneer work, he left for Southern Sudan to explore the possibilities. The arduous nature of this journey may be imagined from the fact that out of 29 donkeys that went on the expedition 25 died. It was on the voyage out that the vision of the Worldwide Evangelization Crusade was born, as God broadened his horizons beyond Africa.

He came back to Britain a man on fire. Once more students were aroused by his meetings. He wrote booklets in his usual hard-hitting, straight-from-the-shoulder style. One-time Editorial Secretary of the Church Missionary Society, Dr Eugene Stock, said that *The Shame of Christ, The Jehad of Jesus*, and *The Chocolate Soldier* are 'the most stirring appeals in modern missionary literature'. In 1913 he set out again, accompanied by a young Cambridge graduate, Alfred Buxton. Together they were the pioneers of the Heart of Africa Mission.

From the coast their way took them through Kenya and Uganda, sometimes in the steps of H. M. Stanley, out of encounters with cannibals, until they reached their destination, Niangara, in north-east Congo (the present Zaire). Within two years three other centres had been established, and during Studd's absence in England to enlist further workers the first baptisms took place at Niangara. While the candidates were immersed shots were fired into the water to keep crocodiles at bay! His stay in Britain was again marked by his unflagging zeal. His physical condition gave cause for alarm, and he was now subject to attacks of malaria. His wife's initial reluctance had now been overcome, and although she was confined to bed because of heart trouble, she was promoting the work tirelessly in the home country. Careless of any comforts and arguments that might be produced to influence him to relax his efforts and consider his health and other circumstances, he summed up his whole attitude in the words:

> Some wish to live within the sound
>   Of Church or Chapel bell,
> I want to run a Rescue Shop
>   Within a yard of hell.

In 1916 he left England for the last time. He took with him a party of eight, including his daughter Edith who was going out to marry Buxton. The work to which he returned was encouraging, with natives being converted and baptized, and launching into evangelism. At the same time they were difficult years with new recruits unable to join them because of the war. At the end of the decade he was cheered by the arrival of another party, this time including another daughter, Pauline, with her husband, Norman Grubb. Within a short period the number of workers had grown to forty. While he moved his home to Ibambi, his wife seemed to leave her invalid days behind her, and the

186

work she accomplished for the Mission at the home end in England was outstanding. Her rousing addresses left an indelible impression upon all who heard them.

Not only was the work expanding in Africa, it was now extending to other areas of the world such as South America and Asia. It was at this time that the title Worldwide Evangelization Crusade was adopted as the movement really spread its wings. However, beneath the surface there were internal disputes, and Buxton and his wife separated from Studd over the question of policy. Letters written at this time indicate something to which he would never have admitted at an earlier stage—the beginnings of weariness. This was to be expected when his strenuous routine is considered. The hours of sleep were minimal—he could never sleep for very long anyway because of asthma—and he worked eighteen-hour days. The Bible was probably his only book, and this he read for hours. Prayer was something into which he poured his heart. There were also the long journeys, the earnest preaching—sometimes to congregations of two thousand—the physical work, all taking their toll. When he was approaching seventy he set himself the task of translating the New Testament. His last two years were overshadowed by news of the death of Mrs Studd, and by fast declining health. He was now having heart attacks, and to his catalogue of infirmities was added gallstones. The combination of all these proved too much even for this gallant and dauntless adventurer, and in July 1931, in a metaphor of which he would have approved, his innings came to an end.

Any portrait of C. T. Studd would be incomplete and a dishonest representation without the warts. Although they may have been present in the earlier period of his life, his time in Africa was to disclose them more fully. His love for Jesus Christ was supreme, and this may well have blinded him to his duties and responsibilities to others. His stubbornness meant that he was inflexible in what he required and demanded of others. There is no doubt that he was controversial; there can be little question that he was eccentric; and it would not be beyond reason to support the claim that he was a fanatic. Certainly his energy, his earnestness, and his single-mindedness made him a most difficult man to work with, as Buxton and Grubb, his own sons-in-law recognized. People were not sure what to make of a man who, in his fifties, could leave behind an ailing wife while he went to be a missionary. He wrote a booklet in which he said he 'didn't care a damn' but to serve Christ and save souls. This language was unacceptable and offensive to many. There were reports that the constant use of morphine to relieve pain had turned him into a morphine addict. On hearing the news associated with his use of morphine, 'the Committee', in Norman Grubb's words, 'decided that the only thing to do was to remove him from the mission'. He was ruthless in the standards he set himself and others, and seems to have interpreted leisure and recreation, for others as well as for himself, as idleness. The mission he had begotten suffered unnecessarily as a result of his own intensity. Thankfully it was rescued and under his successors revived and grew strong.

C. T. Studd unfurled a banner as he responded unconditionally to the uncompromising call of his Master. The Son of God had gone forth to war, and Studd was determined to follow in his train. He laid a powerful emphasis on the need for 'holiness, without which no man shall see the Lord'. If this scripture was not able, and not intended, to bear the weight he placed upon it, his life will always remain a challenge to those who seek an easier path.

25
J. O. Fraser
(1886-1938)

It would be a commonplace to speak of the significance of prayer in the life of a missionary, and no one recognized its value in his work more than J. O. Fraser. What he was to demonstrate and prove was not so much how greatly he relied on his own prayers, but how deeply he was indebted to the important part played by those who were diligently praying for him at home. He laid particular emphasis on the need to have men and women behind him who were constant in remembering him and the task God had appointed him. To this end he organized a group of people to whom he was not merely a missionary for whom they prayed occasionally, but someone for whose success or failure they were in large measure responsible. There was a whole-hearted commitment about the way they supported him, and of this he was never forgetful. He corresponded with them faithfully, writing to each of the eight or ten members individually, and in such a manner that one of them remarked that she felt as if the Lisu people lived in the next street to her. This kind of relationship, built up over many years, was to bear abundant fruit in the remote corner of south-west China where Fraser served.

It was as a student at Imperial College, London that James Fraser realized that religion was to be taken with a seriousness that he had not previously imagined. Before then his life seems to have been comfortable and happy, with one rather incongruous element in it for those Victorian days. His parents separated while he was an adolescent, for reasons of incompatibility. This is not to say that the home was anything but a model of respectability, and his father provided well for his family at St Albans in Hertfordshire. He was President of the Royal College of Veterinary Surgeons, and stood as a parliamentary candidate.

James and his brothers and sisters were brought up to go to church regularly, and the father conducted prayers in the household each evening. But it was with his mother that he developed a particularly close relationship, and if his missionary course could be described as successful, there is no doubt that he would have recognized her before all others as the human agency through whom God accomplished so much. Needless to say she was the corner-stone of the prayer circle upon which he depended so utterly.

James Fraser was a gifted child in a gifted family. All seemed to have a love of music combined with a delight in the improving pursuits of their age. Outdoor interests also played a large part in their early years, James showing a particular strength and power of endurance which was to serve him well in the wastes and mountains that awaited him thousands of miles away. One day he walked to London and back, a distance of 44 miles, while on another occasion he cycled almost two hundred miles without once dismounting. His passion for music developed into an outstanding ability to play the piano, and at the age of twenty he gave his first recital in London. When he finished his college course, a career in engineering, which would have ensured him a very comfortable existence for the remainder of his life, lay open to him. But by then God had intervened in a quiet yet dramatic way in the plans of the young student.

He was facing his last year at college when a fellow student gave him a little booklet entitled, *Do Not Say*. The challenge so clearly presented to him in its pages struck home to his heart. It was a challenge that demanded a response that he could not avoid. Previously he thought God would have been well-satisfied with the kind of life he offered him, a life of church-going and achieving moral standards and practical decency. Did God require anything more than this? Yes! called out the pages before him, much more. He found the arguments in the booklet overwhelming, and he looked upon the experience of those days as his conversion.

His mind turned to missionary concerns immediately, and he took a particular interest in the China Inland Mission. In 1906, at a Christian Training Camp, he met C. T. Studd. No sooner had he graduated than he applied to the CIM. Twice he was rejected because of an ear infection. His determination won through, however, and on his third attempt he was accepted. At the age of 21 he began his formal training to become a missionary. At 22 he had arrived in China, and his hopes and prospects of achievement in this world's terms were as though he had never entertained them. With him he carried a note from his mother in which she confessed herself that day to be 'the happiest woman in London'.

His first home in China was in Tengyueh, not far from the Burma border, in the province of Yunnan. There he worked with his companions, Mr and Mrs Embery. He soon found loneliness and boredom to be powerful enemies against which he had to guard, for Embery was very busy, and had little time to spare. The initial excitement of a novel experience soon passed, but thankfully he was able to apply a rigorous form of discipline to his daily routine. From his language study he would make his way to the market-place and mingle with the crowds gathered there. It was here that he first came across the Lisu tribespeople, a mountain people who spoke among themselves a different language to Chinese. These were to win his affection and give him the name by which he would be known to succeeding generations—Fraser of Lisuland.

There seemed to be no reason why he should be especially drawn to them, but drawn he was, irresistibly. They were scattered throughout the province, and as he knew of a movement of the Spirit of God among the Lisu of the eastern part of the province, he found himself longing for a similar awakening among those of the western. A journey over the mountains to the neighbouring city of Paoshan was the occasion of an incident which was to prove of remarkable significance later on, although he was unaware of it at the time. A six-year-old boy in a town south of Paoshan made off with a copy of Mark's Gospel to take to his father, Moh Ting-Chang, a literate pastrycook who lived in the mountains at Hsiangta. The honesty of the boy in securing the Gospel is open to question. What is not in question is the fact that his action was the means of beginning a work of God among a group of Lisu people. Of this event Fraser was ignorant as he made his way back to Tengyueh. He was still waiting for an opening, an opening that, unknown to him, God had already provided.

Almost a year after arriving in Tengyueh he made his first journey into Lisu country. In the little villages of Pleasant Valley and Trinket Mountain he was given a royal welcome by this very hospitable people. He became early acquainted with some of their customs, which greatly distressed him, and he was introduced to the reality of demon-worship. Here, too, he began to learn their language, and he began to teach them to read Chinese. Most encouraging of all, he was able to tell them of the love of God. The response to this among the Koh family was that they took down the demon shelf on which were arranged the trappings associated with the worship. This was a great step for them to take, and was a gleam of light that cheered him immensely. It was with a full heart that he returned after a few days to Tengyueh, where shortly afterwards he was entrusted with the responsibility for the station.

The critical importance of prayer was already being impressed upon him, as is evidenced in his letters to his mother. Another letter to a friend at home reveals his heart as well as his opinion:

> Solid, lasting missionary work is done on our knees. What I covet more than anything else is earnest, believing prayer, and I write to ask you to continue to put up much prayer for me and the work here in Tengyueh.

His new duties at Tengyueh meant that hopes of further visits to the Lisu were disappointed. He applied himself to open-air work, and found himself involved in discussions over philosophy and politics, which he sought to turn to the advantage of the gospel. The part he played in extinguishing a fire in the city helped to make him a familiar figure. The sense of frustration he felt over his inability to contact the Lisu tribespeople increased when in 1911 the Manchu dynasty was overthrown, and under Sun Yat-Sen a step was taken which was to lead eventually to the establishment of a communist regime in China.

He was forced to take refuge in Burma, where, although he encountered some delightful Christians, for much of the time he was alone, exiled from his adopted country. Here, too, he proved God's goodness in a marvellous way. He was penniless, and needed to pay his coolie for his services. Visits to the Post Office seemed vain, for how was money to come from Shanghai to Tengyueh, itself in deep trouble because of the rebellion, and then over the mountains to Burma? On the day the payment became necessary he made his way to the Post Office once more, to discover that one letter had come in that day. It was for him, had come right across China, and contained money. Shortly after, when another letter reached him from his mother, also containing money, he returned it to her, declaring that her need was greater than his.

His stay in Burma lasted a few months, and after his return to Yunnan, China, he received a double encouragement. He had a fellow worker, American Carl Gowman, and he was invited to make a visit to the Lisu village of Six Family Hollow where the Tsai family were about to celebrate a wedding. Like Moh Ting-Chang, the Tsais were to prove a strategic element in the way the gospel was to work among the Lisu. They confessed themselves to be Christians, and after a week of visiting other villages in the mountains Fraser and Gowman made their way back to Tengyueh. Their homecoming was a happy occasion, for there were four people waiting to be baptized, the nucleus of the first Christian church in that corner of China. Their joy was soon to be tempered, however, with grave sorrow.

One of the foes with which Fraser had to contend among the Lisu was the hold that demon worship exercised upon them. He had seen the demon shelves and had heard the people speak of the awe in which the spirits were held, but he had not yet witnessed the force that the powers of darkness unleashed upon these lovable mountain folk. In the Koh family, prayer for the recovery of one of its members from sickness seemed to have failed, where the efforts of a 'diviner' had succeeded. In the same family, where the gospel had appeared to have taken root, one had gone berserk, the sick brother had eventually died, a wife committed suicide, and her husband had run away. Such devastation was beginning to make Fraser, who had been rather sceptical about the power of demons, think seriously and reconsider his opinions. Later he was to learn that the Tsai family, concerning whom he had entertained such high hopes, with one exception had gone back to their old superstitions. The most significant effect this had on James Fraser was that it drove him back to fervent prayer.

Clearly this was a trying period in Fraser's experience. Explorations of the district revealed to him the immensity of his task and brought him into contact with other people such as the Kachin. This awareness seems to have been the occasion of his writing to his mother asking her to form a prayer circle who would support him in his endeavours. It was at this time that he knew keen disappointment, because his hopes that God was about to bless the Lisu with his abundant grace were not realized. It was at this time that he experienced doubt as to whether he had understood God's leading. It was at this time that clouds of depression gathered around him. But it was also at this time that an important moment in his walk with God occurred when a copy of a magazine called *The Overcomer* fell into his hands. Through this God dealt with him, and it was as a result of reading an article there that he commented:

> It seemed as if God was saying: 'You are crying to me to do a big work among the Lisu; I am wanting to do a big work in you yourself.'

Discouragements still awaited him, as when on returning from a visit to Burma he discovered that untrue rumours about him had been spread among the Lisu by the Chinese. Whereas previously he would have been depressed by the news, now he was able to resist the devil in this assault.

Equally important to him from the trials and questioning of this period was the lesson of what he called the prayer of faith. It was as if God was rebuking him for lack of faith, and challenging him to believe that the prayers of the last five years were already answered. Even while he was coming to terms with this new concept, the tide was beginning to turn.

From Tantsah, where he had settled, he visited a district to the south-west, where he had been five years previously. Awaiting him there was the pastrycook, Moh Ting-Chang. His response to the gospel was such that when Fraser had to leave he told the people that if they needed any teaching about Jesus Christ they should turn to Moh. The circumstances in which he was converted could not fail to hearten Fraser, and yet the following year, 1916, he considered writing to Mr D. E. Hoste, Hudson Taylor's successor as head of the CIM, and one of the Cambridge Seven, to ask for a change of work. The expected breakthrough among the Lisu still had not come. He made his way westward, and after spending the night in one of the villages was about to set off when he was told of a family that wanted to become Christian. The following days saw seven other families similarly affected. As he drew nearer the border of Burma he found others ready and eager to leave their demonolatry. In a few short months 129 families among the Lisu were won to the Saviour. It goes without saying that the letter to Mr Hoste was never written.

Some ten years after his arrival in China he went to Shanghai to rest, but during his stay there he underwent an operation for appendicitis. His love of music remained unquenched and his talent did not appear impaired, for he gave a piano recital there. He also developed a deep and invaluable friendship with Mr Hoste. All the time, he was longing to return to his beloved Lisu. He went back to witness scenes of further encouragement, but as was to be expected problems were beginning to appear. Some of the Lisu were thanking God that since they had become Christians they had made more money than ever out of the opium trade! Obviously further instruction was needed on such matters as the observance of the Lord's Day. With this in mind Fraser set himself to translating the Gospel of Mark into Lisu, and also to preparing a catechism.

In 1923 he was joined by a young American named Allyn Cooke. He proved to be God's provision and was soon in action on his own account. Fraser had committed himself to being among the Kachin, who were turning to Christ, when there came a postcard from Moh at Hsiangta appealing to him to come, for the people in his area wanted

195

to become Christian. Faced with this dilemma Fraser saw that the only way out was to send the novice, Cooke, to the Lisu of the Cold Country where Moh had been telling them of the salvation to be found in Christ.

The effect of Cooke's visit was dramatic. Overwhelmed by the scenes of drunkenness and debauchery he broke down in tears. The first reaction of the people was puzzlement, but when they realized that this was a sign of his care for them they poured away their whisky and listened to him. Within two weeks thirty families had responded to his presentation of the gospel. Some weeks after Cooke returned to Tengyueh, one of the Lisu companions he had taken with him to the Cold Country and left there to teach the Christians, came to Fraser requiring a large number of Gospels, hymn-books, and cate-chisms. When Fraser went to the district he was amazed at the impact made by the gospel. The proportion of believers to unbelievers was astonishing, and in some areas there were scarcely any heathen to be found at all. He returned to Tengyueh to rest and to attend to other duties, only to be uprooted again by further news from the Cold Country. It was as though a second wave of blessing had broken on the people as a result of the evangelism carried out by themselves, and which required his presence there. What this meant for the Lisu and for him is indicated in this extract from a letter that he wrote home:

> Imagine what it is to have between five and six hundred families (repre-senting some three thousand people) looking to you as father, mother, teacher, shepherd, adviser etc. etc. It is a big responsibility.

There was much to encourage him as he left for England on his first furlough.

The return from furlough (during which he visited Canada where the young Isobel Kuhn was called to her work by hearing and meeting him) found him entrusted with a new work in Kansu in the north-west. His time there brought him into danger, and in 1927 the grow-ing communist menace forced him to make a dramatic escape for the second time. A period spent in Shanghai was a mixed blessing, for while he enjoyed the fellowship of D. E. Hoste he was not very happy with plans to keep him there in an administrative role. It was with relief that he was at last allowed to return to Yunnan as superintendent.

196

This was the time when he met Roxie, the daughter of Frank Dymond who had once remarked to her that there was 'a strange chap who lives up in the mountains doing a kind of lone missionary work. No one seems to know much about him.' The strange chap now became his son-in-law. His marriage and the arrival of children provided Fraser with the perfect antidote to the loneliness which he often seemed to feel in his work.

His last years were both active and happy. As well as travelling he was able to play his part in completing the New Testament. The work he had put into the Lisu language meant that this was done in what other translators called the 'Fraser script'. Feeling the burden of supervising such a vast province as Yunnan, he shared his thoughts with others, and it was divided. The Fraser family made their home in Paoshan, where the house was ever open to visitors. This did not shake the missionary from what he had long considered the priorities of his life, and he devoted himself as much as ever to prayer and fasting. Snatches of his conversation with Roxie give the clear impression that he had some kind of premonition of his approaching death. On 21 September 1938 he had a violent headache, the symptom of malignant celebral malaria. Four days later, at the age of 52, he had died.

Devotion to his task brought him his share of suffering and affliction. He contracted pleurisy and typhoid among other illnesses, and he had numerous escapes from death, once at the hands of a pursuing Kachin tribesman, another time being rescued from a swamp in which he was sinking. Emphasis has already been laid on the importance he attached to prayer support. His letters to his circle at home deserve a mention of their own. From them have come many of his observations as to the value of prayer, issuing in the booklet bearing his name, *The Prayer of Faith.*

With the passing years there was an obvious growth in maturity. The work of the Spirit through him was accompanied by the work of the Spirit in him. After a conference which he addressed in 1935 one missionary remarked that it was 'Fraser's zenith'.

Some of his ideas and opinions caused a few flutters in the nest as far as his colleagues were concerned, and not all of his thinking was universally welcomed among the leaders of CIM. While he was not a pioneer in the matter, he was among the first to insist upon the people among whom he worked supporting their own workers and maintaining their own churches. For a time he thought it right to earn his keep by teaching English, as Paul did by making tents. He considered that women on the mission field were not put to the best use since so much of their time was taken up by mundane tasks such as house-keeping. It is easy to see that some of these ideas were very controversial. Looking back it seems beyond argument that he was right in adopting and applying the methods he did. Deeply affected by him as she was, it is hardly fair to expect Isobel Kuhn to be other than partial in her verdict, but in this respect it is well to weigh carefully her estimate that he was '50 years ahead of his time'.

26
Amy Carmichael
(1867-1951)

In one of her books, *God's Missionary*, Amy Carmichael wrote: 'Whatever makes for holiness of life, for the clearing of the glass through which the light shines, this is for us and nothing else.' The record of her life and the testimony of her poems reveal a character so transparent that there can be little excuse for failing to catch a glimpse, and much more, of the Son of God who so captivated her.

She was born at a little village called Millisle, in County Down, on the shore of the Irish Sea. In her veins ran the blood of the Scottish Covenanters and their persecutors. She grew up in very comfortable circumstances, her father and his brother being responsible for developing the Carmichael flour mills in the village. The family wealth was directed to charitable and evangelistic work, and Amy, with her six younger brothers and sisters, was early acquainted with the Bible and the Shorter Catechism. Adventurous, mischievous, gentle and kind, like all children she exhibited in her early days those features that were to play such an important part in her adult years.

For three years she attended a boarding-school at Harrogate, Yorkshire. They appear to have been undistinguished apart from providing her with opportunities to develop her qualities of leadership. And it was also here, probably in 1883, that she made the decision to become a Christian, although she had 'felt the love of the Lord Jesus' from her early childhood.

Her father's generosity proved to be his undoing. The family had moved to Belfast where a new mill was built. Money which had been loaned was not repaid to Mr Carmichael. This did nothing to keep illness at bay, an illness which developed into pneumonia. The result was inevitable, and he died at 54 years of age in 1885. The effect on Amy was dramatic, translating her into womanhood at one bound. Her brothers and sisters came to rely on her almost as much as on their mother. This year also saw another crisis in her life. While helping a poor old lady one Sunday morning in Belfast, she was aware of the disapproval this might arouse in respectable passers-by. Suddenly the passage from 1 Corinthians 3:12-14 was impressed upon her, especially the phrase, 'If any man's work abide'. Her sense of values was revolutionized. That afternoon, records one of her brothers, she 'settled once and for all the pattern of her future life'. The following year, during a visit to Glasgow, she attended a Keswick meeting. Here again God met with her in a startling manner.

Her concern for others at this time was astonishing. Almost all her energy was directed to the benefit of others, and was expressed along the avenues of good works, prayer, and evangelism. Going through the streets of Belfast on Saturday evenings certainly made an impression on her. Her work among the mill-girls was tireless, growing to such a degree that she needed a hall that would seat five hundred. This, called 'The Welcome', came in answer to prayer.

Family circumstances necessitated a change, and Amy found herself with her mother and one of her sisters in Manchester. Here she was asked to do a similar work to that which she had done in Belfast. This did not last very long because of Amy's ill health, but it was evident that she was being prepared for other work. The instrument God used, and a powerful influence in her life, was Robert Wilson. He was one of the founders of the Keswick Convention, and in fact chose as its motto, 'All one in Christ Jesus'. He had become a friend of Amy's family. A widower whose only daughter had died, he was very lonely. Eventually she went to live as his daughter at his home, Broughton Grange, near Cockermouth, Cumberland. References to him in her writings as the 'D. O. M.' indicate the affection she and her family had for him—the Dear Old Man.

At Broughton she had a third experience, equally as significant as those at Harrogate and Glasgow. There on 13 January 1892 she heard God call her. His words were, 'Go ye,' and they were a summons to missionary work. The thought of parting from the D. O. M. put great pressure on her. She used to hear him repeating the words, 'If any man say unto you, Why do ye this? say ye that the Lord hath need of him.' Criticism of her decision came from Mr Wilson's own family, and even from Keswick leaders. However, she was to be the first missionary supported by the Keswick Mission Committee.

Turned down by the China Inland Mission doctor, she knew that was not the end of the story for her, and in March 1893 she set sail for Japan. Her stay here was short, just over a year, but the lessons she learnt and the service she performed proved valuable. Severe bouts of neuralgia necessitated her going to Shanghai for rest. There she thought she ought to work in Ceylon. Some three months after being in that land she received news of Mr Wilson's stroke. There was nothing for it but to return home. It was hardly an auspicious beginning to her missionary vocation.

Her time in England at Broughton in 1895 saw the publication of her first book, *From Sunrise Land*. This comprised her collected letters from Japan. Robert Wilson's recovery freed her to think of the mission field once again. When someone suggested South India rather than China and Japan, she was not impressed because 'it sounded much too easy'. The Church of England Zenana Missionary Society accepted her. She arrived in India in November, and if the length of her first term of service was disappointing, the second more than redressed the balance, for it was also her last. She remained there for 55 years, never once returning to Britain.

Her first year in Bangalore was not a very happy one. She found herself out of sympathy with her colleagues, was distressed that no Muslims were converted, and was disturbed that Hindus, Muslims, and other unconverted teachers were employed in the Mission schools. Relief was at hand, however, for in 1896 she met another man who was to be a tower of strength to her. 'Walker of Tinnevelly', Anglican missionary to South India, was only eight years older than she was, but was already a revered figure in the area. Although at first she did not like him he seems to have recognized something above the ordinary in her and urged her to leave Bangalore for Tinnevelly. South she went to the tip of India, and there she spent the rest of her life.

When Mr and Mrs Walker felt called to a change of work, Amy went with them to the little town of Pannaivilai. Here she was involved in a ministry similar to that which had occupied her in Belfast and Manchester. Here she gathered around her a Women's Band, who were soon given the name 'Starry Cluster'. Her concern for souls was shared by these devout women, who gave themselves to evangelism in and around the town, travelling further afield when weather conditions permitted.

Hostility was aroused, and danger threatened the converts and the missionaries. The caste system was very powerul, and to confess Christ and be baptized brought threats and reproach from the families of those who left this established order. Even little children would be ill-treated by parents for showing any response to the gospel. More than one Christian escaped to the Walkers' bungalow for refuge. Seeing the Mission school burnt down was part of the penalty to be paid. As one village closed, so another opened, where an eleven-year-old girl, destined to be one of Amy's closest friends, became a Christian. Arulai, like so many others was attracted to her. She was not the only one to be so drawn, earning for Amy the name 'child-catching Missie Ammal'.

It was at this time that two significant events occurred. One was the writing of *Things As They Are* which caused a stir because some thought it painted a too discouraging picture of the work. Amy's depiction of the true state of affairs seems to have offended them, and so publication of the book was delayed. Secondly, there was yet another move. Intended to be just for a few months it brought her to the place which was for ever to be associated with her name— Dohnavur.

It was here that she entered the lists in the battle against the evils perpetrated on the Temple children. She had come across this wickedness first through Preena, a Temple child of seven, who had been recaptured after escaping and had had her hands branded with hot irons as a punishment. Temple children were given to a god if a sick member of the family recovered, or if the mother was a widow or a deserted wife. There were other reasons why these girls (and babies) were 'married to the god'. So vile and immoral were the practices related to the traffic in these children that some even in government circles were incredulous. Dohnavur proved an ideal setting as this rescue work developed.

The source of the supply of Temple children was a mystery, and three years elapsed between the arrival at Dohnavur of the first and the second. It was not only those rescued from this danger who found a mother in Amy. In June 1904 she had seventeen in her care, including those saved from such a wretched fate. A pastor succeeded in rescuing a child from a Temple woman and bringing her to Dohnavur. She was just thirteen days old. The arrival of a second baby indicated to her the need for a nursery. The death of another little baby constrained her to observe the anniversary of the day of her death as 'a day of prayer for all imperilled children wherever they may be'.

It would be impossible to set a date upon the origin of the Dohnavur Fellowship, although it was registered under that name in 1927. The Irish woman and her Indian helpers (and by now she was more Indian than Irish) had been for many years drawn very closely together, and the growth of any pattern was almost imperceptible. The writings of such men as Samuel Rutherford, John Bunyan, Thomas à Kempis were a strong influence on her personally, and thus inevitably on the way the work was progressing. Utter dependence on God was foundational to the company: no one received a salary and all needs were met in answer to prayer. In 1908 *The Beginning of a Story* was published, in which she mentioned the need for money. In no way was this intended as an appeal, but she thought it might be so construed, and so the book was withdrawn from circulation.

She was no stranger to the direct and powerful movement of God's Spirit. At the close of a morning service in Dohnavur church, as she was speaking she was obliged to stop. Remarkable scenes followed. A sense of God's presence pervaded the building. Young and old fell to the floor, crying to God. Some pleaded with her to restore order, and as Walker and the pastor were both away she was aware that the responsibility lay with her. She felt, however, that she should do nothing. 'That hurricane of prayer', she writes, 'continued with one short break of a few minutes for over four hours. They passed like four minutes.' In the weeks and months that followed it became clear that God had been at work, with many children converted and workers renewed. The effects were felt in the village, with a number of outstanding conversions, and blessing abounding in the experience of the Christians.

That was in 1905, a year significant for other reasons. A new nursery had been opened at Neyyoor. This was in order to be close to the London Missionary Society hospital, and was in the care of another of Amy's closest friends, Ponnammal. It also saw the death of Mr Wilson, whose loneliness had been a constant strain on her, and whose letters a constant encouragement.

An outbreak of dysentery at Neyyoor in 1907 had devastating effects. Ten children died. Among other lessons it became obvious that more nurseries were required in order to avoid overcrowding. In July a gift of two hundred pounds was received, specifically designated for this very purpose. The need for more helpers was also pressed upon Amy and her band. They came, including Mabel Wade, the first who came from England and settled there. Tamil workers were hard to find, but they came, one of them being Ponnammal's daughter.

The death of Thomas Walker in 1912 was completely unexpected, and was a great grief to Amy, and it brought an awareness of her increased responsibility. Nevertheless God used the occasion. Walker died on 24 August. On Sunday 25 Agnes Naish and her sister Edith arrived to help. They had been preparing for evangelistic work in the Tinnevelly area. Hearing of Amy's predicament they lost no time in coming to her aid. Walker's death had also left a deep imression on some of the older children. The effect was apparent in their changed lives. The deaths of her mother in 1913 and Ponnammal in 1915 were alike heavy losses to her. Suffering from a dangerous illness in the same year as Ponnammal's death, she recorded in her diary: 'Let me die of a battle wound, O my Lord, not of a lingering illness.' Her biography, *Walker of Tinnevelly*, was published at the time. The sad incidents of this decade were relieved for her friends, if not for her, by her being included in 1919 in the Royal Birthday Honours List.

Her concern for the children extended in all directions. Their need of a change of routine and environment led her to prove God once more. Discovering an ideal site for the building of accommodation she was told that the owner was asking for a hundred pounds. With her companions she prayed, and returned to Dohnavur. The next morning she opened the mail that had arrived the previous day, to find that one letter contained notice of a gift of a hundred pounds. The site for the Forest House was theirs.

Her active mind never allowed her to rest content. She was always exploring new possibilities and embarking on new ventures. These included the inauguration of the boys' work (for they too were victims of the darkness of Temple service), and the maintaining of suitable schools—she was not too perturbed about academic standards, but considered correct teaching and diligent conduct of the utmost importance. In 1923 there were thirty nurseries in Dohnavur, and new buildings were always appearing. None of this was at the expense of evangelism. In 1925 a House of Prayer was built, the Three Pavilions housing about seventy girls in need of special care was purchased, and a little house called Joppa was built for tired workers from Dohnavur.

The unique character of her work had long been apparent, and so, in 1926, it seemed a natural step to make the work at Dohnavur independent of the Church of England and its Zenana Missionary Society. It was from this that the Dohnavur Fellowship officially came into being. In the light of this development, three matters of prayer to which she had addressed herself for some time now took on the aspect of urgency. They were the question of a leader for the boys' work, the need for a hospital with someone to be responsible for its building, and the inevitable subject of who was to succeed her, for she was by now approaching sixty. After some remarkable experiences of God in prayer, answers eventually came in the form of two brothers from a family well respected in evangelical circles, Godfrey and Murray Webb-Peploe, whose service she valued very highly.

In October 1931 she sustained an accident from which she never fully recovered. Returning home late one afternoon, in the twilight she fell into a pit and broke her leg. She little knew it, but the course of her ministry, although not ended, was dramatically changed. An invalid for the rest of her life, she rarely left her room for twenty years, and although her existence was not that of a recluse, nonetheless her activities were of necessity curtailed. If she no longer went to people, they constantly came to her. Her room seemed rarely empty during the day as she received visitors, advising, directing, counselling, comforting them. When she was alone she wrote. What came from her pen, in letters and verses and books, has proved of lasting spiritual benefit to Christians without number. And of course there were those precious experiences of prayer, where she grew in intimacy with God, and wrestled for the sake of his kingdom.

Of her thirty-five books, thirteen were written after the accident. That event clearly gave a new character to her writings. Whereas previously they had almost all been 'missionary' books, now less than half were. Her latter writings owe much to her encounter with suffering, and she passed on to thousands the lessons she learnt. Her gift of combining spiritual riches with literary expression is rare indeed. God made abundant use of the talent he had bestowed on his child.

There is a beauty about Amy Carmichael's character that shines in what she said, wrote, and did. She seems fitted for the noble company of 'faithful women' of whom tantalizingly little detail is given in the Bible, but whose partnership with patriarchs, prophets, apostles, and whose devotion to their Master and hers, is inestimable. She was concerned for the children. She was not so concerned for her colleagues in Dohnavur that she forgot those who volunteered but whom she felt constrained to turn away. Rather, for such she requested special prayer as she ached over them. In her were perfectly wedded the mystical and the practical, and if it may be said that her life was spent prodigally for those who looked to her, her treasure without question was in heaven. On being told that she might not live more than another five years or even three, she responded: 'I wonder if ever before you made anyone so happy with just a few words . . . Last night I lay awake too happy to sleep.'

A second fall in 1948 gave reason for her friends to think that her time had at last come. In fact her usefulness continued a further few years. On 18 January 1951 her treasured 'Daily Light' book of excerpts from the Bible contained this scripture: 'It is written, Eye hath not seen, nor ear heard, neither hath entered into the heart of man, the things which God hath prepared for them that love Him.' Amy Carmichael's 'Glory Day' had dawned.

27
Samuel Zwemer
(1867-1952)

The period of the Crusades in the mediaeval age has given rise to a splendid, romantic, and courageous notion of the mission of the Church. It is of course a wholly misguided notion, and that for a very good reason. What lay behind the Crusades was the desire to win territory for the Church rather than the passion to win men for Christ. In spiritual terms the defences of Islam remained unbreached. The first noteworthy attempt to pierce its armoured shell was made in the thirteenth century by Raymond Lull, born in Majorca and converted in his early thirties from an utterly immoral and dissolute life in which he saw no reason why his wife and children should stand in the way of his taking several mistresses. Although not entirely free from certain Roman Catholic ideas his zeal for the gospel brought him severe persecution, including imprisonment and stoning. It was as a result of being stoned, when he was past eighty, that he died in North Africa. For centuries after Lull, Muslim lands were largely neglected. Six hundred years were to pass before anyone ruffled the feathers of the Christian Church by asking, 'What about the Muslims?' One of those who did ask the question, and provide an answer, was Samuel Zwemer, the Apostle of Islam.

He was the thirteenth of fifteen children born in America to Dutch immigrant parents. His first home was, appropriately, near Holland in Michigan where his father was pastor of the Reformed Church. The kind of home it was may be surmised from the fact that four of Samuel's five surviving brothers became missionaries and one of his sisters was a missionary in China for forty years. With such a background it is little wonder that he could not remember a time when he was not a Christian. His preference for books rather than sports gave his brothers occasion to call him 'lazy Sam'. In years to come they must have blushed to think of the glaring inaccuracy of their description. A more industrious man it would have been very difficult to find.

It was during his time at Hope College in Holland, Michigan, that Zwemer first came into contact with Robert Wilder, the moving spirit behind the Student Volunteer Movement, then in its infancy. It was an important contact that was to be renewed over the years and was a significant factor in his becoming a missionary. He was also himself to play a significant role in the work of the movement as it came to assume prominence on the scene of increasing interest in missionary affairs. Throughout his distinguished career he was to attach great importance to the distribution of the Scriptures, and the seeds of this emphasis were already present when in college he undertook work as a colporteur for the American Bible Society.

At the age of twenty he entered a theological seminary in New Jersey, where at the same time he began to study medicine. He played a full part in the local church activities and was also committed to working in the neighbourhood among the poor and disadvantaged. He attended student conferences and himself organized one on missions, at which the speaker was Robert Wilder. Undergirding all this activity was a disciplined approach to his devotional life. At one time during his student days he regularly set aside the hour from twelve to one o'clock as a special time for prayer and devotion. 'Lazy Sam' was already disclaiming that title not so much by his words as by his deeds.

A year ahead of him at seminary was James Cantine. Both men discovered that they had a common interest in missionary work, an interest that God was expressly defining to them in terms of taking the gospel to the followers of Mohammed. As their ideas crystallized they were encouraged by Dr John Lansing, a faculty member who had spent some time in Egypt. There was certainly no question of their determination: not only had they chosen to oppose the only faith that had caused Christianity to beat a retreat, but they also resolved to engage that enemy on the soil of Arabia—birthplace of the Prophet. Plans were set afoot, and not even the negative response of the Reformed Board was allowed to stand in their way. That body had decided that the project was ill-timed, and so the little company formed their own American Arabian Mission. They adopted a rather unique form of fund-raising—Cantine appealing on behalf of Zwemer and Zwemer on behalf of Cantine. Zwemer travelled four thousand miles in the cause, encountering his fair share of the familiar bane of the church, lethargy. Along with this went a due proportion of petty irritations that would be laughable if not so tragic—such as being refused permission to hang up a chart on the wall because it was Sunday!

In 1890 he was reunited at Beirut with Cantine who had gone out the previous year. During his journey he visited Holland, then Scotland and England. It is interesting to note that in London he purchased C. M. Doughty's *Travels in Arabia Deserta*, which remained his constant companion until he sold it many years later in Cairo to another westerner destined to find fame in the east, Lawrence of Arabia. The two missionaries applied themselves to the study of Arabic, an extremely difficult task, and at the close of the year departed for Cairo. Here a kind Providence had purposed that they should meet once more with Dr Lansing. Together the three made plans for the course to be adopted. Since the interior, including Mecca and Medina, was forbidden to Christians, it was decided that between them Zwemer and Cantine should sail along the coast of the peninsula in search of a convenient base. Before they finally settled in Basra in Iraq, Zwemer had visited Sana, the capital of the Yemen, probably the first Christian missionary to do so, and on the strength of this was nominated to the Royal Geographic Society. The danger to which they were exposed was realized when their companion Kamil, a Christian from Syria, died after their arrival at Basra. It was suspected that he had been poisoned.

Never a man to remain idle Zwemer next undertook a voyage up the Tigris to Baghdad, crossed to the Euphrates, then sailed back down the famous river. The fanatical and bloody celebrations of an Islamic festival, forcing him to keep a low profile, could not be forgotten. When he had run the gauntlet of passing through the territory of the river pirates and arrived at Basra once more, he had behind him seven hundred miles of travelling through exciting and exotic places. Supreme in his memory, however, was the impression of such a vast area to be wrested from the grasp of an implacable spiritual foe and so few resources for the accomplishment of the task. Nevertheless he had the satisfaction of knowing that he had been able to pursue his custom, established long ago and observed wherever he went, of distributing copies of the Scriptures. Encouragements were seen in the form of a work being opened in Bahrain, and another in Muscat in the care of his brother Peter.

In 1895 he met a young missionary nurse, Amy Wilkes, and they were married the following year. They made their home in Bahrain where, with the help of his new wife, he continued his study of medicine, and even attained some degree of proficiency as a dentist. Always when the opportunity arose he was on his travels. His second visit to Sana was at the request of the London Jewish Society in order that he might distribute copies of the Hebrew Scriptures. This he was only too glad to do. It was on this occasion that he used his quick wits to good effect. He had taken copies of the Bible in other languages, and when someone suggested that he might sell them to some Turkish officers he lost no time in availing himself of the opportunity. Later some of them returned, wanting their money back. The reason was that a Greek bartender who came from Crete had told them that the versions they had were not genuine, but false imitations produced by the Protestants. Zwemer's response was to turn them to a passage in the New Testament, Titus 1:12—'The Cretians are always liars . . . ' Not only were the Turks happy with their purchase; the bartender bought one for himself!

When Zwemer and his wife returned from furlough in America the prospects for the work seemed bright. They took out two new recruits and other doctors joined the team. Hospitals were being developed in the various stations. Clouds were not very far away, however, and death seized a number of colleagues. Peter Zwemer, his brother, died in 1898. Hardest of all to bear was the loss of two daughters of the Zwemers within eight days in 1904. The smallness of the number of converts added to the weight they were called to bear. All this Samuel faced with his indefatigable hope and confidence. Daring always to gaze beyond the restricted horizons of this life he insisted, 'The harvest is the end of the world.'

His return to the United States in 1905 marked the end of his career as a pioneer missionary. His unquestioned abilities were recognized and required by two parties. Fortunately he saw no conflict between them and so fulfilled what he felt were his obligations in both directions. He became field secretary to the Reformed Board of Foreign Missions, and at the same time travelling secretary to the Student Volunteer Movement. As with all his enterprises he did not take long to find his feet, and was soon making a deep impact in arousing responses to the need for workers on Muslim territory. He also appeared to have a remarkable facility as a fund-raiser, in which capacity he had a reputation for being aggressive rather than demure. 'Coy' was an adjective that would not have sat easily upon him.

His work with students brought him once more into contact with Robert Wilder. It also meant that he was involved with John R. Mott in the famous Edinburgh Missionary Conference in 1910. Prior to this he had been chairman of the first missionary conference on Islam in Cairo in 1906.

The lure of being actually on the field proved very strong, and after the Edinburgh conference he was back in Bahrain. His writing, travelling, and speaking had now placed him in the forefront of authorities on Christian work among Muslims. It was no great surprise when various bodies including the United Presbyterian Mission in Egypt, the Nile Mission Press, and the American University of Cairo, along with others, were involved in urging him to move his base of operations to Cairo. In this he saw the hand of God, and there he set about the mammoth task of co-ordinating the work to the entire Islamic world. If the stream of his activities was now turned in another direction it flowed as fast as ever. The travelling, lecturing, evangelizing, writing continued unabated. Tours included Britain, North and South Africa, China, Indonesia. He was received at the famous universities of Europe. On one visit to America he delivered 151 lectures in 113 days. Some of his meetings in the fastnesses of Islam would be attended by thousands of Muslims. Always, however, opposition was strong and conversions were few. In forty years, actual converts resulting from his ministry probably numbered no more than twelve.

An eager young worker—a kindred spirit—joined him during his first year at Cairo. This was William Borden, himself the subject of a biography by Mrs Howard Taylor, *Borden of Yale*. Wealthy beyond the dreams of most people, he had given away what could be regarded as a fortune, to the benefit of Christian organizations, while he would not allow himself the luxury of a car. Sadly this life so full of promise of fruitful service came to an end after just four months in Cairo, yet another of the seemingly interminable setbacks that Zwemer endured.

During his years at Cairo there was one significant offer that he declined. It was an invitation to teach at Princeton Theological Seminary. The reason for his decision was that he felt the urgency of the task in Egypt outweighed that of the task in America. That was in 1918. When the request came again in 1925 he accepted, and was appointed to the Chair of History of Religion and Christian Missions. Undertaking the academic role did not mean that the pace of life was slackening for him. Travelling and speaking went on much as before, and on one of his visits to England he addressed the world-famous convention at Keswick. Four months after having his appendix removed he was on the back of a mule in the mountains near the Tibetan border! Ministering to missionaries was a priority that would not give way, though the journey might involve ten thousand miles.

Just before he retired, his wife Amy died in January 1937. His friend Cantine introduced him to a lady named Margaret Clarke, and they were married in 1940. She, too, was to die before him in 1950. The year previous to this the mission celebrated its sixtieth anniversary, and Zwemer, accompanied by his wife was able to visit once more the scene of his early adventures and exploits in Bahrain. It was a fitting and graceful way of drawing a long life to a close. In February 1952, after some weeks in hospital the previous year, he suffered a heart attack, and the following April he died aged 84.

There was an energy that simply coursed through Samuel Zwemer. It was as if he did not know how to rest. A colleague who accompanied him on one of his journeys remarked on his return that never again would he go with him. He appeared unable to stay in bed for more than half an hour at a time without putting on the light, making notes, then off with the light for another half hour before it would be on again. From its launching in 1911 he was the editor for forty years of the quarterly *The Moslem World*. He wrote hundreds of tracts and nearly fifty books. Nor was the energy diffuse, lacking concentration. There was an awesome single-mindedness about him as his love for the Muslims drove him to persist in the relentless assault on the unlovely, unyielding gates of the lands where the Koran sways its pitiless sceptre.

The first time William Borden heard Samuel Zwemer was at a convention in Nashville in Tennessee. The student knew that God was speaking to him through the missionary. Among the words he heard were these:

> Leadership in this movement has always been a leadership in suffering. There was Raymond Lull, the first missionary to the Moslems, stoned to

death in Algiers; Henry Martyn, pioneering in Persia with the cry, 'Let me burn out for God'.

The man from Michigan did not meet the cruel death of the Majorcan, nor the agonizing death of the Englishman. His end came peacefully in a New York hospital, but 'lazy Sam' was more than worthy to follow in their train.

28
Isobel Kuhn
(1902-1957)

Isobel Kuhn was dying. Her daughter was about to pursue her course as a missionary and the mother was reluctant to see her go under such circumstances. Could she not delay her departure awhile? In her heart Isobel knew this was impossible. Over thirty years earlier her own mother had stood in her way and vehemently declared that if she insisted on going to China it would be 'over my dead body'. Even her father, who, when she was born had promised God that she should go to China if that was the divine will, had later seemed less eager and refused to offer her any financial help whatsoever. Isobel knew that she owed it to Kathryn to encourage her in every way—to give her, not to keep her; to release, not to hold.

Although born in Toronto, Isobel Miller moved with her parents to homes in a number of places including Pittsburgh, Philadelphia, and St Louis. Despite their disappointing reactions to her decision to become a missionary her parents were both Christians and ensured that Isobel and her brother were taught to respect and honour the values and demands of the gospel. However, although she appeared to others to have been a Christian in her youth the truth was otherwise, and she was content to go through life with nothing more than a high regard for the Bible. Consequently, what faith she had suffered a severe blow in University when one of her teachers accused her and another in her class of believing in the 'myths of Genesis' only on the authority of parents. He maintained that no one any longer accepted the Bible as an infallible record of the works of God and reliable guide to the purposes of God. Finding her unquestioning attitude checked in this unceremonious manner she determined to have done with that path and to walk the way of doubting, whatever religious opinions she had previously encountered. From now on everything to do with her inherited faith would be subjected to rigorous investigation. No more church; no more Bible reading; no more praying. For

all this, she was to discover that God does not give people up as easily as they give him up.

It did not take long for her to lose herself in the round of carefree pleasure normally associated with student life. She was popular with everyone and was elected to a position of influence in student circles. God no longer featured among her priorities, although her moral standards were not lowered. But disillusionment was not too far away. Her engagement to a fellow student was broken by her because of his unfaithfulness, and she found how shallow and empty was the kind of life that she was living. Despair took hold of her to such a degree that she was about to take a dose of poison, a step from which she was kept only by hearing the sound of her father moaning in his sleep. Her deep regard for him was the only reason why she did not carry out her intention. At the end of her tether she sat on her bed and promised to serve God if he would but give her peace. The remainder of that night she slept soundly—something she had not done for a very long time. So the God she had forsaken was not dismissed as easily as she had assumed. She was on her way back.

Now she began what she called 'life at two levels'. While not reforming herself outwardly, inwardly she was searching and waiting. Experiences of God in situations where she least expected to find him further melted the hardness of her heart until one day she went along with her mother to a Bible class. There she found the arguments of liberal scholarship, which had initially led her astray, being met and refuted. From that first occasion she attended that meeting every Sunday afternoon. One level of her life was gradually giving way to the other—and this other, she discovered, could be very lonely.

With college days behind her she became a teacher in Vancouver. This meant boarding with a family who, although very friendly to her, did not share her new way of life. One of the strange results of this acquaintance was the nightly scene of their playing cards to the accompaniment of her playing hymns on the piano! It is clear that by now the great change had taken place for she described herself in this house as being 'the only Christian'. So earnest was she that when the late-night, noisy activity of the family threatened her communion with God she used to rise at 2.0 a.m. in order to read the Bible and pray. Attending a Teachers' Convention at Seattle, in Washington, USA, brought her into contact with a family called Whipple. They were Christians, friends of Isobel's father, and the contact had been arranged by him. Their influence was to be a significant factor in her life and her call to be a missionary, for it was through them that she came to attend The Firs Bible Conference.

Among the many memories she took with her from the conference one stood out. That was her first meeting with J. O. Fraser—Fraser of Lisuland. As she listened to him speak night after night of his work among these tribespeople who lived in China near the Burmese border, but were not really Chinese at all, her heart was stirred. From that moment, she wrote, 'Never did the vision of the Lisu tribe leave me'. When she discovered that her father had invited Mr Fraser to stay at their home she lost no opportunity to share her thoughts with him. One other event arising out of the Firs Conference was to have lasting effect upon her life. That was reading the biography of Hudson Taylor, *The Growth of a Soul*, and later *The Growth of a Work of God*. In this way was her call to work with the China Inland Mission among the Lisu confirmed.

In September 1924 she enrolled as a student at the Moody Bible Institute, in Chicago. Before the year ended her mother had died. The awful threat regarding Isobel's intention had been realized. There were other happier events, chief of which was meeting the man who was to be her husband, John Kuhn. When her course ended she spent some time as a candidate at the CIM Toronto Home. Here she was utterly dismayed to be told that one of her referees had described her as 'proud, disobedient and likely to be a trouble maker'. Nevertheless the Mission did show confidence in her and although anti-foreign feeling in China meant that it was unwise to send missionaries there she would be allowed to go there provided she conquered these unpleasant features. Later Isobel discovered the identity of the referee and recognized that the opinion volunteered was a result of malice. However, she did give attention to the allegations that were levelled against her. The time until she could go to China was spent very profitably as Superintendent of the Vancouver Girls Corner Club, an organization of Christian girls devoted to evangelistic work. Eventually the great day dawned, and she sailed for China in October 1928.

John had been in China since 1926. The one obstacle to their getting married was that they both felt called to vastly different parts of the country. He was interested in the north-west but was eventually appointed to Yunnan province—and that was where the Lisu were. It appeared that the way was clear, and so in November 1928 they were married at Kunming. However, other interests were involved. Mr Fraser was superintendent of Yunnan and entertained hopes that John would be his successor. This may have been one reason, along with concern for her health, why he was reluctant to give Isobel her heart's desire to work among the tribe. The young couple moved from home to home, and a daughter, Kathryn, was born to them in Tali. Isobel began to wonder if she would ever visit her beloved but unseen Lisu. Then came a letter from the superintendent asking for help. In the Upper Salween canyon there were two Lisu churches with only one missionary couple to care for them. John and Isobel offered themselves and were instructed to go there 'for a trip'. They moved there, wrote to Mr Fraser expressing their happiness, and were allowed to stay until their furlough. When illness struck her, one of her great concerns was that Mr Fraser would forbid her to remain there.

They came to Canada and the USA in 1937, and despite the outbreak of war between Japan and China were able to return the following year. The first shock they received was to learn that Kathryn would be separated from them. She was to go to school at Chefoo. Like many another missionary mother Isobel knew the heartache that so often is part of the education of their children. She was aware that, 'in one sense, it was giving her up for life'. The pain and grief which she experienced bear a character that only those who have been placed in similar circumstances can share. There is no doubt that the pain and grief would have been multiplied had she known what lay in store. How grateful she was for the strength she received in the patient understanding of her husband! Her burden was only increased when she was told that they were not to return to the Lisu. Her health, and plans for John to become superintendent were the factors behind Mr Fraser's thinking. They were to be stationed at Paoshan.

It was impossible for her to forget the Lisu people, and one day while she was reading her Bible she received a promise from God that was to her unmistakable. She knew that she would go back. Barely a month after arriving in Paoshan they received a letter from Mr Fraser asking them to go back to the Lisu village of Oak Flat. This, he added, was to be for just a short period. She confessed to gloating, 'So says you, my dearly beloved Super. So says you!' They made their way to the tribe and set about resolving the confusion that had arisen. A Rainy Season Bible School, the first, was established, and continued for three months. Her confidence in the promise was proved in a very sad way: in September 1938 came the distressing news that J. O. Fraser was dead. With his death all missionaries remained where they were. No one missed him more than Isobel Kuhn.

The year 1942 was one in which her faith was really put to the test. Helpers were unable to do what they had done formerly; she was separated from her husband; and news came that Kathryn's school had been taken by the Japanese. She was not one to succumb easily to setbacks, but a raging toothache drove her to make the long journey to Kunming to the dentist. This meant a round trip of a month. It was as well that she took it. The toothache was found to be symptomatic of a poison in her system, and the dentist told her that if she had delayed her coming by another day she would have died. It was also in this year that the Japanese threat drew nearer and panic was spreading through Yunnan province. Along with many others Isobel fled. She was uneasy about taking this course without a clear word from God. Later, on hearing that Yunnan had not fallen, she knew she had been wrong to run away. John was in Yunnan; news from Kathryn was scarce; and she had little hope of returning to her husband. The biggest problem was that she did not have enough money for the journey. The answer to her prayer for this was amazing. The Monday after she prayed two letters arrived in the same mail from the same girl. Each letter contained $50.00, and they had been posted six months apart! The way home was fraught with danger but accomplished safely. On arrival Isobel and John found that refugee missionaries had occupied their house. Her disappointment was afterward a cause of shame to her. All these afflictions served only to draw her nearer to the Lord. In them she learnt the practical lesson she had been taught in theory previously—'Keep your treasures on the open palm of your hand.'

The return to Oak Flat was a return to the danger zone. God honoured faith and steadfastness in the face of fresh perils. The shadow of the presence of the Japanese was cast over them constantly but they held their ground. Illnesses overtook them both, and the baby who had been born to them. Even so the Bible Schools were held, and flourished. Perhaps best of all they learnt that Kathryn had been released and was being cared for.

Their second furlough beckoned and with it the opportunity of being reunited as a family. It was to be an extended furlough with John taking a refresher course at Dallas Theological Seminary, but with the end of the war came a change of plans. He and the other superintendents were required to return to China a year ahead of their families. So January 1946 brought the experience of parting which was becoming very familiar, yet no more welcome. Isobel and young Danny joined him later, Kathryn this time being left with friends in Philadelphia.

Some of the leaders of the church in Oak Flat Village were a tragic disappointment in terms of their conduct and had to be disciplined. One of them made common cause with the leader of a band of Communist brigands. Providentially Isobel had moved from the village before the Communist leader came looking for her. It seemed that having been delivered from the Japanese threat the missionaries now had to face another. There was one occasion when John was away when Isobel found herself defenceless as an alliance of Communists and heathen Lisu robbers contested the issue with the local powerful landowner—the Laird. Once again the temptation was to escape: but the scripture she was given that morning was, 'Leave not thy place.' When John returned he agreed that she must take Danny to America, not only because of the physical danger but also the spiritual. First, they decided to hold one more Bible School. The result was remarkable. When the students went out to evangelize hundreds professed conversion each week-end.

By now Yunnan was under Communist rule, and the only way out for Isobel and Danny was over the Pienma Pass into Burma. The prospect was awesome. The pass was almost 11,000 feet above sea level; there was always the possibility that snow would have closed it; and the sound of rain falling on the lower slopes made it almost certain that there would indeed be snow as they climbed higher. The crossing, made with certain of the Lisu as helpers, was truly heroic. After numerous adventures they came through Rangoon and Bangkok to Hong Kong before making the long sea voyage home. It was 1950, and Isobel Kuhn knew she would not return to China.

One more chapter remained to be written in her story. When John came home they turned their attention to Thailand, where they went in 1952. On one of their expeditions in search of the tribes they faced many obstacles that seemed to them to come from the devil. The company gathered on the side of the mountain and claimed God's protection. Apparently it was not to be as they expected. Isobel suffered a severe blow in her chest. Several months later she was injured in the very same part of her body. Further examination revealed nothing harmful, but over a year later an operation became necessary. When she had been discharged from hospital for about a week the news she had been half expecting was broken to her. It was estimated that she had just a year to live, and in 1954 she returned home. Much of her closing years was spent in writing of her experiences, and among her many books produced at this time was *Ascent to the Tribes*, the account of their call to Thailand, *By Searching* and *In the Arena*. John came home in the summer of 1955 and was with her when she died in March 1957. Of that occasion he said: 'If ever I was near heaven, and if ever I was conscious that death had lost its sting, it was then.'

Isobel Kuhn had searched, and been found by God. The service she returned him is testimony not to the diligence of her effort in seeking, but to the abundance of his grace in saving.

29
Ida Scudder
(1870-1960)

Dr John Scudder picked up a pamphlet in the home of one of his wealthy patients in New York City, and by that casual act set in motion a train of events that can scarcely be equalled in missionary history.

The year was 1819, and the article that caught the eye of Dr Scudder concerned the plight of 600 million of the inhabitants of the earth. His response was to recognize the claim that he felt some of that number exercised on him. To the horror of his father he left his comfortable and successful practice for India in order to become his country's first medical missionary to a foreign country. From that moment the name 'Scudder' came to be the most noble and renowned in medical missions. In four generations 42 of the family became missionaries, giving a total of over a thousand years of service in India. 'Scudder' and 'missionary' were almost interchangeable terms, and when a baby was born into the family the odds were that the child would grow up into a medical missionary. To be born a Scudder was to be cast into a certain mould. Ida Scudder, however, determined to break the mould.

Raised in India, she was acquainted with its charm and its anguish, and there is no doubt that it was the anguish and suffering that left the greater impression upon her. It was not an impression that constrained her, like her grandfather, to come to the aid of the people, but rather drove her away from their hunger and disease. Her father, Dr John Scudder II, served in a number of capacities in various towns and villages around Madras, on the south-east coast. Apart from his work as a doctor, he was responsible for a boarding school of a hundred boys, Hindu as well as Christian; he was pastor of a little church; he toured surrounding communities encouraging the Christians, and in the Great Famine of 1877 he ran a relief camp at Vellore, nearby. In the records he kept he noted that deaths as a result of the famine were estimated at over five million. Ida had clear memories of the harrowing scenes of those days, but the deepest psychological mark she bore from childhood was the spirit of resentment begotten in her when her parents left her in the care of relatives in America, while they returned to India. The sobbing, the grief, the anger were not easily forgotten. It was a wound that took years to heal.

During her time in America she attended a seminary for ladies, founded by D. L. Moody in Northfield, Massachusetts. She developed into an attractive, vivacious, ambitious young woman, busy planning her life. Those plans were destined to be overthrown when in 1890 she received word from India that her mother was ill and needed her. This she saw as a necessary but inconvenient intrusion into the pursuit of the course she had mapped out for herself. Any suggestion by her friends that she would stay out there as a missionary was greeted with fury. She was certainly not going the way of her family simply because her name was Scudder. Just as soon as she could see she was no longer required in India she would be back in the USA. No amount of pressure was going to turn her into a missionary.

She found India to be no better than she expected. The haunting sights and sounds of hunger and poverty with their attendant evils met her as she made her way to her parents' home. The sooner this was over the better. She applied herself to her duties, some with more enthusiasm than others, and settled into a routine. The routine itself was disturbed one unforgettable night, with lifelong effects on her, and immense consequences for the sub-continent. At different times during that night she received visits from three men, two of them Hindus, one a Muslim. Each one had a wife dying in childbirth, and each one was desperate for help. Ida explained that there was nothing she could do, but she would call her father to accompany them. The men were dismayed at such a suggestion. Their religions would never tolerate the outrage of having a man attend to the needs of their wives. It was better that the women should die. She pleaded with them, but to no avail. Helpless, she waited for the morning, and sent to discover the outcome of the drama of the night. It was the worst possible: all three women had died. Ida Scudder found herself shut up to one inescapable conclusion. However hard she ran away, God had overtaken her. She was left with no option but one—to return to America to study medicine in order to minister to the needs of India.

Her eagerness to go home was the same, but now her motive was different. It was not to forget India, but to serve her. No sooner had she qualified as a doctor than she was confronted with her first task. She was to go out to Vellore where a hospital for women was to be built, but before she went she was charged with the responsibility of raising the money for it, the sum of eight thousand dollars. She set to her work with great enthusiasm, but as the time of her departure drew near she had succeeded in collecting just a few hundred. Shortly before sailing, her fears were allayed when she received a cheque for the hospital from a Mr Schell in memory of his wife. The cheque was for ten thousand dollars. Not content with this she presented to various friends and groups the need for an evangelistic worker among the women. She knew just the person to go, her friend Annie Hancock. From a Miss Gertrude Dodd and her sisters came the money to pay for her expenses. With these encouragements Ida and Annie arrived in Vellore at the turn of the century.

Within months Ida sustained a severe blow in the death of her tough, kindly father, upon whom she was going to depend so much, and from whom she was going to learn so much. His final pain drew from him only the quiet murmur, 'Oh, Master, let the light go out.' It did, only to kindle a different light in his daughter. Overwhelmed by what had happened, she came to herself, and in the same spirit that he manifested, one day she began moving furniture about with the terse announcement to her mother, 'My dispensary.' Ida Scudder had taken up the torch that her father had so lately laid down. Prejudices and superstitions about women doctors died hard, but soon she found herself incredibly busy. An additional room in the bungalow was needed to cope with the increasing demand for her services. Cataracts, cancer, typhoid, tuberculosis, venereal diseases were just a few of the conditions she had to treat. Average life expectancy was less than 27, and one out of every four babies did not see its first birthday. In the two years since opening the dispensary she had treated over five thousand patients.

In 1902 the Mary Taber Schell Memorial Hospital was opened with fewer than thirty beds, and it was soon in commission. Unaccustomed to lying in beds raised from the floor, some patients preferred to sleep under the beds. Then, so many were coming for attention that people were sleeping on and under the beds! The opening of the hospital meant that she was able to deal with more people, and during the whole of the year she treated over twelve thousand patients. Individual, local, and national tragedies seemed to follow fast on each other. Towards the end of 1901 famine struck, affecting an area of 200,000 square miles, and 1903 began with an outbreak of bubonic plague. Statistics soon acquired their usual horrifying, yet meaningless, significance. Before the plague abated it had covered India, and had claimed a million victims. Her work load was nothing short of phenomenal, for there were days when she saw 150 patients—and then went on to make her round of the hospital and performed operations. Homes in the town were then visited. Nor was this all. Nights before operations were usually broken as she rose to supervise the sterilization process. 'Often', writes Dorothy Clarke Wilson, 'her working hours stretched around the clock.'

In no way could her day be described as stereotyped, but even in a routine where the unusual was normal, she was aware of incidents which could not be accounted for other than by the direct intervention of God. On one occasion she was seeing patients in her dispensary when, on impulse, she rose, hurried to the hospital, becoming more agitated as she approached one particular bed. Running across the room she pushed aside the screen around one of the beds to find the grandmother and aunt of a newly born girl pressing a pillow over the face of the child. Seconds later and the baby would have died, and all because it had been born on an 'unlucky day'. The family gave the child away there and then to Ida. If she was so concerned, let her look after her. She did, naming her Mary Taber, after the hospital, and raising her as her own child. In later years the number was to grow, for Ida could never turn away any destitute or forsaken.

The longer she stayed in India the more impressed did she become with the massive need of the women of the country. The vicious and degrading accompaniments of ignorance, superstition, and child marriage were enough to break any but the hardest heart. Frequently her patients included girls of twelve or thirteen who were brought to her for help in giving birth. She began to realize how small, how pathetically small, had been her original vision of a hospital at Vellore. It was all very well to think of the service such a hospital could provide for those who came. But she was merely scratching the surface. There was a need to make the facilities available to a wider constituency;

225

there was a need for more nurses; there was a need to teach the women of India to care for themselves; there was a need to visit the surrounding villages; most of all there was a need for a school of nursing in Vellore. She had to be more involved. There had to be more money, more time. All this was essential. Impossible but essential. Fired with these ideals she went home on furlough, to inspire others with her ideals and to enlist their aid.

On her return to India in 1908 she lost no time in bringing her plans to fruition. As with so many of her attempts to improve the lot of the country, it proved to be an uphill task. Nursing was not considered to be a very proper profession for girls of any intelligence and ability. In spite of this applications came. The other venture upon which she entered was making regular visits to new dispensaries that had been opened at neighbouring Gudiyattam, and at her brother's station, Punganur. With the arrival of a car the following year she hoped to be able to go to more remote areas. From this grew 'Roadside', the scheme whereby she visited the villages around Vellore, setting up a mobile dispensary where the people gathered by the side of the road. Often she would be stopped as she was being driven along, and on one occasion she was required to treat a sick bullock. This was more important than might appear at first sight considering the sacred light in which the animal is regarded.

The initial reluctance with which she had been met was now a thing of the past. The needs and demands were growing, and with them her vision was growing. The hospital was already too small, and so she thought of adding to it. Scope for training needed to be enlarged. She realized that it was not addition to the hospital that was needed but a new hospital. Even beyond that, what was really the answer was the medical college she dreamed of. Encouraged by an influential and authoritative visitor to Vellore, Mrs Lucy Peabody, she set herself the goal of a medical college for women in Vellore. With this in mind, and full of enthusiasm, she sailed for America in 1914. Before she arrived her plans had received a severe blow with the outbreak of war. In financial terms her stay in America was far from being successful, as people were more concerned with the need in Europe than in India.

God's most profitable servants become so, not by waiting for things to happen, but rather by making them happen. Thus when Ida

Scudder went back to India in 1915 she was undismayed by lack of funds. Plans for the building of the medical school went ahead. In fact the school was opened in 1918 without a building, the seventeen members of the first year being accommodated in rented premises and taught at various venues in Vellore. To these seventeen and to their successors she was instructor, counsellor, mother, and much else beside. Among the most valuable contributions she made to their lives were the Bible studies that she conducted every Tuesday. She did not seem to sacrifice the previous activities for the new demands made upon her; rather she applied herself to the added responsibilities involved. Perhaps it was a seal on her venture, as well as a testimony to her industry, when the results of the exams at the end of the year were issued. She had been advised, somewhat patronizingly, not to be disappointed if none of her girls passed since the standard was very high. Women could not be expected to do very well. How could she with her unsophisticated efforts and facilities compete with the men who came from first-class government institutions? When it emerged that only one in five of the men had passed, Ida's feelings sank with those of the girls. In the event they achieved complete success—theirs was the best school of all.

She was attracting staff as the building was going on, providing her with further encouragement. Furlough in 1922 afforded her a change of labour, not a rest from it. She spent it along with Mrs Peabody, raising the astonishing sum of two million dollars. Her delight at this achievement was tempered by the deaths in 1924 and 1925 of two of the people who were most close to her, Annie Hancock and her mother. Sophia Scudder died 63 years after being denied support by the mission board when she came out to India with Dr John because her health gave cause for concern. She had outlived her husband by 25 years. In 1927 the hospital numbered the great national leader and social reformer, Mahatma Gandhi, among its visitors, and the following year the new hospital buildings were dedicated. The college buildings were opened in 1932. It appeared to some that she had reached the pinnacle of her achievements. Not so; there was more to come.

Like most major goals, hers were accomplished in the face of many difficulties. There was the depression of the thirties, the strained relations between Britain and India, and in 1937 the highest obstacle of all. The medical school had been granting diplomas, but now the government, with a commendable eye on higher standards, ruled that no students would be admitted to such institutions unless they were candidates for a degree. This meant for Vellore affiliation with the University of Madras. At least twelve new members of staff were needed. Those already teaching at the school were inadequately qualified. New equipment and laboratories were required. The number of beds had to be almost doubled to five hundred. In their present straitened circumstances Ida Scudder and her colleagues saw no way forward, and the prospect of the closure of the school stared them in the face. Once again God met with her in a remarkable way, this time through the dream of one of her pupils. As a result she wrote:

> First ponder, then dare. Know your facts. Count the cost. Money is not the most important thing. What you are building is not a medical school. It is the Kingdom of God. Don't err on the side of being too small. If this is the will of God that we should find some way to keep the college open, it has to be done.

A solution presented itself and it was one she accepted only after much agonizing. The opportunity came to proceed along the lines marked out by the authorities, but it meant making the facilities at Vellore available to men, thus revising the original intention of having a college exclusively for women, so that the institution became co-educational. She was happy to take this step, but faced stern opposition from her good friend Mrs Peabody. Torn in two directions Ida felt she was left with no option but to pursue the only logical course. During the years when the Second World War was occupying the attention of men and women everywhere, she was fighting her own personal battle. In 1942 she knew she could delay her decision no longer. It would be criminal to decline the opportunity. Vellore was to be open to male and female. That same year 27 girls began their course, each intent on becoming a Bachelor of Medicine, Bachelor of Surgery.

She retired at the age of 75, but maintained a keen interest in the work to the end of her life, and was privileged to see the young Dr Paul Brand, pioneer of the treatment of leprosy, develop his skills in Vellore. She had come to India as an unwilling visitor who regarded the period to be spent there as a minor irritant, an annoying, but thankfully temporary, inconvenience compelling the postponement of her plans. Ten years later she had returned with a settled purpose and a dominant mission. In the jubilee year of that occasion she rejoiced that Vellore Christian Medical College was permanently affiliated to Madras University. Her long life was spent in laying the foundations. In her closing years she saw others build upon them, for since her retirement in 1946 the hospital grew out of all recognition. Its place in the health care of India may be measured by the fact that her creation became the greatest medical centre throughout Asia, and that today it has a staff of about three thousand. Her own reputation is acknowledged by the fact that a letter addressed to Dr Ida, India, was safely delivered. She died in Vellore in 1960.

She had a life-long passion for tennis, and was still playing at the age of 83! She approached the game in the same spirit as that with which she met all the problems and obstacles that she encountered in her work. Aged 65 she entered a competition and was drawn against a teenager, who cried in derision, 'I've pulled a grannie!' Ida was unimpressed when reports of the remark reached her. When the two opponents faced each other across the net it looked as though the result was never in doubt.

It wasn't. The grannie won, two sets to love.

30
Gladys Aylward
(1902-1970)

The stage-struck parlourmaid worked hard at realizing her ambition. Sunday-school classes gave way to drama classes as she strove to attain her goal. The early influences of a Christian upbringing were losing their grip as she became consumed with the dreams of the theatre.

Such dreams were not unusual for a young London girl, and no doubt Gladys Aylward shared them with hundreds of others of her age, but while most idly entertained these aims, Gladys diligently pursued them. Fame did eventually come to her, though along a very different path from that which she had anticipated, when her experiences were portrayed in a film, but by that time she had long put aside the frail and brittle prospects held out by an acting career. Nevertheless there is a certain irony in the fact that she, who had once intended to portray others, found herself portrayed by one of the most famous actresses of the screen.

Edmonton in north London was her birthplace, a short distance from where another great missionary, John Williams, was born. It was a working-class home typical of that time, her father a postman and her mother a housewife. She left school at the age of fourteen, 'never, as far as I can find out, having passed one exam'. Also typical of the period was her entry 'into service', becoming a maid or servant to one of the wealthier families. It was here in the evenings that she expressed her lively nature by preparing herself for the stage.

Her course altered dramatically in her twenties when she became a Christian. Before long her mind was taken up with the needs of China, and she sought to stir up interest in others, and even to persuade her brother to go there. Faced with their lack of concern it became clear that she could hardly expect others to respond if all she did was to tell them that someone should do something about it. Gradually but surely the truth was beginning to dawn on her. God had chosen a role for her and she was to play it on a huge stage thousands of miles away.

A three-month probationary period in a missionary college was sufficient to prove to the committee of the college that whatever God had in store for her it was certainly not a career in China. She showed no appreciation of theology, and already at the age of 26 she would be too old when she reached China to acquire the language. Brutal as it seemed, it was as well for them to point these matters out to her then, rather than mislead her by allowing her to continue with her studies.

She went to be housekeeper to two retired missionaries in Bristol, moving from there to Swansea where she worked among the prostitutes who frequented the dockland area. Next she returned to London to be housemaid at the home of Sir Francis Younghusband, noted soldier, author, and explorer. If all this seemed rather aimless it was not so to her. The name 'China' had been burnt into her heart. It would not be erased, and nothing was permitted to divert her from her intention of going there in order to make known the glorious gospel of Jesus Christ. It was this that caused her to move from her work in South Wales back to London, for she was saving up for the journey, and the best way open for her to make money was in the kind of service to which she was accustomed. Each week she went along to the travel agent and paid something toward the fare. She had no idea what she was to do when she arrived in China, until one day she heard of Jeannie Lawson. This was a 73-year-old widow who had come home to retire, found she could not settle, and had gone back to China and was looking for a companion. Gladys Aylward's response was immediate: 'That's me!'

Never did the departure of a missionary present a more incongruous sight than that which took place on Liverpool Street Station one October Saturday morning in 1930. Such farewells are usually taken in an atmosphere of sadness mixed with joy. To the casual observer this particular valediction had the element of the comical as well, for along with Gladys's luggage, containing corned beef, baked beans, hard-boiled eggs, and tea, were tied together a kettle and a saucepan. Thus equipped she set out on the long train journey to China, through Germany, Poland and Moscow, across the vast distances of Siberia, skirting the northern borders of Mongolia and Manchuria and at last to the sea at Vladivostok.

Her destination was Tientsin, where she would be met by a guide who would take her to Mrs Lawson. If there was any charm in the prospect of the long journey it was soon lost as the train took her through the very unfriendly countryside of Russia and Siberia. The chilling climate fitted the chilling sight of poor, under-fed, and miserable people. She was delivered from dangers many times before she reached China. On one occasion she had to walk along the railway track at night for miles. As she followed the line she complained to herself at the owners of the dogs she could hear howling nearby. Later she discovered that the noise came from a pack of wolves. Her perils increased as she passed through the Manchurian-Siberian border where Chinese and Russian powers were contesting the issue. Her problems were complicated by the fact that the officials and authorities she met kept mistaking the innocuous word 'missionary' on her passport for the prestigious description 'machinist'. The confusion was responsible for bringing her into more than one tight corner, for the skills of anyone capable of handling a machine were very much in demand in bleak and struggling Russia. In all her difficulties she came across mysterious figures who helped her, and in them she recognized the provision of God.

Arriving at last at the port of Vladivostok she managed to get a ship to Japan, travelled by bus down to Kobe, and from there she sailed to China. When she reached Tientsin, some ninety miles from Peking (modern Beijing), she met some European Christians who said 'they had heard of Mrs Lawson'. On she went through Peking to Tsehchow where she expected to meet her companion, only to be told that a two-day journey by mule track awaited her, taking her to the small walled town of Yangcheng. There at last among the mountain fastnesses the two ladies met. Perhaps the most farcical element in the whole venture was reserved to this moment, for Gladys could hardly have expected to be greeted with, 'Well, and who are you?' If the words of welcome were lacking in warmth, at least they did not flatter to deceive. Jeannie Lawson was a fierce, uncompromising, Scots Christian, and Gladys, grateful for the opportunity the older lady had given her, learned as far as possible to adapt to her unusual ways. From this strange, and sometimes strained, relationship evolved 'The Inn of Eight Happinesses.'

The inns were the stopping places for the mule trains that travelled through China. They provided food and shelter for the men and the animals as they halted for the night. Together the two missionaries saw the strategic importance of using their premises for this purpose—with an added benefit. The Chinese loved stories, and these travellers would be told gospel stories at no extra charge. Once the fear of being entertained by 'foreign devils' was overcome the venture proved to be hugely successful, with their inn crowded, and gaining a reputation for hospitality of a different kind. The partnership was short-lived, however, for eight months after the opening of the inn Jeannie Lawson died. It was a crucial time for Gladys, but she had no intention of abandoning the inn, and with her growing fluency in the local Chinese dialect, she determined to carry on her primitive but valuable ministry.

The day the Mandarin of Yangcheng visited her was another significant occasion in her life and work in China. It marked the beginning of a deep and respectful relationship between the little Londoner and the cultured dignitary. The Central Government had issued a decree that the ancient custom of foot-binding was to cease, and the mandarin had come to ask her help in finding a woman who would travel about inspecting the feet of women and girls. In the event Gladys herself was appointed to the office. She would be given some payment, a mule would be provided to carry her, and she would be accompanied by a guard. She saw in this an outstanding opportunity to take the gospel out among the villages, and when she pointed out to the mandarin that this was her intention he raised no objection whatever. Thus it was that Gladys Aylward, who had turned the time-honoured occupation of inn-keeper into that of an evangelist, now did the same for the role of inspector of feet. In looking back she declared:

> I had longed to go to China, but never in my wildest dreams had I imagined that God would overrule in such a way that I would be given entrance into every village home; have authority to banish a cruel, horrible custom; have government protection; and be paid to preach the gospel of Jesus Christ as I inspected feet!

Conversions were recorded, the beginnings of churches appeared, and a testimony to the gospel was established among the mountain peoples. The determined parlourmaid knew that it was for this that she had been intended.

There was no telling where her influence might be felt. Frequently events overtook her, and without making any specific plans she found herself having to deal with situations that had been thrust upon her. So it proved when she was called upon to deal with a prison riot in Yangcheng—and quelled it! So, too, when confronted with the practice of child dealing, the buying and selling of children. One child was rescued by her for the price of ninepence, and so acquired the name Ninepence. She became the first member of a constantly growing family. Care for children was to play an increasing part in her work. Her identification with the Chinese people was completed when she was given the name Ai-weh-deh, which meant 'the virtuous one'. It was the name she took for herself when she became a naturalized Chinese citizen in 1936.

China had known turbulent times over the centuries, and the period Gladys Aylward spent there ranked with the worst. It coincided with the enormous growth in power of Mao Tse-tung, particularly when he became the dominant force in the Chinese Communist Party in 1936. The country also had reason to fear the expansionist ideas of Japan. The name of Genghis Khan is forever associated with unspeakable butchery and cruelty in China, and the ferocity of the attacks of his hordes may well be equalled by that of the Japanese.

They were dark days indeed for this ancient civilization, and inevitably Gladys found herself caught up in the warfare. Occasionally, Japanese soldiers would pass through Yangcheng without causing more than a flutter of interest—after all, of what importance could Yangcheng be to either side? However, the order of life in the city was shattered one morning in 1938 with a terrifying suddenness. The sight and sound of the Japanese planes brought the people hurrying out in excitement, for many of them had never seen a plane before. It was a pathetic scene as they pointed up at the metal objects that were falling from the bellies of these strange machines. Within seconds Yangcheng was a place of devastation. The Inn of Eight Happinesses belied the simple charm of its name as it failed to escape the aim of the invaders. Amazingly the little missionary was not killed, and was soon running about attending to the wounded and seeking to organize some form of rescue work. She was tireless in her efforts to help others, comforting the bereaved, inspiring the dazed, burying the dead. This was a different face from the charming one Japan had presented eight years previously when she passed through the country on her way to China.

The days of the war brought joy, heartache, and dilemma for her. Shortly before the air attack, a convention for the believers was held in Yangcheng, and people attended from a wide area. It might have seemed a foolish idea to proceed with arrangements at such a perilous time but everything went ahead as planned. In the event it proved a time of remarkable blessing. One morning she awoke to a strange noise, and rushing out with the children into the courtyard she was confronted with an astonishing sight:

> Hundreds of men and women were praying—some kneeling, some stand-ing. A power that I can only liken to that of Pentecost swept over that place. In a moment I, too, was on my knees, awed and full of great rever-ence. Beside me was a woman who, with tears running down her face, was pleading with God for her husband. Suddenly the dawn began to break and over the compound was a great 'Hallelujah Sam Mei Chu' (Praise the Lord).

Romance was also in the air when she met a soldier in the Chinese Nationalist Army whose name was Linnan. They were both very much in love, but it was a bitter-sweet affair, for, as with so many couples in times of war, their duties and responsibilities meant that marriage plans had to be postponed and eventually they came to nothing.

The dilemma, which she was able to resolve without too much dif-ficulty, arose from the privilege she enjoyed in being able to travel about the countryside in comparative freedom. She found that some-times she would visit villages that were occupied by Japanese forces. On her return she would report the strength and movements of the enemy soldiers to the Chinese military authorities. It was not always easy to still her conscience regarding her spying activities, but she justified them by reminding herself that she was a Chinese citizen, and if she had been in England and London was threatened she would have behaved in precisely the same way.

Four times Yangcheng changed hands, and Gladys had to fly with Ninepence and her other young charges to the caves in the hills. She also found a tower of strength in two missionaries who had come to Tsehchow, Welshman David Davies and his Scots wife, Jean. It was while she was in Tsehchow on one occasion that she was presented with a leaflet, representative of many that were being posted in the surrounding villages and which were soon to appear in the city itself. In the leaflets three people were named with a price of a hundred dollars each on their heads. One was the Mandarin of Tsehchow, another was a well-known businessman, the third was, 'The Small Woman, known as Ai-weh-deh'! Gladys Aylward with a 'Wanted' notice out for her! It became plain that she would have to escape.

As she raced from Tsehchow in the sight of Japanese soldiers she was literally running for her life—and barely succeeded, when a bullet tore along her back leaving a graze mark along her right shoulder-blade. In two days she was back at the Inn of Eight Happinesses, but not to stay. Her plan was formed, and it was to involve her in the most astounding episode in her adventurous career. In 1934-5 Mao with his communist allies had completed their incredible Long March of six thousand miles. If Gladys Aylward is known for anything it is for her own long march of twelve days over the mountains, leading a hundred children to safety out of the clutches of the enemy. The one was more spectacular in the sight of men: more significant was the other to the eye of God.

There is something epic about the journey they undertook, the little English woman with her brood of homeless orphans, some as young as four, the oldest fifteen. Her faithful friend, the Mandarin of Yangcheng, who had expressed his wish to become a Christian, aided her with such provisions as he could, but she knew they would be hopelessly inadequate. The excitement and energy of the little ones at the prospect of a 'walk' soon disappeared as they made their way through the cold, inhospitable, threatening mountains, scuttling for cover when it seemed soldiers might appear, finding shelter in caves and among the rocks. Gladys's spirit came near breaking-point more than once as she saw the older ones care for and carry the younger. Constantly she heard the piping cries, 'Ai-weh-deh, I'm tired,' 'My feet hurt,' 'I'm hungry,' 'Can we go home?' 'How much further?' She felt the sickening disappointment when there was no boat to take them across the Yellow River, and when trains failed to fulfil their promise. When they reached Sian where they had been assured of a haven, she was told to go away. The gates of the city were closed. There was no room. Another train journey had to be made to Fufeng where she was able to hand the children over to others to care for them. Then came physical collapse.

The march may well have been the climax of her stay in China but it was by no means the end. After recovery from her exhaustion and illness she was at her work of evangelism once more. This was to take her into a prison and even a lamasery, a monastery for Tibetan priests. She saw the fierce attack of Communist tyranny on a university which resulted in two hundred students being beheaded in one day. Dr Olin Stockwell, an American missionary imprisoned by the Communists wrote this:

> I remember a little pint-sized missionary lady from England who had been with us out in West China for a year or so. She went into a leper colony to minister to lepers' needs. She found a Christian man there who worked with her. She preached and served with such enthusiasm that she brought new hope to that whole group of lepers. Before she came, the lepers had been quarrelsome and jealous, fighting among themselves. Many of them felt that life was hopeless. She came to tell them of a God who loved them. The tone of that colony changed . . . God had used this little missionary as his Barnabas to them.

When after twenty years she went back to England it was to work in a different capacity among the Chinese who were to be found there. Although mainland China was closed to her she did go to Hong Kong where she established the 'Hope Mission', working among refugees and orphans. From there in 1957 she moved to Taiwan, once more devoting herself to orphaned and abandoned babies. As she looked over the years she had the incomparable satisfaction of seeing so many who had passed through her hands dedicated to the work of the gospel. She spent the remaining years of her life on the island, obviously very happy and contented in her ministry. Her death occurred in 1970 at the age of 67 as a result of pneumonia.

With such a spirit of determination who is to say that she would not have made her name on the stage? But the bright lights of the theatre were willingly surrendered for the dark recesses of a vast land mass. She had no ideas of grandeur after God called her—she affirmed that she was not his 'first choice'. That appears to confirm the opinion of those in the missionary college that her theology was weak. Accuracy in points of doctrine, however, although important and necessary, is not the sole criterion God applies when calling men and women into his service. She is better judged by the extract from the letter she wrote to her mother:

> Do not wish me out of this or in any way seek to get me out, for I will not be got out while this trial is on. These are my people; God has given them to me, and I will live or die with them for Him and His Glory.

31
Jim Elliot
(1927-56)

In the long and often bloody annals of missionary endeavour few accounts can have captured the imaginations, as well as the hearts of the Christian Church, as the exploits of five young Americans which reached a savage climax at a time of day when most people are beginning to prepare themselves for evening worship. From a human perspective the record is sad and heart-rending: their lives were short; their hopes were high; their deaths were violent. From a divine perspective faith asserts with the historian that the blood of the martyrs is the seed of the Church. Almost two thousand years after the words were written Jim Elliot and his friends were numbered among 'the souls of them that were slain for the word of God'. His life is recounted here as representative of the other four as well as for its own worth.

Six years after his birth to godly parents in Portland, Oregon in 1927, he became a Christian. An earnest witness from the start, 'preaching' from the swing on the lawn to his little companions, his singlemindedness was to remain an outstanding feature of his character. Schooldays found him ready to enter unreservedly upon the activities that occupied others in the school, without his ever having to compromise through lowering his standards. He seems particularly to have distinguished himself in oratory and drama. Missionary desires were already being formed in him.

His student years were spent at Wheaton College in the state of Illinois where his purposeful attitude impressed itself upon others. Nothing was allowed to turn him aside from his commitment to God and his determination to realize that intent. On one occasion when his grades were not what they ought to have been he admitted that he had not worked as hard as he should have. This was because he had been more concerned with the study of the Bible in which he sought 'the degree A.U.G., "approved unto God" '. The missionary call appears to have been confirmed about this time. A notebook found by his dead body contains notes made at this period, including statistics showing the enormous spiritual needs in those parts of the world where the gospel had not come. The question he seems to have posed for himself was not did he have a call to go, but rather was he justified in staying at home. What did need settling in his mind was where he should go. Mexico, Peru, Brazil, India, all passed through his mind as possible destinations. Nor was his waiting and preparation merely theoretical—his activity in praying, preaching, literature work, arranging meetings and so on was endless. He was involved in sending packages to missionaries and Sunday afternoons would find him in Chicago witnessing at the railway station to those waiting for trains. All this while being a prominent member of the college wrestling team!

Wheaton had one other claim of significance in his life for it was here that he met his future wife. It was a mark of his—and her—devotion to God that although they knew that they loved each other, both determined to remain single for the sake of the gospel until God made it perfectly plain that they were to marry each other.

The years after leaving college, although full, were very trying ones as he waited for God's direction. There was criticism from some because he was not seen to be working and this naturally brought him the temptation to justify himself. His time, however, was not wasted and he seems to have been constantly occupied with evangelism and preaching. For a while he taught in a Christian school, but all the time he was straining at the leash, longing for service in a foreign land. He had little time for those who suggested that there was work at home to be done. For such an attitude he barely concealed his scorn. To his mother he wrote:

> Please let's not have any more of this talk about staying home, telling people of the 'need'. That would be augmenting the need. There are too many good preachers berating people night after night about a lost world who have never faced the challenge of sacrificial foreign service themselves. I feel as if I haven't got any excuse whatsoever to let a body such as you have given me get fat leaning on pulpits.

In February 1949 his brother Bert went to Peru as missionary Reading a letter to him from Wilfred Tidmarsh, an older missionary who was already there, moved Jim to write a letter offering himself for service in Ecuador. He found himself in a dilemma when a missionary in India was obviously keen for him to go there. Where was he to go? How was he to decide? Confirmation and further guidance came at the Summer Institute of Linguistics which he attended in 1950. It was here that he first heard of the Auca Indians. 'Jim's heart was immediately set on fire', writes his wife Elisabeth. His parents showed some reluctance at the thought of his leaving home, but his response was typical. Referring to Psalm 127 where the psalmist speaks of children as arrows, he asked, 'What are arrows for but to shoot?' Jesus once rebuked his mother when she appeared to be a hindrance to him while still a boy. Jim Elliot would have hated the comparison, but the same spirit impelled him as he considered the will of his Father.

Renewed contact with a friend, Ed McCully, gave him hope that he would accompany him to South America. Both were busy with evangelistic work, including being responsible for a radio programme. Hopes of going out together were frustrated when his friend became engaged, but prayers for an unmarried companion were answered in the person of Pete Fleming. He and Elisabeth had received no further guidance regarding marriage although her intention to go to the South Seas had come to nothing. The obvious course was that they should marry and go together to Ecuador. Jim Elliot, however, was not a man to do even the obvious without a word from God. Therefore even though she now would follow him to South America, wedding plans were not in their minds. So the two young men set sail on a voyage from which they were never to return. On 4 February 1952 the *Santa Juana* carried them away from the harbour in California. Three weeks later they were taken by plane from the Ecuadorian coast high up the Andes mountains to the capital, Quito.

With characteristic eagerness he threw himself into the work. His heart had for long been set upon the Aucas and now he did all he could to hasten the day when he could make contact with them. Their reputation was fearsome—that of 'savage Stone Age killers'. Time spent at Missionary Aviation Fellowship headquarters at Shell Mera making jungle surveys gave little cause for optimism. Had there been any friendly relations at all established between the southern Quichua Indians and the Aucas? The answer was grim. The Aucas had just killed five of their enemies in the area. Flights over the jungle

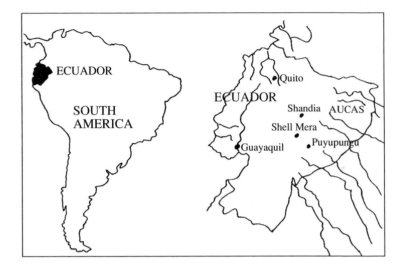

revealed very little. There appeared to be no trace of them and they seemed totally inaccessible.

There was other work to be done while they waited for their opportunity. After running a boys' camp he moved with Pete Fleming and Dr Tidmarsh to Shandia where there was an airstrip to be constructed, buildings to be erected, medical work to be pursued, and a language to be learned. There was also a school which needed their attention. Discouragements were inevitable and interruptions to the work were a regular feature. However, the beginning of 1953 saw the arrival in Ecuador of Ed McCully and his wife, and the engagement of Jim and Elisabeth. He was making headway with the Quichua language and a few months later was sufficiently competent to preach in it. Midway through the year came the rainy season. This occasioned a severe setback with the destruction of Shandia by the floods. A further handicap was an attack of malaria which he suffered.

He and the others were heartened by a visit to one of the surrounding areas when a group of Indians begged them to come and establish a school among them. The decision by the missionaries to accept the invitation was not a particularly hard one, and so Jim Elliot moved to his new home in Puyupungu—with his new bride. Their stay here was short-lived since he was needed for the rebuilding of Shandia which they had decided to make a main centre, while places like Puyupungu would serve as outstations. Back at Shandia Indians were baptized, the number of those breaking bread increased, and his daughter Valerie was born. Then came the news he had been waiting for: in September 1955 Ed McCully and Nate Saint, the missionary pilot, had seen some houses belonging to the Aucas.

Some Auca phrases were learnt from Dayuma, an escaped Auca girl. Flights were made to establish some sort of contact with them. Phrases such as 'We are your friends' were shouted to them, and gifts were exchanged by means of a bucket being lowered and raised. By Christmas the team had been completed with the arrival of Roger Youderian. Before actually going among them momentous issues had to be faced. The Aucas were killers. The missionaries had work to do among those with whom they had settled. And some of them had wives and children. The decision was made. They had to go.

Early in January 1956 the plane landed by the Curaray river. Jim Elliot, Ed McCully, Nate Saint, Roger Youderian and Pete Fleming met their first Aucas. All seemed to go well. Two days later they waited eagerly for them to return bringing others with them. The missionaries had their lunch, sang the hymn, 'We rest on Thee, our Shield and our Defender', and waited. Their last messages to their loved ones had been sent. It was a Sunday afternoon. Before the evening came they had entered into their Sabbath of rest, speared by the Aucas.

It is a matter of gratitude that Jim Elliot wrote so many letters and kept a journal, for they contain so much of spiritual wealth. In them there is a perfect record of a soul's walk with God as well as a mine of instruction and counsel. The man was aflame—with contempt for hypocrites, with compassion for those who had not heard of Jesus and his love, with holy fire for God. From many passages that could be cited the following must suffice:

> Ah, generation that hears, but feels not, listens, but aches not, harks, but knows not pain nor the pleasurable healing balm thereof. Tell me, does all fire extinguish save in Hell? Damned be this tepidity. Have we no fire to hate? Does no flame seize our prophets? Show me one burning heart. Let me see a single worldling afire with true passion, one Heavenling consumed with his God's eternal burnings. In them I would find excuse for you, my cheating, shamming, joyless generation. Well has your own poet said, you live and die 'ox-like, limp, and leaden-eyed'.

I do not understand why I have never seen in America what missionaries write of—that sense of swords being drawn, the smell of war with demon-powers. Corresponding is the unity among Christians on the mission-field, forced by the onslaught of a very real foe. Satan is not real—though we talk much of belief in a 'personal devil'. As a result, our warfare takes on this sham-fight with shadows, a cold war of weary words. There is no shouting; rather, yawning. Laughter long ago stifled sobs in our assemblings together. Woe, woe, woe unto us. We have not submitted to sacrifice. We have not guessed the power of the calling to which God has called—its power to ruin and to revive, its strength to slay.

And perhaps best known and wisest of all:

He is no fool who gives what he cannot keep to gain what he cannot lose.

32
Cameron Townsend
(1896-1982)

Los Angeles is a name with associations of the glitz and glamour of Hollywood, and does not spring readily to mind in the context of Christian matters. Yet, in its neighbourhood was born a child who was to become, in the opinion of Billy Graham, 'the greatest missionary of our time'. When he died, Ralph Winter of the United States Centre for World Mission considered him one of the three greatest missionaries of the last two centuries. He was in exalted company indeed, for the other two were William Carey and Hudson Taylor. Opinions had changed since someone had remarked on his first excursion to Guatemala as a seller of Bibles, 'that skinny Townsend won't last two months.'

William Cameron Townsend grew up in a close-knit, happy family with Christian parents. His father was a scrupulously honest man who spent his life struggling to make a livelihood and keeping out of the grasping fingers of debt. His example and standards were not lost on his children. When someone told the young Cameron that his father's word was enough for all the merchants who bought his farm produce, a surge of pride ran through him. There were not many traces of sophistication on the Townsend hearth, but there was no lack of evidence of godliness. Each day the Bible was read in the family circle, a hymn was sung, and a prayer offered. Will Townsend's prayers always ended, 'May the knowledge of the Lord cover the earth as the waters cover the sea.' What could be more appropriate than that his son should be a mighty instrument in the hand of God to promote the realization of that desire?

He became a member of the local Presbyterian Church at the age of twelve, and while still a youth was inclined towards the ministry. During his time at college he was drawn to the Student Volunteer Movement with its powerful missionary incentive. His interest intensified on hearing the presiding genius of the organization, John R.

Mott, and again on reading the story of Hudson Taylor. In 1916, when America had still not entered the First World War, and when hostilities seemed remote, he enlisted in the National Guard. In January 1917 he took his first steps towards serving in a foreign country when he applied to become a Bible salesman in Guatemala, thinking that if accepted there would be little difficulty in resigning from the Guard. Meanwhile America had declared war in April of that year, and his situation had thereby changed. However, on being called a coward by a female missionary for leaving all the work on the field to women, he applied for a discharge from his military responsibilities. Astonishingly this was granted, the captain commenting that he would probably do more good selling Bibles in Central America than serving on the battlefields of France. So it was that in September 1917, together with a friend of his, Elbert Robinson, he found himself on his way to Guatemala.

His assignment was to work around two Indian towns among a group of Cakchiquel Indians. It was an invaluable introduction to his life's work. He was escorted in his travels by a Cakchiquel Christian named Francisco. He learnt to endure hardships and how to approach the Indians on their own level. When an earthquake struck Guatemala City he was involved in distribution of tracts and also bringing relief to those who had suffered loss or injury. His journeys took him to the neighbouring countries of El Salvador, Honduras, and Nicaragua, but the most significant observation he made was in Guatemala itself, seeing the difference between the Indians and the *ladinos*. These were people of mixed Spanish and Indian heritage, and regarded themselves as the superior of the two groupings. Francisco was an Indian and resented the way in which the *ladinos* were given preference, even by the evangelical missionaries. This was because the *ladinos* could be addressed in Spanish, whereas no one could speak the Indian language. Francisco pleaded with his friend to learn the Cakchiquel language so that he could teach the Indians. Cameron Townsend did not need much persuading. Already his mind was entertaining the enormous possibilities that lay open to him. If he could learn the language, what was to stop him then translating the Bible?

In 1919 he opened a school for the Indians. It was held in a room loaned by one of the chiefs, it had a Cakchiquel teacher who could teach in Spanish and Cakchiquel, and it had 25 students, some of whom were boarders. It was a giant step to take and marked him out as a pioneer in the field of Indian education. For a long time his contemporaries would be 'shackled to the melting pot philosophy of offering schooling to minority linguistic groups in the language of the majority'.

His own work of learning the language was proving difficult. One of the reasons for this was that he was trying to force Cakchiquel into the pattern of languages with which he was already familiar, such as English and Spanish. Slowly the task went on, while he mastered this new and unruly tongue. An additional benefit from all this hard work was that he was not only learning a particular language; he was learning about language in general. This was to stand him in good stead when his unique contribution to translation work was to profit the helpers God would give him. In the same eventful year he was married, but this was to prove something of a mixed blessing, for his wife would give vent to violent emotional and physical outbursts. It was obvious that she was unwell, but her attacks upon him did not stop him from loving her deeply. A great blow to him at this time was the death of Francisco to whom he owed so much and from whom he expected so much.

Developments came rapidly, and with the developments came further visions of expansion. He was able to present a translation of the first four chapters of the Gospel of Mark; the boarding school soon had a hundred scholars; his brother Paul and his wife arrived as helpers; a coffee manufacturer provided the Indians with the means to run their own co-operative; and a volunteer offered his services in establishing a Bible Institute that had been planned. Sadly, Elbert Robinson who had played such a major role in the planning of the Institute, had died before this development. In his honour it was named after him.

Even with these encouragements it was not all plain sailing for Cameron Townsend, and he found that not all his helpers and colleagues were of the same mind as he was. The Central American Mission which he and his wife had joined were by no means persuaded of the value of translating the Bible into the minority language, believing this would drive a wedge between the Indians and the *ladinos*. His determination won the day, however, in spite of indifference and opposition. In 1926 he had completed the Cakchiquel grammar.

Although only 49 pages it marked another important step along the path that was opening before him. Three years later the New Testament was finished.

Never one to stand back and simply watch the seed he had planted grow, he always was on the look-out for new opportunities. His eyes and his mind seemed to work in perfect co-ordination to further the cause of the gospel. Thus when he read in the newspapers of US Navy planes visiting Guatemala, he immediately thought of harnessing aviation in reaching tribes in Amazonia. CAM were less than enthusiastic, and believed that he should remain among the Cakchiquels. He was convinced he must move on, and so at the suggestion of a friend, L. L. Legters, he left Guatemala for Mexico. Another seed was beginning to germinate at the same time—a summer training school where personnel from all missions could come and learn the skill of reducing a language to writing and then translating the Scriptures. In 1934 he organized a 'Summer Training Camp for Prospective Bible Translators' with about half a dozen lecturers. Then he set out to search for students. He was only moderately successful—the faculty outnumbered the students! He was not to know that he had played the midwife or even father to a movement that was to become world-wide in its influence. The birth had occurred; the new arrival was known as Camp Wycliffe; a further two years were to elapse before it received its formal name: Summer Institute of Linguistics. Contracting T. B., and caring for his wife who had a heart condition, hampered his activities—but not much.

Cameron Townsend was never slow to make contacts and to use them to gain an entry for the gospel. By this means he was able to begin a work in Mexico when the door seemed to be firmly shut in his face. He made his home in Tetelcingo, a very backward Aztec settlement. There he came to know the mayor, and there also began a friendship with the president of Mexico. He envisaged the basic work of literacy campaigns and Bible translation being undergirded with a programme for social improvement. This included helping drug addicts, alcoholics, prostitutes, and expediting irrigation and reforestation. Like all true missionaries of the Son of God he identified himself as fully as possible with the people whom he served, even taking Mexico's part in political dispute with the USA. The increasing co-operation with governments aroused suspicions among some fellow missionaries and alienated him from them. At the same time, in view of the speed and manner of the expansion of the work, with the complexities that were involved, it was decided that some division was required. The Summer Institute of Linguistics was to have a twin organization, the Wycliffe Bible Translators.

His personal and domestic problems continued until the death of his wife in 1944. Two years later he remarried. The period of widowhood did nothing to cloud his vision or hinder his plans for expansion. Amazonia, India, Borneo, Siberia were all finding a lodging place in his mind and heart. When an opening for Peru was in the offing he made arrangements for the responsibility of the work in Mexico—he had no intention of allowing someone else to lead the advance into the new field! With the Amazon jungle now waiting he acquired his first plane. This in turn was to lead to a third development. SIL/WBT was now joined by JAARS—Jungle Aviation And Radio Service. An almost fatal plane crash illustrates the way he turned everything to advantage. With his leg broken he called for a camera so that photographs could be taken to show people how badly they needed safe aviation for jungle work. On another level, the same commitment that he had shown in Guatemala and Mexico earned him the Order of Distinguished Service of Peru.

In 1952 one of his colleagues began a work in the Philippines. Another worker went to Ecuador. Invitations came from Africa. He had hopes of Venezuela and Colombia. In 1957 a couple went to Vietnam. The waves of expansion continued, and the Bible was being translated into more and more languages. The names 'linguistics' and 'Bible translators' by no means give the whole picture; 'Uncle Cam', as he was fondly known, was always ready to help in terms of agriculture, carpentry, mechanics and so on. Over the years the work had gained the respect of distinguished people and institutions. Historian Arnold Toynbee commended it. Wycliffe personnel were working alongside acknowledged experts in their fields. Cameron Townsend himself was offered honorary doctorates, but declined them all except · for one from the University of San Marcos in Peru, which he accepted out of affection for the country he loved so much. Along with so much to cheer, criticism went on mounting, and this culminated in 1959 in resignation from the International Foreign Missions Association. The charges, from anonymous sources, centred in the allegation that their work was 'scientific and cultural, not spiritual'. It seemed that Townsend himself was always having to answer the question, 'Are you a missionary or a linguist?'

As he realized aims and ambitions they were constantly replaced by new ones. The last of these was to initiate a work in Russia. His appetite was whetted on learning that there were more than a hundred languages spoken in the Caucasus. In 1968 he made his first visit there and was impressed with what he saw. He was never content to go simply to 'give'. He was always prepared to learn from his experiences, and this was no less true of the time he spent in the USSR. His return to America was certainly not to rest. Travelling, planning, encouraging took up as much of his time as it had ever done. When asked in 1969 about his schedule he responded that he was going back to work in Russia for a month, then going on to India, Nepal, the Philippines, New Guinea, Australia and New Zealand. By now he had been told that he had an irregular heartbeat, but he refused to let that stand in the way of his intentions.

His devotion to his work was matched by his love for his colleagues. At the age of 84 he insisted on flying down to Colombia to comfort the friends of one of the Wycliffe translators who had been murdered by terrorists. In that sad visit he did not allow them to lose sight of the task that faced them, and encouraged them in their share of the work to ensure that 'every single language group on the face of the earth has heard the good news of God's love'. His reminder that his time was drawing to a close was in itself a spur to them. It was not misplaced, for a year following, in April 1982, he died. He had seen many dreams come true, but a man with so many dreams cannot see them all realized. His latest dream was of the day when ethnic minorities in the USSR would read the Bible in their own tongue. And if he had seen that longing fulfilled, he would only have exchanged the dream for another.

No missionary can have been dogged by more controversy than Cameron Townsend. This was not because he sought trouble but because he showed such eagerness in the pursuit of his objective. There are four questions that may be indicated here, and it is easy to understand why so much passion should have been generated in the disputes. Some of the issues have lost none of their relevance today.

The first rose out of his friendship with President Cárdenas of

Mexico. He was so impressed with the man and with what he had achieved that he felt he should write a biography of him. Many thought it unwise to be occupied with the life of a radical statesman with so many spiritual demands to be met.

Closely allied to this was his involvement in politics. Should he have concerned himself so much with, for example, the matter of Mexico's oil dispute with the United States? He did not regard this as 'dabbling in politics' but as something affecting the integrity of his work.

There were those who were uneasy at the fact that he was prepared to accept Pentecostals in the work. Opinions were so strong on this that he threatened to resign if a couple from the Assemblies of God were refused membership.

Perhaps most testing of all was his readiness to work alongside Roman Catholics, and even to receive them as members of SIL/WBT. One young man who was engaged to a Salvation Army girl was given his wholehearted support, and was denied membership only by the majority of those who had voting rights. The lengths to which he was prepared to go to accommodate Catholics was alarming, and surprising, when one considers that he had seen evidence of the way Catholicism itself had accommodated pagan Aztec worship.

Controversy did not disappear with his death. In recent years criticism has come from fresh quarters, and this is in no way justifiable. SIL has become the object of attacks in books and newspapers from those professing to be concerned with the environment and with preserving primitive cultures. Missionaries have been accused of various crimes including greed, hypocrisy, enslaving Indians, reducing them to the status of peasants, acting as a cover for CIA activities, drug trafficking, along with much else besides. This is not the place to deal with such malicious allegations, the evidence for which is tenuous in the extreme. The words of UN Secretary-General Perez de Cuellar will suffice to help put the record straight:

> Your mission as ambassadors of literacy deserves high praise. By transcribing into writing mother tongues that were previously unwritten . . . you are facilitating the preservation of ethnic cultures and building bridges for those cultures to the rest of humanity. Your work complements our own . . . promoting peace through increased communication.

No doubt the controversy will continue, and Christian missionaries will have to ride the storms of angry criticisms for many years. When words have drifted into their long silence and arguments finally stilled, the compelling testimony and enduring contribution of Cameron Townsend will be his own apologia and God's vindication.

33
Clarence Jones
(1900-1986)

It goes without saying that missionaries frequently face stern opposition from enemies of the gospel. What is not so often recognized, however, is the fact that the criticism can sometimes come from other Christians. Particularly is this the case when a new and untried step is ventured. Clarence Jones found this to be true on his way to becoming the pioneer of missionary radio. Radio was still regarded in some ultra-conservative circles as the 'tool of the devil', and Jones's vision as 'Jones's folly'. Ultimately it would be acknowledged as Jones's triumph.

Clarence Wesley Jones was born to Salvation Army parents in the state of Illinois in December 1900. As he grew up he was to show that he had inherited something of the spirit of his father, who as a young man had chosen to leave home rather than heed his family's instructions to leave the Army. Poverty was the order of the day, with the boy Clarence having newspapers wrapped around his legs to keep them warm in the Chicago cold. A high-spirited, athletic child, gifted with his hands, he soon revealed a standard of musicianship that enabled him to play every instrument in the Salvation Army band except the tuba. His mastery of the trombone became complete and was to stand him in good stead on many occasions. He loved to play in the band on the street corners, there being only one drawback—he had no experience of Christ. When the leader of the group asked each member to give a testimony, Clarence was reduced to a feeble 'Same goes for me' after the previous speaker.

Conversion became a reality to him as he approached his eighteenth birthday, while attending the Moody Memorial Tabernacle. There, under the ministry of the unconventional Paul Rader, he trusted the Saviour and received forgiveness of sins. Within weeks he had enrolled at the Moody Bible Institute, and three years later on the day after he had graduated he was on an evangelistic tour. Clarence Jones was not a man to let the grass grow under his feet.

In 1924 he was married, and spent his honeymoon preparing for a series of meetings for Rader. He was by now gaining a reputation as a song leader in campaigns and also for his solos on the trombone. When Rader had left the Moody Tabernacle to establish the Chicago Gospel Tabernacle Jones had accepted an invitation to join three friends in forming a brass quartet. Other gifted musicians at the Tabernacle helped to swell the congregation to five thousand. When Chicago's new radio station opened Rader and his companions were asked to help with the music. He needed no second invitation and in June 1922 Clarence Jones had his first encounter with radio ministry. On the roof of the old City Hall he and the other members of the quartet were set in front of a small rough construction with a hole in the side. From inside came a hand holding a telephone and they followed their instructions: 'Point your instruments at that hole, and when we say play, you play.' Similar lack of sophistication was to accompany many of Jones's early endeavours to proclaim the gospel over the air.

His proficiency and skill developed quickly, largely owing to the demands that Rader made upon him and his colleagues. It was precisely the kind of training that was needed for the work that lay in store for him. Within a few years the nature of that work was disclosed to him through the ministry of Paul Rader and also through hearing the testimony of a missionary couple whose work in Tibet had cost them the lives of their two young children as the family came home. He distinctly heard the call of God, so clearly that he thought others had heard it as well. It was a summons to go south, just as Philip had been directed in the book of Acts. In Jones's case two words had been added: 'with radio'. So it was that in 1928 he went south—to Venezuela, to see if there were openings and opportunities there. President Gomez gave him short shrift. Although Jones pointed out to him the benefits, the President was suspicious, and saw the dangers to his position posed by such power. The same response was met in Colombia, Panama, and Cuba. Clarence Jones's confused comment summed up the reaction of many servants of God at home and abroad, before and since:

> I went to Venezuela so sure they'd come running to me because the Lord had called me there. Instead they ran the other way.

Unknown to him his wife, Kath, now with two little children to care for, had lost her interest in the mission field. At that moment the future was looking far from bright for him.

Eighteen months went by with little if anything to show. Discouragement fell upon him heavily at times, on one occasion causing him to attempt to join the navy. Only his defective eyesight prevented him from being successful in his bid. Late in 1929 he and Kath came into contact with two missionaries from Ecuador, J. D. and Ruth Clark. Conversation with them and with two other missionaries, Reuben and Grace Larson soon revived Clarence's interest in the work on which his heart had been set. From the Larsons he was assured that his trip to South America had not been a waste of time, that 'he had simply gone to the wrong countries'. When Larsen returned to Ecuador it was on the understanding that Jones would raise funds in the United States for the projected radio work, and then follow him. Happily by this time husband and wife both had their hearts in the work. For his part Larsen was busily engaged in arranging the contract with the Ecuadorian government. With some notable exceptions, there was a distinct lack of enthusiasm, if not of approval, among the Christians at home. What was the point, they asked, of setting up a radio network in a country where there were only six receiving sets? And where was

255

the money to come from, for this was the year of the notorious Wall Street crash? Undismayed, in August 1930 Clarence Jones was on his way.

No sooner had he arrived in Ecuador than he was greeted with facts concerning the utter unsuitability of the country and especially of Quito the capital where they had decided to establish the station. Ecuador, as the name implies, was too near the equator, and Quito, at over 9000 feet was surrounded by mountains. The advice of the experts was to stay away from the equator and from the mountains, yet here they were committed to both. Other adverse circumstances arose which affected him keenly. Nevertheless, armed with the confidence that he was in God's will, he and his companions pressed on with their plans. On 3 October they had decided on the name for the new radio station. 'HC' were the international call letters allocated to Ecuador. They thought of a slogan which could be represented by those intitials, and because most of the broadcasting would be in Spanish, decided upon 'Hoy Cristo Jesus Bendice'—today Jesus Christ blesses. They also came up with an English counterpart, 'Heralding Christ Jesus' Blessings'. So HCJB was born. There was still much to be done before they actually went on the air—support to be encouraged, funds to be gathered, programmes to be arranged, the World Radio Missionary Fellowship to be formed as a legal corporation, and not least, a transmitter to be taken out from the States to Quito. Jones had planned for a 5,000 watt transmitter; he had to make do with a 250 watt version. All along it seemed that his vision was too great for his resources, but he, or rather God, was to have the last word.

Excitement grew as Christmas Day 1931 approached, for this was to be the day when the new station was launched. The equipment, studio, control room, antenna, all bore a very primitive appearance but were the pride and joy of all concerned. Then on Christmas Eve Clarence had to make a six-hour 120-mile journey for a replacement item that had failed them on that very day. At three o'clock on Christmas Day, accompanied by Ruth Clark on a portable organ, he played on the trombone the signature tune, 'Great is Thy faithfulness'. Reuben Larsen announced into the microphone, 'This is the Voice of the Andes, HCJB'. The very first missionary radio broadcast was under way. Half an hour later they breathed a sigh of relief as telephone calls came in congratulating them. Christmas dinner later that day had never tasted so sweet to any of them.

The policy of HCJB was laid down at the outset. It would be 'first educational, second cultural, and then religious'. It was obviously important not to antagonize Roman Catholic opinion while at the same time presenting the gospel clearly. So successful were they in this that even when they came across a sign warning Protestants that they were not welcome, from behind the door could be heard the sound of 'Voice of the Andes'. Diligent, punctual, authoritarian even, Clarence Jones was conscientious in everything and expected the same high standards from those who worked around him. One announcer who turned up blithely two and a half hours late was rebuked and told, 'If you are not fifteen minutes early, you're late!' The pace at which he worked and the demands he made upon himself were bound to bring pressures upon him and his family. He sold radios, taught English in the school for a few hours a day, but his children were still reduced to wearing cardboard inside their shoes to keep out the damp. The tension inevitably showed in the relationship between him and Kath and had to be honestly resolved. A crisis point was reached one day in 1933 when he was faced with an electricity bill and had nothing with which to pay. He spent the day praying and fasting in the toolshed at the bottom of the garden. There God met with him, and the crisis passed. God used a verse that had often been a force in Jones's life, Jeremiah 33:3: 'Call unto me, and I will answer thee, and shew thee great and mighty things, which thou knowest not.'

HCJB certainly stood for variety. The government was encouraged to use 20% of the broadcasting time. Then there was 'Radio Rodante', a van or truck that was fitted out with a public address system and broadcasting equipment. This was used for taking the gospel to various villages and townships. The poverty of Ecuador meant that not all could afford receivers, so Jones supplied fifty to strategic places through the country. These were in the charge of Christians whose neighbours were eager to avail themselves of the opportunity of listening to 'the little magic box that sings'. South America's notoriety for revolutions meant that the station came in useful for conveying information. On one occasion an armoured car drew up. The occupants wished to listen to the radio to find out which side was winning!

257

In 1941 it was Clarence Jones who informed the American Embassy of the bombing of Pearl Harbour. Pan American Airways celebrated their twenty-thousandth flight across the Equator with a broadcast from an aircraft flying over Quito. Their pilots had relied on the radio beam of HCJB to ensure safe guidance. The reputation of HCJB was on the increase.

In 1937 a new 1,000 watt transmitter had come into use, meaning that now eighty or ninety million people in South and Central America provided a potential audience. The generosity of R. G. Le Tourneau, a Christian businessman, meant that two years later Quito had a brand new 10,000 watt transmitter. President Andres Cordova switched this on for the first time. The response was astonishing with letters coming in from Japan, New Zealand, India, Germany, and Russia. HCJB was being heard in Sumatra and in Alaska. As its circle of influence was being extended it obviously became necessary for the number of languages employed to multiply, and so it was that from 1945 the number of missionaries grew from fifteen to eighty-seven in ten years. Strange that Quito, which the missionaries had initially been told was to be avoided, now turned out to be 'the best site on earth!' The World Radio Missionary Fellowship was beginning to live up to its name.

Clarence Jones grasped radio with both hands and used it in every way he could to the advantage of the gospel. He initiated Summer Schools of Christian Radio in 1946. The Bible Institute of the Air was another of his schemes. He saw the enormous use to which television could be put. When the government renewed the contract of HCJB eight years before the old one expired, he saw the time had come to increase the power from 10,000 watts to 50,000. Always ready to think big he planned the construction of a dam and the installation of a hydroelectric plant. In 1965 he saw the realization of this dream, which was to provide them with two million watts of power. Serious setbacks were not allowed to detract him from his calling. An accident to himself and Kath which almost proved fatal, and a tragedy in which their son Dick, who worked with his father, died, saw him return with immense and undiminished vigour to the task.

His constant activity did not blind him to the fact that he was not indispensable, and he was wise enough to retire from leadership after making sure of his successor. Retirement was not for him an opportunity for indulging himself. He made extensive journeys to the growing number of missionary radio stations around the world, and was always a means of encouragement to the staff. He in turn was cheered by such accounts as that of three Red Army officers on a remote Siberian base, searching for a Russian language broadcast, finding a gospel service in that language, and through that finding the Saviour.

In 1975 he suffered a cerebral thrombosis, from which he recovered in spite of the doctor's predictions. A happy and full eleven years remained to him before his death occurred in April, 1986. The Salvationist without a testimony had harnessed the massive energy of the radio waves to provide millions with a testiomony of their own. When a missionary with HCJB wanted to argue with him about her persuasion that they ought to be treating subjects such as solidarity, rights and revolution, his reply was a perfect epitome of what his life had emphasised:

> There is only one message you need to give out on your radio programs: the Blood, the Book and the Blessed Hope.

In retrospect she thanked him 'for having demonstrated for me a life that was redeemed by the Blood, guided by the Book and anchored in the Blessed Hope.'

INDEX

261